C000088758

797,885 Books

are available to read at

Forgotten Books

www.ForgottenBooks.com

Forgotten Books' App
Available for mobile, tablet & eReader

Download on the
App Store

ANDROID APP ON
Google play

ISBN 978-1-330-30297-2
PIBN 10019820

This book is a reproduction of an important historical work. Forgotten Books uses
state-of-the-art technology to digitally reconstruct the work, preserving the original format
whilst repairing imperfections present in the aged copy. In rare cases, an imperfection in
the original, such as a blemish or missing page, may be replicated in our edition. We do,
however, repair the vast majority of imperfections successfully; any imperfections that
remain are intentionally left to preserve the state of such historical works.

Forgotten Books is a registered trademark of FB &c Ltd.
Copyright © 2017 FB &c Ltd.
FB &c Ltd, Dalton House, 60 Windsor Avenue, London, SW19 2RR.
Company number 08720141. Registered in England and Wales.

For support please visit www.forgottenbooks.com

1 MONTH OF
FREE
READING

at

www.ForgottenBooks.com

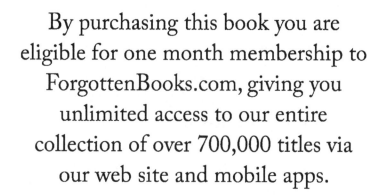

By purchasing this book you are
eligible for one month membership to
ForgottenBooks.com, giving you
unlimited access to our entire
collection of over 700,000 titles via
our web site and mobile apps.

To claim your free month visit:

www.forgottenbooks.com/free19820

* Offer is valid for 45 days from date of purchase. Terms and conditions apply.

English
Français
Deutsche
Italiano
Español
Português

www.forgottenbooks.com

Mythology Photography **Fiction**
Fishing Christianity **Art** Cooking
Essays Buddhism Freemasonry
Medicine **Biology** Music **Ancient
Egypt** Evolution Carpentry Physics
Dance Geology **Mathematics** Fitness
Shakespeare **Folklore** Yoga Marketing
Confidence Immortality Biographies
Poetry **Psychology** Witchcraft
Electronics Chemistry History **Law**
Accounting **Philosophy** Anthropology
Alchemy Drama Quantum Mechanics
Atheism Sexual Health **Ancient History**
Entrepreneurship Languages Sport
Paleontology Needlework Islam
Metaphysics Investment Archaeology
Parenting Statistics Criminology
Motivational

HOMESTEAD: THE HOUSEHOLDS OF A MILL TOWN

RUSSELL SAGE FOUNDATION PUBLICATIONS

—

THE STANDARD OF LIVING AMONG WORKINGMEN'S FAMILIES IN NEW YORK CITY. By ROBERT COIT CHAPIN, Ph.D. 388 pages. 131 tables. 16 diagrams. Price, postpaid, $2.00.

MEDICAL INSPECTION OF SCHOOLS. By LUTHER HALSEY GULICK, M.D., and LEONARD P. AYRES, Ph.D. 286 pages. Third edition. Price, postpaid, $1.00.

LAGGARDS IN OUR SCHOOLS: A Study of Retardation and Elimination. By LEONARD P. AYRES, Ph.D. 252 pages. 106 tables. 38 diagrams. Third edition. Price, postpaid, $1.50.

CORRECTION AND PREVENTION. Four volumes prepared for the Eighth International Prison Congress. Edited by CHARLES RICHMOND HENDERSON, Ph.D. Price per set, postpaid, $10; per volume, net, $2.50. Titles: PRISON REFORM; PENAL AND REFORMATORY INSTITUTIONS; PREVENTIVE AGENCIES AND METHODS; PREVENTIVE TREATMENT OF NEGLECTED CHILDREN.

JUVENILE COURT LAWS IN THE UNITED STATES: SUMMARIZED. 160 pages. Price, postpaid, $1.50.

THE PITTSBURGH SURVEY. Six volumes. Fully illustrated. Price per set, postpaid, $10; per volume, net, $1.50.

WOMEN AND THE TRADES. By Elizabeth Beardsley Butler. Price, postpaid, $1.72.

WORK-ACCIDENTS AND THE LAW. By Crystal Eastman. Price, postpaid, $1.71.

THE STEEL WORKERS. By John A. Fitch, New York Dept. of Labor. Price, postpaid, $1.71.

HOMESTEAD: THE HOUSEHOLDS OF A MILL TOWN. By Margaret F. Byington. Price, postpaid, $1.70.

THE PITTSBURGH DISTRICT. Symposium by John R. Commons, Robert A. Woods, Florence Kelley, Charles Mulford Robinson and others. (In preparation.)

PITTSBURGH: THE GIST OF THE SURVEY. By Paul U. Kellogg. (In preparation.)

HOUSING REFORM. A Handbook for Practical Use in American Cities. By LAWRENCE VEILLER. 220 pages. 5 schedules. Price, postpaid, $1.25.

A MODEL TENEMENT HOUSE LAW. By LAWRENCE VEILLER. 130 pages. Price, postpaid, $1.25.

AMONG SCHOOL GARDENS. By M. LOUISE GREENE, M.Pd., Ph.D. Illustrated. 380 pages. Price, postpaid, $1.25.

WORKINGMEN'S INSURANCE IN EUROPE. By LEE K. FRANKEL and MILES M. DAWSON, with the co-operation of LOUIS I. DUBLIN. 450 pages. 145 tables. Price, postpaid, $2.70.

THE CAMPAIGN AGAINST TUBERCULOSIS IN THE UNITED STATES: Including a Directory of Institutions. Compiled under direction of the National Association for Study and Prevention of Tuberculosis. By PHILIP P. JACOBS. 467 pages. Price, postpaid, $1.00.

REPORT ON THE DESIRABILITY OF ESTABLISHING AN EMPLOYMENT BUREAU IN THE CITY OF NEW YORK. By EDWARD T. DEVINE, Ph.D., LL.D. 238 pages. Price, postpaid, $1.00.

WIDER USE OF THE SCHOOL PLANT. By CLARENCE A. PERRY. Illustrated. 404 pages. Price, postpaid, $1.25.

—

CHARITIES PUBLICATION COMMITTEE
105 EAST 22D STREET, NEW YORK

The Homestead Plant, Carnegie Steel Company
To these mills and furnaces, the households of the community look for their livelihood

RUSSELL SAGE
FOUNDATION

HOMESTEAD
THE HOUSEHOLDS OF A MILL TOWN

BY

MARGARET F. BYINGTON
FORMERLY DISTRICT AGENT, BOSTON ASSOCIATED CHARITIES, ASSISTANT
SECRETARY, CHARITY ORGANIZATION DEPARTMENT,
RUSSELL SAGE FOUNDATION

THE PITTSBURGH SURVEY
FINDINGS IN SIX VOLUMES

EDITED BY

PAUL UNDERWOOD KELLOGG

NEW YORK
CHARITIES PUBLICATION
COMMITTEE . . . . MCMX

RUSSELL SAGE
FOUNDATION

—

⌐HOMESTEAD

THE HOUSEHOLDS OF A
MILL TOWN⌐

By

MARGARET F. BYINGTON

FORMERLY DISTRICT AGENT, BOSTON ASSOCIATED CHARITIES; ASSISTANT
SECRETARY, CHARITY ORGANIZATION DEPARTMENT,
RUSSELL SAGE FOUNDATION

THE PITTSBURGH SURVEY

FINDINGS IN SIX VOLUMES

EDITED BY

PAUL UNDERWOOD KELLOGG

NEW YORK
CHARITIES PUBLICATION
COMMITTEE . . . . . MCMX (1910)

d UCB ENVI

5   1986

531 36925

Envi.

Copyright, 1910, by

THE RUSSELL SAGE FOUNDATION

EDITOR'S FOREWORD

THE family as a social unit takes us back into shadows beyond where history begins; the town carries with it a thousand written memories of walled boroughs, county markets and communes, where self-government had its beginnings. But the mill with its acres of tracks and sheds, its continuous operation, its intricate plan of discipline, of interlocking processes, of insistent demands upon human nature, is a newer institution. Factory production is less than two centuries old. The power transmission through which the modern plant with its thousands of workmen has expanded and developed, is scarcely as many generations old. Electrically charged wires have become the binding nervous cords of industrial mechanism well within the memory of living men.

Miss Byington's study is essentially a portrayal of these two older social institutions, the family and the town, as they are brought into contact with this new insurgent third. Has their development and equipment kept pace with mechanical invention? Have they held their own against the mill? Is the balance of life and work preserved? Or have we, in the industrial town of twentieth century America, not a "deserted village" such as Goldsmith lamented in eighteenth century England, but a more serious, antithetical problem in an overcrowded, overwrought aggregate of households. The query is, not shall "every rood of ground maintain its man," but shall the day's work afford an adequate basis for American livelihood?

Such a description, however modest in scope and put forth in the homely imagery of domestic life, deals thus with the forces which are wrenching at the very structure of society. There are other, perhaps more obvious circumstances, which give this book a distinctive place in the general scheme of these volumes. The colleagues in the field work of the Pittsburgh Survey took up special factors affecting the welfare of the wage-earning population—such as sanitation, housing and public education; Miss Byington's commission was to analyze these factors as they enter jointly into the life of one of the small industrial communities which are characteristic of the Pittsburgh District, and especially to analyze them as they bear upon the well-being of family groups. Her book also complements Mr. Fitch's volume on wages and the general labor conditions in the steel industry.

In carrying out this commission, Miss Byington made an intimate case study of 90 households, employing methods of budget taking which have been developed for standard of living inquiries. She brought to her work, as basis for comparisons, an acquaintance with tenement conditions in New York and Boston. The resulting data have some rather obvious statistical shortcomings, which are explained in the appendix; but as a transcript of everyday economic existence, they served at once to re-enforce and to check up the impressions which grew out of her personal contact with the people who earned the money, and ate the food, and lived in the houses, and worshipped in the churches of this town. If the book inevitably brings out sharply the odds of life with which many industrial communities have to reckon, we trust that the loyalty of Homestead residents will not take offense that theirs should have been the town thus singled out for study. "The rank and file of the people are with you," said an old mill man. To housekeepers and steel workers, to professional and business people, who gave freely of their time and information, we cannot offer thanks, for the book is partly theirs. Theirs, also, are the two irrepressible, grim interrogations which underlie both the statistical tables and the bits of neighborly gossip with which the author has enlivened her narrative. In their bearings upon contemporary economic and social conditions, these are questions for a nation as well as for this community.

The first has to do with the town: how shall local self-government keep abreast of a nationalized industry?

The second has to do with the family: here is a town dependent upon one of the great industries of America, which has profited by brilliant invention, by organizing genius, by a national policy of tariff protection. It was studied at the close of the longest period of prosperity which has been known by our generation. What has that prosperity brought to the rank and file of the people whose waking hours are put into the industry?

Miss Byington has summed up in a single phrase the negative aspects of the situation so far as the men are concerned, who "turn daily from twelve hours in the din of the huge mills to home, supper, a smoke and bed." What steel production holds out to the families of these men she sets forth within the covers of this book.

PAUL U. KELLOGG
Director Pittsburgh Survey

TABLE OF CONTENTS

ix

LIST OF ILLUSTRATIONS

xi

LIST OF TABLES

LIST OF TABLES

LIST OF TABLES

XV

PITTSBURGH SURVEY
MAPS UNDER DIRECTION OF
SHELBY M. HARRISON
1905

MONONGAHELA RIVER

✝ CHURCHES

WEST HOMESTEAD

PART I

THE MILL AND THE TOWN

CHAPTER I

HOMESTEAD AND THE GREAT STRIKE

HOMESTEAD gives at the first a sense of the stress of industry rather than of the old time household cheer which its name suggests. The banks of the brown Monongahela are preëmpted on one side by the railroad, on the other by unsightly stretches of mill yards. Gray plumes of smoke hang heavily from the stacks of the long, low mill buildings, and noise and effort dominate what once were quiet pasture lands.

On the slope which rises steeply behind the mill are the Carnegie Library and the "mansion" of the mill superintendent, with the larger and more attractive dwellings of the town grouped about two small parks. Here and there the towers of a church rise in relief. The green of the parks modifies the first impression of dreariness by one of prosperity such as is not infrequent in American industrial towns. Turn up a side street, however, and you pass uniform frame houses, closely built and dulled by the smoke; and below, on the flats behind the mill, are cluttered alleys, unsightly and unsanitary, the dwelling place of the Slavic laborers. The trees are dwarfed and the foliage withered by the fumes; the air is gray, and only from the top of the hill above the smoke is the sky clear blue.

There is more to tell, however, than can be gained by first impressions. The Homestead I would interpret in detail is neither the mill nor the town, but is made up of the households of working people, the sturdy Scotch and Welsh and German of the early immigration, the sons of Yankee "buckwheats," and the daughters of Pennsylvania Dutch farmers. Set off against the hill streets, lined with these English-speaking homes, are the courts where all Austria-Hungary seems gathered afresh. Here are lodging houses filled with single men, where the " boarding bosses" keep accounts in Russian, Slovak or Hungarian; alley dwellings where immigrant families are venturing a permanent home in one or two rooms, near by the Slavic church where their children are christened and receive their first communion. It is the home life the mill town leads on the wages the mill pays that has been the subject of my study.

The glaring evils and startling injustices found on every hand in the congested sections of large cities supplied the first and strongest impetus toward social reform in this country. But many of the unwholesome living conditions which we associate with the poorer city neighborhoods are repeated in the average mill town with less excuse and with as bitter effects. Furthermore, industrial conditions, such as low wages and long hours of labor, have as direct an influence upon home life as high rents and bad sanitation, and their influence can be studied in a community which grows up about a single plant more easily than in one which presents the complications of a great city. With a knowledge of tenement districts in New York and Boston as a basis of comparison, I spent the greater part of a year in Homestead, studying the family side of the labor problem as presented there.

Homestead* is a community of approximately 25,000 people, chiefly mill workers and their families. There is today no labor organization among them. Trade unionism belonged to an earlier chapter in the history of the town. A generation of boys has now grown up and entered the mills without knowing by personal experience what unionism is, or, except by hearsay, what the great strike of 1892 was about. Yet, as the history of the town has been largely the history of the mill, I must first sketch the development of both, and the labor struggle which fifteen years ago determined the relations between them.

As late as 1870, two farms, the old McClure and West homesteads, occupied the site of the present mill and town. Scattered along the river on smaller holdings were the simple homes of a farming population. To get to Pittsburgh, seven miles down stream, the people had either to travel the distance by road or cross the river and take the Baltimore and Ohio Railroad at Brad-

---

* Politically, as will be noted later, Homestead is made up of three independent boroughs: in common speech the one term covers them all.

dock, two miles away.   In 1871, the Homestead Bank and Life
Insurance Company, which had bought the farms, cut them up into
building lots and put them on the market, intending that Homestead should be a residential suburb.   With the building of the
Pittsburgh, Virginia and Charleston Railroad in 1872, it became
possible for people doing business in the city to live in Homestead.
In 1874 the first church, St. John's Lutheran, was erected, and
the little village began to have a social life of its own.   In 1878,
when its population was about 600, Bryce and Highbie opened a
glass factory and the town's industrial history began.   Ten houses,
the first to be built for rent, were erected on Fifth Avenue for
the married workmen.   The land above the works was still an
open field where farmers from the nearby country drove their cows
to graze.

   In 1881, when Klomans built a steel mill on the banks
of the river, the step definitely determining the future of Homestead was taken.   The Klomans mill was absorbed by the Carnegie
Steel Company in 1886, and became in turn one of the most important plants of the United States Steel Corporation on its organization in 1901.   The site of Homestead made its part in this industrial development almost inevitable.   Situated on the Monongahela River, six miles below its confluence with the Youghiogheny
and seven miles above the point where with the Allegheny it
forms the Ohio, the town has unusual facilities for water carriage,
as well as the supply of water necessary for the processes of steel
manufacture.   Railroad and lake routes bring iron ores from
the mines of Michigan to meet here the fuel needed to reduce
them.   The river, which is navigable from Fairmont, West
Virginia,—a distance of over one hundred miles,—runs through a
region of bituminous mines.   It has been this nearness to the
coal beds which has made the Pittsburgh District a steel center,
and the level space in the bend of the river at Homestead the
floor of a great steel mill.

   By 1892, 8000 people had gathered at Homestead, though
the town still kept many of its village characteristics.   The
population was composed of a fairly homogeneous group,
most of them speaking the same language and mingling freely
in school, church and neighborhood life, as well as within the

mill. While it is impossible to secure any definite figures as to the make-up of the population in those days, certain facts give us a general picture of the earlier situation. Among the families visited for this study, half of the Americans and about half of the foreign born, who came from Great Britain and Western Europe, had been 15 years in Homestead; of 264 Slavs, however, only 31 were living here before the strike of 1892.

The churches founded before 1892 were Lutheran, Presbyterian, Methodist, Baptist, United Presbyterian, Episcopal, and German Evangelical. It was not until 1896 that a Slavic church was built. During the ten years following the starting of the mill, there was still much immigration to the United States from Great Britain and Germany, and the growing town was in a large measure recruited from these peoples. The good pay offered in the mills attracted also American boys. Apparently, the officials fostered this natural gravitation to the industry.

In a letter written in the early days, Captain Jones, of the Edgar Thomson Works, said, "My experience has shown that Germans, Irish, Swedes and 'buckwheats' (young American country boys), judiciously mixed, make the most effective, tractable force you can find. Scotsmen do very well, are honest and faithful. Welsh can be used in limited quantities. But Englishmen have been the worst class of men—sticklers for high wages, small production and strikes."*

According to an old resident, the men of each nationality often grouped themselves in separate mills, and, when there were good openings, sent to the old country for their friends. The ties thus created had their share in making possible an early development of trade unionism, for along with uniform standards of living, existed the opportunity to organize in order to secure conditions which would make those standards possible. Almost immediately after the opening of the mill the men formed a lodge of the Amalgamated Association of Iron and Steel Workers, and within a year there was a small, quickly settled strike.

The Homestead lodges grew steadily in power until they held an assured place. The wage scale was each year fixed by agreement between committees representing the Amalgamated Associa-

* Bridge, J. H.: Inside History of the Carnegie Steel Company, p. 81.

6

tion and the employers in the industry. Within the mill also the men had much influence, and in many minor points controlled the action even of the superintendents. There developed, however, a diversity of interest, not between the different races but between two main wage groups,—the less skilled men, many of whom are paid by the day, and the highly skilled workers upon whom the output of the mills depends, who are paid by the ton. The lodges of the Amalgamated Association, consisting almost entirely of the tonnage men, were charged with ignoring the interests of the day men. A man employed there at the time told me that some of the highly skilled workers, such as rollers,— who were really sub-bosses and were paid on the basis of the output of the gang under them,—made as much as $300 in two weeks. The rank and file felt with some bitterness that not only were the capitalists securing far more than their share of the proceeds of labor, but that these few among the workers were also unduly favored. False standards in some cases were developed by the abnormally high pay, and the tendency of the few to spend carelessly what had been earned thus easily gave the town a reputation for extravagance. A woman said, "My father used to earn $300 in two weeks and yet he never saved anything, and never tried to buy a house; that was because he drank. Why, now we have paid for our house and have money in the bank and the 'mister' never makes more than $25 a week." The reckless expenditure of the exceptionally paid men, however, apparently no more than reflected the general spirit of the Pittsburgh District in days when new processes were doubling output and money was easily made.

This, then, was the situation at the time of the great strike in 1892, which in so many ways influenced the future of Homestead. Within the five years preceding, the Carnegie Steel Company had doubled its capital and had increased the number of employes in Homestead alone to about 4000, 800 of whom were members of the Amalgamated Association. In 1889, a sliding scale had been introduced by which the rate of pay per ton varied with the market price of steel, under the proviso, however, that if the latter fell below $25 per ton no further reduction in wages was to be made. This agreement did not affect the wages of the day men. In the spring of 1892, the Association voted to renew the contract on the old terms, but the company demanded that the base should be $22 instead of $25 and that the contract should expire in January instead of July. After a number of conferences, the company advanced its minimum to $23 and the men reduced theirs to $24, but no concessions at all were made in regard to the date of expiration of the contract. The men felt that in case of disagreement and strike they would be at a far greater disadvantage in the winter when lack of work would be more keenly felt. The company, on the other hand, claimed that as its commercial contracts were frequently made to date from January 1, it was necessary to know at that time what was to be the labor cost for the ensuing year.

Behind these ostensible points of disagreement, however, lay one fundamental issue which, though seldom mentioned, was the keynote of the strike,—trade unionism. The Amalgamated Association had been taking to itself more and more power. A small group secured the desirable positions; the permission of the Association had to be obtained before any of its members could be discharged. It stood in the way of lowering individual wage rates, and in general not only obstructed the free hand which the company wanted but interfered with many details of operation.

In 1889, H. C. Frick became chairman of Carnegie Brothers and Company. As he had aroused the antagonism of the labor world through his suppression of the strike in the coke region a few years before, the mill men feared that he would crush the Amalgamated Association. More keen, therefore, than their interest in the points at issue was the belief that if they failed in this strike, the power, if not the very existence of the union, would go. This fear accounts for the pertinacity with which the struggle was fought to the finish and for the deep-seated bitterness which followed the men's defeat.

The strike began June 30. The Association, which had been so recently indifferent to the condition of the day men, now realized, since many of the latter could be put into the skilled positions, that the strike could not be won without their assistance. A call was thereupon issued for them to strike, and the day men, with everything to lose and almost nothing to gain, went out too, and

8

Photo by Emil J. Kloes

HOMESTEAD FROM THE PITTSBURGH SIDE OF THE MONONGAHELA

remained faithful supporters to the end. A committee of fifty men, called the advisory board, conducted the strike.

Shortly after the trouble began, the company attempted to bring into the mill some 300 men in charge of Pinkerton detectives. The strikers had feared that the company would do this, since Mr. Frick had called in the Pinkertons at the Connellsville coke strike and bloodshed had followed. The detectives started up the river in boats in the early morning of July 6, and a scout who had been stationed by the strikers came on horseback to warn the town. The story of that morning, as it is retold among the people of Homestead, suggests vividly the ride of Paul Revere to rouse other insurgents more than a century earlier. Men and women hurried to the mill, weapons were hunted up and barricades erected. Which side fired the first shot is still a debated question, but a miniature battle followed in which seven persons were killed and others wounded. The Pinkertons finally surrendered, were brought into the town and later were returned to Pittsburgh. There are conflicting stories as to the incidents of the day, stories of bloodshed and cruelty. The one clear fact is that the mob fury latent in most men was wakened by that first shot. It is hard to believe that the sober, self-contained workmen who told me the story fifteen years afterward had been part of the frenzied crowd on the river bank.

As is so often the case, however, that July morning overshadowed in the minds of the public the true character and significance of the determined struggle, which under conservative leadership lasted four or five months. For after the first clash the question became one of endurance, and though the state militia were called in no further disturbance of any magnitude arose. One woman, the owner of a number of small houses, told me that in the latter part of the strike she rented some of them to non-union men, but that contrary to her expectation she experienced no personal annoyance. Quietly, stubbornly, the men continued the fight. The contributions which poured in from fellow workmen and the public prevented physical suffering; sympathetic strikes kept up their courage, as did the difficulty of the company in finding men to take their places. In the meantime the life of the town went on, changed but little by the in-

9

dustrial conflict.   The local papers tell of weddings, of picnics, of church suppers and of the casual comings and goings of the townspeople, while in the mill below was being contested, though in a waiting game, the issue which was to determine in many respects the future of the village.

Since the whole town was in one way or another dependent on the mill, the interest even of small merchants and others not directly concerned was of course intense.   While some of the people appreciated the weak points in the claims of the Amalgamated Association, the general feeling was so strong that no one would express an opinion unfavorable to the union.   The mild tone of the local papers leads one to believe that they did not reflect the state of the public mind, with its resentment at the presence of the soldiers and its alternations of hope and despair as to the outcome of the summer.   About the middle of October the men realized that they had failed, and went back —those who could get their old jobs—at a wage determined by the company.   A few were refused positions, and many others who found that their places in the mill had been taken by the strike breakers had either to take inferior positions or go elsewhere. The resulting bitterness made itself felt for years in the relation of the men to the Carnegie Company.   When you talk with a skilled and intelligent man who is still refused work in any mill of the United States Steel Corporation because of the part he played in that strike, over fifteen years ago, you realize why the passions it aroused have not died out.   For most of the town, life resumed its normal course.   Newspapers in New Orleans and St. Paul and San Francisco ceased to discuss Homestead; it dropped back to its place among industrial towns, facing for good or ill the problems which this changed labor situation created.

Looking back from the vantage ground of the present, one is impressed by the vital character of the questions at issue.   The particular change in the wage scale which was ostensibly the point under dispute, was, comparatively speaking, a small matter; the significant fact is that every cut since has been accepted by the men without hope and with no effective protest.

There was involved a question of social equity apart from

whether the union carried its interference in mill administration to unwarranted lengths, or whether the company had grounds for adopting its inflexible policy of suppressing any labor organizations among the men. This question was whether the workmen in the industry were to profit in the long run by improved and cheapened processes of production; in other words, was mechanical progress to mean a real increase of prosperity to the community as the years passed. If the Homestead strike had been won by the men, the company would have continued to recognize that settled employes have some claims with respect to the terms of their employment, and to grant them a voice in the wage adjustments which from time to time determine what share of the proceeds of production belongs to labor. It may well be questioned whether the standards of living for steel employes would have settled to their present levels.

The union ceased to exist, and since that date those common factors in employment which circumscribe a man's life,—his hours, his wages, and the conditions under which he works,—and which in turn vitally affect the well-being of his family; these he was to have less and less share in determining.

CHAPTER II

THE MAKE-UP OF THE TOWN

THE strike ended, mill and town continued their rapid growth until little is now left to suggest the village which in 1870 we saw developing on the farms beside the river. The changes of the intervening years, however, except for the influx of the Slavs, have been gradual and unnoticed. Their history is unwritten, and our real interest lies rather in the present development, in the type of town which the great plant and its 7000 employes have created at Homestead. The population is typical of the newer American industrial centers as distinguished from the New England village or the western county seat. It is a town primarily of workingmen—a town of many transients. It is, moreover, strikingly representative of the two waves of immigration,—the first, of Teutons and Celts, the later, of Slavs—and of the great social cleavage between them.

While at the date of this study there were no detailed statistics of nationalities making up the population, the census of 1900 reported for the borough of Homestead, 4528 native white of native parents, 3781 native white of foreign parents, 3594 foreign born white, 640 Negroes, and 11 Chinese; that is, about 36 per cent of the population was native white of native parents. This percentage is fairly typical of mill towns in the steel district, as shown by a comparison with nearby industrial boroughs (Table 2).

Facts obtained as to the birthplace of men employed in the mill in July, 1907, the greater number of whom live in Homestead, give with fair accuracy the racial groups represented in the present foreign born population. Of 6772 employes, 1925, or 28.4 per cent, were native white, 121 colored, 398 English, 259 Irish, 129 Scotch, 176 German, 3603 Slavs,* and 161 other European

* In this book "Slav" is used as a general term to include Magyars and Lithuanians, as well as those belonging to the Slavic race. For an exhaustive and thoroughly interesting account of the immigration to this country from Austro-Hungary see Balch, Emily Greene: Our Slavic Fellow Citizens. New York, Charities Publication Committee, 1910.

12

Drawn by Joseph Stella

TABLE 1.—TOTAL POPULATION, AND NUMBER AND PER CENT OF NATIVE AND FOREIGN BORN IN HOMESTEAD, 1900

Total Population	Native White of Native Parents		Native White of Foreign Parents		Foreign Born White		Colored	
	Number	Per cent	Number	Per cent	Number	Per cent	Number	Per cent
12,554	4528	36.0	3781	30.1	3594	28.6	651	5.2

TABLE 2.—TOTAL POPULATION, AND PER CENT OF NATIVE WHITE AND FOREIGN BORN IN FOUR BOROUGHS OF ALLEGHENY COUNTY, 1900*

Borough	Total Population	Native White of Native Parents		Native White of Foreign Parents		Foreign Born White		Colored	
		Number	Per cent	Number	Per cent	Number	Per cent	Number	Per cent
Braddock	15654	4887	31.2	5098	32.6	5105	32.6	564	3.6
Duquesne	9036	2765	30.6	2628	29.1	3448	38.2	195	2.2
Millvale	6736	2088	31.0	3056	45.4	1581	23.5	11	0.2
Sharpsburg	6842	2766	40.4	2539	37.1	1279	18.7	258	3.8

TABLE 3.—TOTAL EMPLOYES, AND NUMBER AND PER CENT OF VARIOUS RACIAL GROUPS IN THE HOMESTEAD PLANT, CARNEGIE STEEL CO., JULY, 1907

Total Employes	Number and Per cent of							
	Native White	English	Irish	Scotch	German	Other Europeans	Slav	Colored
6772	1925	398	259	129	176	161	3603	121
100.0	28.4	16.6					53.2	1.8

*Twelfth U. S. Census, 1900.

13

nationalities. These figures show the absence of Italians as a factor in the labor situation in the mills, and the predominance of Slavs, who form over 53 per cent of the total number employed.

As Germans and British tend to amalgamate with the native whites the community has fallen more or less naturally into two major groups,—the English-speaking and the Slavs.

The Negroes form a third group, much fewer in numbers, allied to the first group by a common speech, but resembling the second in the attitude toward them in the earlier days when they were looked down upon as intruders of alien blood. In Homestead, Negroes are not engaged in domestic service as in most northern cities, but are employed in the mill or in the building trades. Of those who are now in the mills, some came in the first instance as strike breakers and have advanced to well-paid positions. I call to mind especially a man who, starting as a laborer, is now a roller, the highest skilled of the steel workers. These men have in the main come to adopt the same standards as their white neighbors, and are usually treated with genuine respect by the latter, but there is still some sense of resentment roused by the success of the Negroes or their pretensions to gentility. An interesting instance of this attitude came to my attention. A white woman who had been for many years a resident of Homestead was especially vexed because a nearby house had been sold to a Negro. Some weeks later I visited the wife of this colored property owner, who had been ill, and she told me feelingly how good her white neighbors had been to her. She spoke especially of this older resident who had complained to me, and mentioned how she had brought dainties and finally helped persuade her to go to the hospital. Thus, though social distinctions still exist and the colored people have their own lodges and churches, the more prosperous among them are winning respect.*

The break between the Slavs and the rest of the community is on the whole more absolute than that between the whites and

*There is a totally different class of colored people, who run houses of ill fame and gambling resorts on Sixth Avenue; a "sporty" element which is much in evidence and creates for the race an unpleasant notoriety. These people frequently appear in police courts and form a low element in the town's life.

the Negroes. Neither in lodge nor in church, nor, with a few exceptions, in school, do the two mingle. Even their living places are separated; the Second Ward, except for those who owned homes there in earlier years, has been largely abandoned to the newer immigrants. This sharp division, while partly due to the barrier which differences in language and custom create, is intensified by a feeling of scorn for the newcomers on the part of the older residents. They are "Hunkies," that is all, and many an American workman who earns but a few cents a day more looks upon them with an utter absence of kinship. The more intelligent Slavs, who desire better things for their people, feel this lack of understanding keenly, for they realize the handicap it means in their upward struggle.

The change from the early homogeneous group of workmen in Homestead is due in part to the fact that the general tide of immigrants now setting toward the United States comes from the Slavic countries, and in part to the increasing demand for manual laborers able to do the hard, unskilled work in the mills. This heavy labor the English-speaking group is now less willing to perform and here the Slav finds his opportunity.

The population of the town has also been affected by the fact that the steel industry calls for the work of men only. In the census for 1900, we find that of the 12,554 people in Homestead borough, 7,141, or 56.9 per cent, were males, while in Allegheny County as a whole the males formed 52 per cent, and in the entire United States but 51.2. The preponderance of males was even greater among the immigrant population in Homestead, constituting 63.4 per cent of the foreign born. Furthermore, of the men employed in the mill, 35.3 per cent are unmarried, though only 10.2 per cent are under twenty. The large transient body of single men, as we shall see in Chapter XI, constitutes a serious menace to home life among the Slavs. Other transients are also numerous, and their presence lessens the effective civic force of the community. Among them are many young college graduates employed in the mechanical departments of the mill, who do not consider themselves permanent residents. My acquaintance with those met in two boarding houses in Homestead showed me that their interest in the town was casual. Few take any active share either in local politics or in movements to improve local conditions.

The families of the English-speaking workers, however, are bound together by common interests and common ties. They live near enough to see each other easily, their lives are molded by similar forces and as a result a more than usual degree of sympathy exists among them. This is shown perhaps most strikingly in the great kindnesses of neighbor to neighbor in times of distress. Such acts are not looked upon as charity. If a man is ill, the men in his mill take up a collection for his needs as friend for friend, knowing that when the need is theirs he will return the kindness. A man told me of his experience when he was laid up four months with rheumatism. He had begun to worry about bills, for when pay day came no pay was due him. But his "buddy" walked in with an envelope containing a sum of money. Later, when this was exhausted, the men made another gift. He accepted it very simply, almost as a matter of course, the thought of similar gifts he had made, and others he would make, keeping him from feeling any sense of obligation. This sense of community of interest I found helped greatly to strengthen the fraternal organizations.

In the main, then, this is a town of wage-earners. None of those extremes of wealth and social position that exist in cities are found here. There is a small social circle composed of business and professional men and the officials in the mill. As some of the most skilled workmen earn more than the minor officials over them, the line between workmen and superintendents is not a sharp one. In the days of small industries the mill owner lived in the mill town, maintaining there his social as well as economic leadership, stimulating its activities and playing his part in movements for its well-being. But the individual mill owner is a thing of the past. Stockholders have taken his place. They are scattered all over the country and know their property only as a source of dividends, giving in return neither interest nor stimulus to the workers; and managers and superintendents, however public spirited, shift and change.

Drawn by Joseph Stella

HEAD: SLAVIC DAY LABORER

These are some of the changes in the social make-up of the borough which have come with that business development which has made the Homestead mills part of a national industry, and with that labor policy which has opened the doors to all comers and has tolerated no control of the situation by the men on the ground. Under such conditions of growth it is well to ask how adequately the physical difficulties of building a town on the river bank have been mastered; what has been the development of civic and political institutions to meet the needs of the changing community; and what the economic development of the borough, outside of the great industry itself.

My inquiry into these things has been limited intentionally to certain aspects of the situation as reflected in the household life.

We have seen that industrial factors—easy access to ores, water, transportation, etc.—made Homestead an ideal mill site. As a site for a town it is not ideal.* The river in hollowing its way through the hills sometimes left a narrow rim along its banks, but more often the descent to the water's edge is abrupt. The larger level space at a sharp bend was chosen as the site for the mill. As the plant was at first small the buildings did not monopolize the entire river front, and the low ground then open to the river furnished ample room for the homes of the workers. The mill, however, grew rapidly and spread over more and more of the level, till now its buildings stretch for a mile along the water. In its growth it has encroached on some of the territory already occupied by houses. The last to go were the rows of little shanties inside the mill grounds erected to shelter the strike breakers of 1892,—a settlement called Potterville, after the superintendent in charge during the strike. These houses were demolished some four years ago and the tenants had to move to the already crowded districts just outside. This congestion, due to the desire of the employes for homes near their work, is increased by the steepness of the hill behind, a weary climb after the labor of the day. As the site of the mill was extended up the river, houses were built further along the hillside and also along the ravines where the slope was more gradual. In this way the town pushed

* See map, facing page 1.

out beyond the narrow triangle with its base on the river, which formed the original borough. Instead, however, of extending the boundaries of Homestead to cover this new territory two additional boroughs were created, Munhall on the east and West Homestead on the west. Consequently we have the curious anomaly of a town that is a social and industrial unit parceled off into three politically independent boroughs.

Munhall, the eastern part of the hill, was originally separated from Homestead by a ravine, and was largely the property of John Munhall, one of the oldest residents of the town. Adjoining was the site of the Pittsburgh City Poor Farm. It was here that the state militia were quartered in 1892. Soon after the strike, the property was bought up by the Carnegie Land Company, now a constituent part of the United States Steel Corporation. Before any lots were offered for sale, streets were laid out, sewers, running water and electricity put in, and houses planned and erected. The majority of the larger houses were sold to mill employes, and those that the company still owns can only be rented by them. In 1901, on application of the property owners, the borough was incorporated.* It included not only the land owned by the Carnegie Land Company, but three-quarters of the mill property itself. Munhall thus forms a geographical triangle similar to Homestead, the mill occupying the base on the river and the residence portion lying on the hill above.

Beyond Munhall lies the "Hollow," a deep ravine with a meandering stream at the bottom and with irregular rows of houses, often hardly more than shanties, on either hand. Forty-four acres of land hang upon the sides of the two abrupt hills. The land is owned by the John Munhall Estate; and the 250 frame, box-like houses, many of them no larger than two rooms,

* This action was taken under a provision of the state constitution that any section of a township may, with the approval of the county court, be formed into a borough on the vote of a majority of its electors. The site of the Carnegie steel plant at Homestead was formerly part of Mifflin township and the township collected all the tax. It was found that the tax rate on other parts of the township was being reduced to a minimum while the bulk of the tax receipts coming from the steel plant was being used in rural parts and very little spent in the neighborhood of the works. The new borough of Munhall was organized and the taxes paid by the works were thereafter expended within its boundaries.

Photo by Hine

Detached Dwellings of the Better Type, Sixteenth Avenue, Munhall

These were originally built by the Carnegie Land Company

are owned mostly by unskilled laborers in the mills. The Munhall Estate lets the land upon which the workers build their houses on ten-year leases. Like the Cabbage Patch in which the Wiggses lived, it is a "queer neighborhood where ramshackle cottages play hop-scotch" over the crooked ditch and up the hillsides. The property is not surveyed into streets, there being only one public thoroughfare, an unpaved dirt road running lengthwise of the hollow; and, along most of the road, the owner seems in building his house to have "faced it any way his fancy prompted." The borough has installed street lights along this road, and has placed perhaps half a dozen upon the private property of the estate; but there are no sewers nor other public improvements.

A branch line of street cars running through the Hollow connects with a rather promising suburb called Homeville, built on the hill slopes at the end of the ravine. Another branch line runs straight back from the river over the top of the hill to Homestead Park and Lincoln Place, suburbs attractively situated on high ground. Whitaker, which adjoins Munhall to the east, has a population of about 2000, largely wage-earners. As these men work in the mill, and their families shop in Homestead, they might fairly be included in the Homestead census. Hays, toward Pittsburgh, is another borough that is at least in a measure a part of the Homestead community.

Nearer by, formed by the extension of Homestead to the west, in much the same way that Munhall was created to the east, is West Homestead. Disregarding the outlying settlements, these three boroughs may be said to make up the fairly compact but politically divided community which has been gathered together by the Homestead mill. Though West Homestead contains less wealth than Munhall, it includes the plant of the Mesta Machine Company, the only other considerable industry in the town. Each of these separate boroughs elects its own officials, makes its own ordinances, and provides through taxation for its own needs. Through this division the taxable properties of the great industries are separated from the central borough, which has by far the largest population and which, with the exception of Munhall Hollow, includes the sections where the poorest workers live. On this point, I can quote from Shelby M. Harrison, a

colleague in the work of the Pittsburgh Survey, who compares
the fiscal situation in Homestead and Munhall as follows:

> The mill-worker resident in Homestead is affected by
> the tax question from at least two directions. First, over
> three-fourths of the mill property is located in Munhall
> borough where, except in 1907, the tax rate has never
> been over half that in Homestead, the borough in which a
> majority of the mill workers live. In 1907, property in
> Munhall paid a total borough and school tax of 8¼ mills
> on the dollar, while in the same year Homestead property
> paid 15 mills.* This artificial division into separate taxing
> districts of a community which is in practically all senses a

TABLE 4.—HOMESTEAD AND MUNHALL TAXES, 1907

| Boroughs | Assessed Valuation of Property | MILLAGE | | | Total Tax |
		Borough	School	Total	
Munhall	$6,957,630	3⅛	4¾	8¼	$ 57,400.45
Homestead . . .	9,120,765	8	7	15	136,811.48
Total	$16,078,395				$194,211.93

unit, however that division may have come about, relieves
the Steel Corporation from much of its local responsibility
as a property holder. Its relief means a heavier burden
upon the residents of Homestead; some one must build
and maintain schools and public works, protect person and
property, and support local government. The burden is
further accentuated by the tendency among assessors, common in all industrial centers, to value small properties at
much nearer their full market value than they do large
properties—especially large manufacturing plants. Conservative estimates by persons familiar with the situation

* In 1908, the rates were, Munhall, 8¼ mills, Homestead, 16 mills; in 1909,
Munhall, 8¼ mills, Homestead, 18 mills. In 1910, with no statement or explanation to the taxpayers, the Homestead borough council jumped the borough millage
from 10 to 13. The school tax for 1910 is 9 mills, the total local rate thus reaching
22 mills, or 2.2 per cent of the assessed value of property, a rate 2¾ times that in
Munhall.

indicate that the mill property in both boroughs is not assessed upon more than 30 per cent of its actual value, whereas Homestead residence property will average an assessed valuation equal to 80 per cent of its market value. Thus, in reality, the tax rate upon much the greater part of the mill property must be more than cut in two for purposes of comparison. A rate of 8¼ mills on a 30 per cent valuation is equal to 2.5 mills on full valuation; and 15 mills on an 80 per cent valuation equals 12 mills on full value; so that the real tax rates closely approximate 2.5 mills for the corporation against 12 mills, practically five times as much, for the everyday Homestead taxpayer. The same percentages would hold with respect to county taxes.

On the other hand, if this social and industrial unit were made a municipal unit, then instead of Munhall paying a tax of 8¼ mills on the dollar, as in 1907, and Homestead paying 15 mills on the dollar, the united boroughs could receive the same total revenues as before by paying 12 mills upon the same valuations. This would reduce the tax rate for the Homestead householder by three mills, or 20 per cent less than his present rates. It would raise the tax rate on a majority of the corporation property 3¾ mills, or 45 per cent. Raising the assessed valuation of the property of the steel company to the general level would reduce the householders' rates still further.

Second, the Homestead borough government aggravates this heavy burden of taxation instead of lightening it. In direct contrast to conditions in Munhall, where the influence of the Carnegie Steel Company practically dominates borough action and has made the local government efficient and without suspicion of graft, an appreciable part of Homestead's public funds has been squandered upon enterprises that have failed, the cost of improvements is excessive, and the city's finances are looked after in an utterly haphazard fashion. In 1907–8, $95,000 was outstanding as delinquent taxes—much over half the sum annually assessed in taxes for the borough. Although the borough bears a big debt burden, and although its bonds stipulate that a sinking fund must be established for their retirement, no sinking fund has existed for a number of years. Yet borrowing is resorted to with small concern. In 1907 the bonded debt amounted to $441,500, and the current debt to $16,933,—$458,000 in all.* The borough

---

* In March, 1910, the borough was $621,776.03 in debt,—certainly near, if not actually beyond, the limit of its borrowing privilege,—and was arranging to

21

has been selling bonds from time to time to pay current expenses—a broad, easy, spendthrift course, paved with engraved promises, which, if persisted in, must lead to ultimate loss of credit and bankruptcy."

The mill's escape, then, from the local government burden, and the town's aggravation of that burden, come down on the families of working people, either as house-owners or as payers of the high rents current in the borough.

HOMESTEAD AS A CIVIC UNIT

It is with Homestead borough in 1907–8 that this household study is primarily concerned, and in judging its public activities we must consider the limitations of borough resources noted, and the state restrictions upon borough authority, coupled with the industrial conditions which, as we shall see, circumscribe the effective citizenship of the mill workers. These have had a part in the failures in self-government which have characterized this community, along with many others in America. For while the town has grown steadily both in population and territory, civic interest and the well-being resulting from sound political organization have not kept pace with this growth. The school board and the board of health have the respect of the town, and men of standing are willing to serve on them. But the borough legislature, a council of fifteen members, has been controlled in Homestead by the type of small politician to be found in office wherever wholesale liquor dealers dominate politics and where the local government is used merely as a feeder for a state political machine.* Townspeople with whom I talked had apparently ceased to expect intelligent action on their part. Serious charges of dishonesty in

float $45,000 additional bonds. The borough clerk's published estimates of municipal assets total only $509,874.28 —over $100,000 less than its total indebtedness. In authorizing the new bonds a resolution was adopted providing for the maintenance of a sinking fund in the future. Homestead borough's system of public accounting is neither a system nor accounting; the borough treasurer was not only without a personal bond for several months recently, but he allowed several thousand dollars of certificates to go to protest while the books of the clerk showed that the treasurer had money of the borough in his possession sufficient to pay them. Some years the borough auditors have not audited the accounts of the treasurer giving as a reason that the treasurer kept no books.

* John F. Cox, the Republican "boss" of the borough, was in 1908 speaker of the Pennsylvania House of Representatives, which has long since ceased to represent the people of Pennsylvania.

Photo by Hine

"THE MANSION"

The company-owned home of the Superintendent. The purpose in providing it is, of course, to make it practicable for the responsible executive to be within call of the works.

Photo by Hine

THE STREET

Homestead's only outdoor playground in 1907. These children, through no will of their own, live within sound of the mill. There was as yet no provision for their simplest recreational needs in the scheme of things laid out by their elders.

awarding bids for a garbage plant and of bribery in connection with other matters had been brought against members in 1904. While the testimony given at the investigation leaves no doubt in the mind of the reader that there had been crooked dealings, it was suppressed and led to no action.

Apart from these allegations of dishonesty, the council has acquired a reputation for general inefficiency. It has been slow to insist on sanitary regulations necessitated by the increasing density of population. The first forward step from the primitive sanitation of village days was taken the year after the strike, when the streets were paved, and sewers and town water put in. A large percentage of the houses, especially the cheaper ones, nevertheless had neither running water nor toilets in them in 1907–8.*

The water supply of the borough is drawn from the Monongahela River. This stream is contaminated by the sewage of many small towns, as well as of two cities, McKeesport and Connellsville, the former with a population of about 40,000 and the latter of 10,000. In addition the water, some of which drains from the mines, has been used over and over for the processes of steel and coke manufacture, and is impregnated with chemicals, especially sulphuric acid. One Homestead resident said, "No respectable microbe would live in it." In this probably lies the explanation of why the typhoid death rate in Homestead has been low (6 deaths in 1907) in contrast to Pittsburgh. While these chemicals may destroy the bacteria to a considerable extent, they are not in themselves ingredients of good drinking water. This water was formerly pumped directly from the river into the reservoir, but in 1904–5 a number of wells were driven at a short distance from the river, with the idea that the water draining into them would thus be gravel-filtered before it was pumped into the reservoir. I was told, however, by a physician and a town official that these wells do not supply enough water, and that when they give out the reservoir is again filled directly from the stream. After this plant was constructed the water was analyzed by the

---

*I am told that there has been a marked increase in these sanitary improvements since. (See Appendix VI. p. 222. Report, Homestead Board of Health For comment on the Pittsburgh Survey, see p. 224.)

state board of health and reported safe for drinking. When I first went to live in Homestead I attempted to use water that had been boiled but not filtered, and found it exceedingly distasteful. Local physicians forbid people to drink the borough water unless it has been boiled and filtered, and many refuse to use it at all for drinking purposes.

Most residents seemed to accept such a situation as a matter of course. Until recently conditions in Pittsburgh and McKeesport have been equally bad,* so that Homestead had no compelling nearby example to make its people realize that a satisfactory water system was possible. Instead of attempting to improve the town supply, many have drawn their drinking water from wells. No ordinances govern the location of these wells. In the courts of Slavic dwellings they are often near drains which carry waste water to the privy vaults, and when the pavements are broken this water must leak into the wells with but little filtration. Moreover, the board of health does not inspect the wells nor analyze the water from them, except at private expense. One outbreak of typhoid was traced directly to a well which had been used by a number of families because the water was supposed to be particularly good.

Not only is the quality of the water supplied by the borough of Homestead poor, but there is no ordinance requiring running water in tenements. The borough clerk does not know how many houses are without it since he charges the water tax to each property holder in a lump sum with no indication as to the number of families supplied. The landlords, who seem to be influential with the council, naturally oppose such a requirement, and becaus: of a shortage in dwelling houses have been under no pressure to put in water taps in order to rent the older or cheaper buildings. The men with larger wages and more influence move into houses which at least have running water in the kitchens. Immigrant laborers continue to carry water in and out from a common hydrant in the court. In different sections, also, I found young American families who had no running water in the house, and

* Munhall borough today purchases filtered water from the South Pittsburgh Water Company. McKeesport treats and mechanically filters its water; Pittsburgh has built huge sand filtration beds. These plants have been put into operation within the last three years.

Photo by Hine

GLEN ALLEY, A FEW BLOCKS FROM FRICK PARK HOMESTEAD

who complained that they could not afford to move to better quarters. But though the husbands had votes and had friends with votes, it apparently never occurred to them to attempt to secure what they wanted through public action.

More serious is the indifference of many of the residents, including the officials, to the evils resulting from unflushed privy vaults. Though a borough ordinance requires that vaults be connected with the sewer, it demands no adequate means of flushing them. Physicians felt that conditions in the Second Ward near the mill were so bad that the council should pass an ordinance requiring that all closets be placed within the house and properly flushed; yet no steps were taken to secure it. There are, furthermore, no building laws, except one which requires that buildings on the business streets shall be fireproof. In regulating overcrowding or other unsanitary conditions the board of health has authority to act in cases which can be classed as nuisances.* Under the authority thus granted it has insisted in many instances upon the cleansing of vaults, the destruction of particularly unsanitary closets, and upon turning some of the boarders out of especially overcrowded tenements. Thus, in 1907 the sanitary officers reported that they had compelled the cleaning of 848 yards and 176 cellars, and the opening of 254 closets; forced owners to abandon 42 outside closets and place new ones in houses; had 201 stopped sewers cleaned and 48 new sewer connections made; removed 64 boarders from overcrowded houses and compelled the cleaning of 48 rooms found in unsanitary condition and the windows of 161 rooms in residences and of 12 in schools. There are, however, no municipal regulations as to overcrowding, ventilation or sanitation that would create specific standards which all property owners might be compelled to meet.

The death rate for 1907, 24 per 1000, indicated the need of

---

*Borough Ordinance:—Whatever is dangerous to human life or health; whatever renders the air or food or water or other drinks unwholesome; and whatever building, erection or part or cellar thereof is overcrowded or not provided with adequate means of ingress and egress, or is not sufficiently supported, ventilated, sewered, drained, cleaned or lighted, are declared to be nuisances, and to be illegal, and every person having aided in creating or contributing to the same, or who may support, continue or retain any of them, shall be deemed guilty of a violation of this ordinance, and also be liable for the expense of the abatement and remedy thereof.

further sanitary precautions. Of the 416 deaths, 94, or 22.6 per cent, were from pneumonia and tuberculosis, and 65, or 15.6 per cent, were from marasmus, cholera infantum and convulsions. That is, 38.2 per cent of the total number of deaths were from diseases closely connected with lack of sufficient air, good food and intelligent care of children.

Altogether, the public seems to take little active interest in the situation. The burgess,* in 1908, reported that the results of an investigation of overcrowding in the lodging houses, which he himself had made, aroused no general interest.

Inefficient as the local government may be in dealing with sanitary problems, the general run of landlords give no evidence of a greater sense of responsibility for solving them. This is illustrated in the conditions permitted by the big private estate in the adjoining borough of Munhall. The "run" in Munhall Hollow amounts to an open sewer bringing down filth and débris from other settlements farther up the valley through which its tributaries pass. In the hot summer months, the stench becomes almost unbearable, making it frequently necessary to haul lime in by the wagon load, to be dumped along the bed of the creek. When the rains are heavy in the spring, the valley is often so flooded that the water fills many of the cellars and even comes in much above the first floors of the houses at the lower end of the hollow.

It may be well to note how this peculiar form of landlordism affects the home life of a considerable group of mill employes. The system of leasing followed by the Munhall Estate makes it more or less easy to shift responsibility for the continuance of primitive conditions in the Hollow. By the terms of the short-time leases, the tenants agree to pay a stipulated land rent, and all taxes and water rates in addition. The local rule is that public improvements, such as paving, sewers, etc., shall be assessed one-third against the borough and two-thirds against abutting property owners; and naturally improvements are not made unless there is a demand among property owners for them. Since the agreement of the tenants to pay taxes includes the two-thirds of the cost of public improvements, they do not urge the building of public works which will benefit the Munhall Estate and might only tend to raise rents every ten years.

* The burgess is the chief executive officer of the borough.

The agent, on the other hand, maintains that the houses do not belong to the Estate, and that it is not responsible for bad conditions inside a tenant's lot and house; the land rents are low and the tenant should take enough interest in his home to improve it. Furthermore, the most serious sanitary problem, as the Estate sees it, and the one to be dealt with first, is the brook, both when it keeps within its banks and when it overflows them. The agent feels that this is not even a Munhall borough problem; for since the stream and its tributaries drain a wide area, the state of Pennsylvania is best fitted to act and the responsibility is laid at its door, and until it acts other things must wait.

Munhall Borough in turn clears its skirts of responsibility for the Hollow on the ground that the land is private property and that its condition is the concern of the Munhall Estate. The borough has not yet regarded the condition of the Hollow as a possible menace to the health of the whole community.

Meanwhile, a very appreciable proportion of the residents of Munhall, those with the scantiest resources of health and pocketbook, live in this damp, odorous gap between the hills, contending with disease, floods and an occasional fire.

To turn from questions of public health to those of good order, we find the situation if anything less promising. The borough police force has for years failed to enforce the liquor laws. The man who was chief in 1908 formerly ran a gambling place under the guise of a club,* and while he was held to be capable, it was commonly reported that he owed his position to the liquor interests. I was told that the numerous "speakeasies" were left undisturbed as long as they bought from the wholesalers in power. In Munhall there are no saloons; in Homestead, over 50, eight being in a single block on Eighth Avenue next the mill entrance. A Homesteader summed up the situation in this way: "We have at least 65 saloons, 10 wholesale liquor stores, a number of beer

---

* In 1908 this place, the Colonial Club, was closed, and a new chief of police was elected. There is also a new burgess, Thomas L. Davis, superintendent of a mill in the Jones and Laughlin Steel Co., the largest independent plant in Pittsburgh. He is a Welshman, but has lived in Homestead for many years. A general toning up of the police situation has accompanied his administration. Moreover, the Taxpayers' League, which was organized to carry on a good government campaign, succeeded in electing one member of the Council, M. P. Schooley, a man of personal independence and civic spirit.

27

agents, innumerable 'speakeasies,' and a dozen or more drug stores,"—and this in a community of 25,000.

In common with the whole industrial district, Homestead suffers from a system of aldermanic courts which prevails throughout Pennsylvania, and is ill devised to serve other than rural communities. The system is especially open to petty tyranny and corruption in dealing with an immigrant population. All misdemeanors are tried before local "squires" or justices of the peace, who can impose fines or short terms of imprisonment, and can also act in civil suits involving amounts of less than $300. These justices and the constables who serve under them are elected by the voters of the borough and serve for a period of five years. They receive no salary but are paid certain fees; for example, the fee for issuing a warrant is fifty cents and the same sum for a hearing in a criminal case or for taking bail in such a case. The constable receives one dollar for executing a warrant or for conveying the defendant to jail. These men are often uneducated, with no training in the law, and dependent for income on the number of arrests made. Obviously, many fail to comprehend the importance of dealing equitably with minor offenders. Of the cases of disorderly conduct reported in the newspapers from January 1 to March 31, 1908, there were 121 in which sentence was pronounced. Of these, 80 were either discharged, or fined costs or $1.00 and costs. Ten out of the 121 were sent to the jail or workhouse, and four of these were sent at their own request because they had no home to go to. Such treatment by magistrates and constables of course has little deterrent effect.

On one point the borough government cannot act because of its legislative limitations. In dealing with disorderly houses, for example, the owners can be arraigned only on a charge of disorderly conduct, for which a small fine or a short period in the workhouse is the maximum penalty. No local action can be brought against them on a criminal charge. In 1907 the district attorney of Allegheny County raided a number of houses in Homestead. Without his co-operation, however, the borough is unable to take thoroughgoing measures to eradicate them.

The limitations of borough autonomy are brought out in even sharper relief in its relation to an outside corporation, the

Photo by Hine

DOUBLE GRADE CROSSING NEAR THE HEART OF HOMESTEAD

Photo by Hine

AN UNPAVED ALLEY

railroad. The ordinance, for example, which requires that the speed of trains inside borough limits shall be limited to six miles an hour, is almost totally disregarded. One fast train which goes through late in the evening, makes but little reduction in speed, merely sending out a prolonged shriek of warning to the passer-by. Two railroads run through Homestead parallel to the main street, one two blocks and one three blocks from it. Many children on their way to school must cross the tracks, and the same is true of all the traffic going from the main street to Pittsburgh. Yet until 1908 the crossings, all level with the street, were without gates, and flagmen stationed at them left at 6 p. m.* The Pennsylvania courts had declared that a borough has no power to enact ordinances affecting outside corporations, can neither enforce a speed limit, nor require a railroad to put safety gates at the crossings nearest its business centers.

HOMESTEAD'S ECONOMIC STATUS

Enough has been said to indicate that politically the citizens of Homestead have not succeeded in creating an altogether wholesome sanitary or civic environment for their homes. Of equal influence upon household life is the economic development of a community of 25,000 people. Here we find the dominance of the one industry and the nearness of Homestead to Pittsburgh important factors.

Homestead is now the market for the three boroughs and also for the outlying districts. Since the branch car lines into the surrounding country have made it possible for women living back from Homestead to shop here, the demand for good local stores has increased. The main thoroughfare, Eighth Avenue, is a typical two- and three-story business street with banks, real estate offices, numerous butcher shops and bakeries, grocery and furnishing stores, the latter displaying modish garments on sale for cash or "credit." A low white building bears the imposing sign "Home-

---

* The Pittsburgh and Lake Erie tracks (New York Central System) have since been guarded with gates; the tracks of the Pittsburgh, Virginia and Charleston (Pennsylvania lines) are without gates. Gatemen and flagmen alike are as heretofore off duty at night. See Appendix VII, p. 233, for list of casualties.

stead's Department Stores." At frequent intervals saloons and nickelodeons offer entertainment after their kind. The few shabby looking hotels, obviously making more money from their bars than from their rooms, are characteristic of any town so near a great city. The row of shops offers all the necessities of life and the housekeeper need not journey to the city unless she wishes. Pittsburgh, to be sure, is near. It takes only fifteen minutes on the railroad and forty-five on a street car, and as the fare in the latter case is only five cents, many women make their more important purchases from the greater variety of goods and the bargains offered by the big stores. For the most part, however, they rely on the local dealers.

Business interests have not adequately met certain other needs of the town, notably the provisions for amusement. These are meagre and in winter monotonous and not inspiriting. In summer opportunities for relaxation are afforded by two parks owned by the street railway company, each situated within a five-cent fare of the town. On the line to the suburb Lincoln Place is Homestead Park. Here is a baseball ground which a league of business men utilize for games after business hours; swings, roller skating and a dancing pavilion offer their attractions to the young. Kennywood Park, on the hills beyond Homestead toward Duquesne, is the liveliest outdoor pleasure ground within reach of Pittsburgh. It is the popular place for large picnics. There is, too, a small park on the hill in Homestead which was given to the town by Mr. Henry C. Frick. It is attractively laid out in lawns and flower beds and offers a refreshing glimpse of green to the passer-by. With these parks and the numerous trolley lines into the country, the needs of summer recreation are fairly provided for, but, as has been said, when winter comes people must return to a limited range of amusements. The number and character of these are affected by the nearness of Pittsburgh. People with leisure or those who desire a better class of entertainment naturally prefer to attend lectures, concerts and theatres in the city, where they can have the best. Most towns of the size of Homestead have a local theatre where fairly good companies come for a one-night stand. In Homestead, public amusements, aside from the entertainments offered by the Carnegie Library, have been limited largely to skating rinks and nickelodeons.

Of the business enterprises, those which doubtless most closely affect the lives of the residents are the real estate companies. Real estate, except in Munhall, is largely in the hands of local firms, who recognize that they have a definite part in building up the town and who take a genuine pride in it. By making it possible for those with small incomes to buy houses and by creating a sense of confidence through fair dealing (such as considerateness when purchasers strike hard times), the real estate men have helped to increase the number of house-owners. Even in this form of enterprise, in which the business life of Homestead is at its best, the resources of the community have not been sufficient to meet the demands of its growth. Houses have not been built fast enough, and in 1907 rents were high and people found difficulty in securing suitable homes.

The town's lack of economic self-dependence is serious and fundamental. A large machine manufactory and the steel mill employ practically all the inhabitants except those who provide for the needs of the workers. Financially, therefore, Homestead is almost entirely dependent on the outsiders who own these industries,—non-residents who for the most part lack any interest in the future development of the town as distinguished from the mill. Some few may make gifts,—even notable ones, as in the case of the park, the library and the manual training school,—and small building loans may be granted employes; but the profits of the industries are not in any large sense re-invested in the town.

The setting of the average Homestead household is now fairly complete before us. On the one hand is the inexorable mill, offering wages and work under such conditions as it pleases; on the other is a town politically failing to maintain a sound environment for its inhabitants and not possessed of independent business resources sufficient to serve them.

It may well be questioned whether, with labor organization among the working people, the civic conditions would today be any better than they are. Democracy has pretty much the same weaknesses in small cities as in large. Certain it is, however, that the employers in Homestead who have assumed entire authority within the mill gates, have not assumed positive responsibilities toward the well-being of the community which has grown up outside them. And of the indirect and too often negative influences of the industry upon the normal life of the community, there are, as we shall see, many evidences.

In reviewing the relations of the mill to its employes in the first chapter, I pointed out that the strike, which shut the men off from any part in the terms of their work, left them still two vantage grounds from which they could control much that entered into everyday living,—the town and the home. We now see how and where the town fails to create those civic and sanitary conditions which should make for mental and physical efficiency. The problem then becomes largely one of the home. It is in the individual household, supported on the customary wages paid by the mill, that we must seek the meaning of life in Homestead.

PART II
THE ENGLISH-SPEAKING HOUSEHOLDS

CHAPTER III

WORK, WAGES, AND THE COST OF LIVING

IF YOU are near the mill in the late afternoon you will see a procession, an almost steady stream of men, each carrying the inevitable bucket, hurrying towards the great buildings for the night's work. A little later the tide turns and back come the day men, walking slowly and wearily towards home and supper.

Thus the life of the town keeps time with the rhythm of the mill. This is brought out also by the way the town reckons dates from the year of the great strike; by the trend of its development, conditioned by dependence upon one industrial enterprise owned by outsiders; and most clearly of all by the part the mill work plays in the lives of the men themselves.

While I shall not attempt to go into the technique of steel making, the general process can be stated in a few words. The crude iron brought to Homestead in huge ladles from the "Carrie" blast furnaces across the river, is taken to the open-hearth department where it is put into the furnaces, mixed with scrap iron, ore, and certain chemicals, and brought to a melting heat. The open-hearth furnaces are then tapped and the metal is poured into ingot molds to cool. As the steel is needed for use the ingots are reheated and go to the "rolls," ponderous and wonderful machines, which turn out steel rails, sheets of plate for war vessels, beams for constructing skyscrapers.

The conditions under which the work is carried on seem to an outsider fairly intolerable. The din in the great vaulted sheds makes speech hard. Men who have worked near the engines, though their organs of hearing remain in physically good condition, sometimes become almost oblivious to ordinary sound. Some work where the heat is intense; and before the open doors

35

of furnaces full of white-hot metal they must wear smoked glasses to temper the glare. This heat, exhausting in summer, makes a man in winter doubly susceptible to the cold without. While for the men directing the processes the physical exertion is often not great, most of the laborers perform heavy manual toil. And everywhere is the danger of accident from constantly moving machinery, from bars of glowing steel, from engines moving along the tracks in the yard. The men, of course, grow used to these dangers, but a new peril lies in the carelessness that results from such familiarity, for human nature cannot be eternally on guard; men would be unable to do their work if they became too cautious.

The nature of the work, with the heat and its inherent hazard, makes much of it exhausting. Yet these men for the most part keep it up twelve hours a day. It is uneconomical to have the plant shut down. In order that the mills may run practically continuously, the twenty-four hours is divided between two shifts. The greater number of men employed in making steel (as distinct from the clerical staff) work half of the time at night, the usual arrangement being for a man to work one week on the day and the next on the night shift. At the request of the men, the night turn is made longer, so that they can have the full evening to themselves the other week. Their hours on the day turn, therefore, are from 7 a. m. to 5:30 p. m.; this leaves thirteen and one-half hours for the night shift. In certain departments the regular processes are continued straight through Sunday and the crews work the full seven days out of seven; this is the case, for instance, in the blast furnaces, such as the Carrie group which are practically a part of the Homestead plant. The officials claimed in 1908 that in the rolling mills only necessary labor, such as repairing, was done on Sunday. Yet my colleague, Mr. Fitch, estimated that for Allegheny County as a whole one steel worker out of five worked seven days in a week. Moreover, a majority of the men have to be on duty either Saturday night or Sunday night, thus breaking into the day of rest.*

* Mechanics, and day laborers in the yards work ten hours a day. For a full discussion of the extent of twelve-hour and Sunday work see Fitch, John A.: The Steel Workers, a companion volume in the series of The Pittsburgh Survey, p. 166 ff. For recent action of the United States Steel Corporation curtailing some kinds of Sunday work, see Appendix VIII, p. 236.

Photo by Hine

Where the Mill Meets the Town

These are the demands which the mill makes on the Homestead men. Even the details of family life depend on whether "the mister" is working day turn or night turn; and the long shifts determine the part the steel worker plays in his household and also in his community. Financially, all time is marked off by the fortnightly "pay Friday." On that night stores are open all the evening. The streets are filled with music, and the German bands go from saloon to saloon reaping a generous harvest when times are good. Beggars besiege the gates of the mill bearing pathetic signs, "I am injured and blind—my eyes were destroyed by hot steel," and the full pocketbook is opened. It is the night for settling scores, and the bills which have accumulated for two weeks are paid and a fresh household account opened.

The influence of mill work upon the home is most direct of all through the wages themselves, since wages, by limiting expenditures, set bounds to the attainment of a family's ideals.

As a means of interpreting the household life of Homestead, therefore, I studied the everyday life of families who represented different earning and racial groups in the town's population. Ninety of the families visited kept a detailed account of all purchases for four weeks or more. The inquiry was not, however, primarily statistical, but rather a study at first hand of family life. It was not easy to become acquainted with the mill employes since there were no agencies, such as settlements or trade unions, to put a stranger confidentially in touch with them. Introductions, secured mainly from clergymen, made it possible, however, to approach people, and paved the way for more familiar relationships as the weeks went on. Suspicion was often aroused and some refused to assist in the investigation. Keeping personal accounts is arduous (many of us have abandoned the praiseworthy habit), and it was not surprising that busy women declined to add this task to their burdens, or else failed to keep up the daily entries once they had begun. My 90 families were thus the residue of a much larger number; some of them dropped out; the entries of others could not be depended upon. Repeated visits to "see how the book is getting on," gave an opportunity to secure that intimate knowledge of family life which most of all was desired. One of my assistants, an American, became a resident of the town, living like other residents and sending her son to the Homestead schools. The young widow of a Slavic mill worker secured the budgets from the immigrants. As an interpreter in the Homestead courts she held to a marked degree the confidence of her people, and from her I gained an insight into Slavic customs and points of view which was invaluable. The fairly complete picture of the households thus obtained made the budgets more significant and also threw light on the community life.

TABLE 5.—ANALYSIS OF 90 BUDGET FAMILIES.—BY RACIAL GROUP
AND NORMAL WEEKLY WAGE OF MAN*

Racial Group	Number of families	Under $12.00	$12.00–$14.99	$15.00–$19.99	$20.00 and over	Per cent earning under $12.00
Slav . . .	29	21	2	4	2	72.4
Eng. sp. Eur.† .	13	1	6	4	2	7.7
Nat. white . .	25	..	4	6	15	0.0
Colored . .	23	2	9	8	4	8.7
Total . .	90	24	21	22	23	26.6

* For detailed analysis, see Appendix I, Table 1, p. 200.
† This group included English, Scotch, Irish and German families.

A few words of personal description from these individual studies will illustrate the make-up of the representative groupings of the table. The men earning less than $12 a week were largely Slavic day laborers, many of them newcomers, although three had been here fifteen years or more. Some were lately married, starting life in a single room, and some had families of four or five children to maintain.

The group of men earning $12 to $14.99 a week included more varied types; such as a middle-aged Englishman, semi-skilled, whose thrifty wife was managing on this wage to bring up their six children; two Americans with equally large families (one of six children, the other of seven), whose work also demanded little skill, and who also had wives who to some extent made up for the low wages by skilful housekeeping; a third American, unambitious, who held a poorly paid "pencil" job,* and who

* Clerical or semi-clerical position.

already counted on his fourteen-year-old son to help provide for the household; a colored teamster, who with three children to support, called on his wife to earn a little, by cleaning for her neighbors; and, in contrast to these, a Slav who had worked seven years in the mill and was now an engineer. This group and the succeeding one were drawn from the better paid day men and the lower paid tonnage men.

Among the steel workers earning $15 to $19.99 were two Slavs and a Scotchman who were helpers at the open-hearth furnaces, an Irish machinist, one American with a good "pencil job" and another who did semi-skilled work at the rolls. The part which personal choice plays in spending when incomes are large enough to give some margin, was illustrated by the families of the men in this group. Here, an American on the clerical staff of the mill with a clever wife and two small children, saved little, for they had chosen instead to have an attractive five-room house; there, a Slav with the same income and the same sized family lived in two rooms which were shared by two lodgers, and already had a bank account of $400; another, an Irish machinist, drank up part of his wages, and his wife had not the gift of home-making.

The group of men earning $20 and over were good workmen and good providers as well. For instance, one was a Slav who came to America over twenty years ago to begin life here as a miner, and who now is a citizen and has a comfortable four-room home; another, a Scotchman, intelligent and interesting, whose home is a model of thrift, and whose four children are to have the best that American public schools can give. Nine out of 15 of the steel workers in this group were tonnage men.

There are two main factors which determine the standards of living of such wage-earning families: one, external circumstances which the family cannot control, such as money-wages, location, educational and social opportunities; the other, the ideals which it is continually struggling to reach. No account of individuals or families which fails to take both external circumstances and personal ideals into consideration can be complete; both are necessary to reveal the latent power in the people of a community. The problem presents itself to the mind of the wage-earner in simpler English: "How much can I make? What shall I spend it for?" As the second question is always that of a choice of wants, the decision as to which seem worth working and paying for is perhaps the clearest mark of a family's mental development. If we collect data as to family expenditures and compare the answers thus made to these two questions, we can estimate the character and self-dependence of a laboring community; and, in turn, can measure what home life the wage-earner's pay makes possible. What in the first place then are the wages paid in Homestead?

As a background to the study of the 90 budget families, we were fortunate in securing an authoritative statement regarding the men employed in the Homestead plant in March, 1907, classified by racial group, degree of skill, etc. Of the total 6,772 men, 1,266, or 18.7 per cent, were skilled; 1,556, or 23 per cent, semi-skilled; and 3,950, or 58.3 per cent, unskilled.

TABLE 6.—MEN EMPLOYED IN THE HOMESTEAD MILL IN MARCH, 1907. NUMBER AND PERCENTAGES.—BY RACIAL GROUPS AND DEGREE OF SKILL

Racial Group	Skilled	Semi-skilled	Unskilled	Total	Per cent Unskilled
Slav	80	459	3064	3603	85.0
Eng. sp. Eur. . .	398	358	367	1123	32.7
Nat. white . . .	767	707	451	1925	23.4
Colored . . .	21	32	68	121	56.2
Total . . .	1266	1556	3950	6772	
Per cent . .	18.7	23.0	58.3		

A careful study of wages showed that unskilled laborers received $ .16½ an hour for a ten- or twelve-hour day; the semi-skilled, including both day and tonnage workers, earn $2.00 or $3.00 a day, and the skilled, $2.50 to $5.00, a small percentage earning more than that.*

*Beginning May 1, 1910, the prevailing rate for common labor was raised to 17½ cents an hour in Homestead. This was part of a general advance put into effect by the United States Steel Corporation, equal, it was announced, to an average of somewhat over 6 per cent on the rates previously paid.

Photo by Hine

SLAVIC LABORERS

These figures represent earnings, moreover, at the height of a long period of prosperity. The first and most important fact revealed by them is that the pay of over half the men in the Homestead mills in 1907 was that of common laborers. Eighty-five per cent of the Slavs, 23.4 per cent of the native whites, 32.7 per cent of the English-speaking Europeans and 56.2 per cent of the colored were classed as unskilled, receiving less than $12 a week. This will reveal the situation as it actually is to those who have heard only that wages in the steel industry are high. Its reputation for big wages is based on the earnings, especially in the early years of the industry, of the rollers, heaters and other skilled men, a fraction of the total force. The new machine processes call for an increasing number of unskilled positions, and however much the personnel of these workers shifts, this group with a low maximum wage must be considered a constant factor in Homestead life.

Even among the English-speaking employes, unskilled work with its low wage is not always a merely temporary stage in mill work, a period of apprenticeship, to be endured until time and promotion bring a larger income. For instance, among the men over forty years of age in the families keeping budgets, 16 earned over $15 and 12 earned less than that sum. About a fourth of the total number of those earning less than $15 were over forty. Of the men earning $12 to $14.99 a week, the six English-speaking Europeans were on an average forty-five years old; the four native whites, forty-five.

A second fact is scarcely less distinctive from an economic point of view. Family life in Homestead depends for its support almost entirely upon the men's earnings; women and chidren rarely work outside the home since the steel plant and machine works cannot use them and there are no other industries in the town. Of the 90 budget families there were only nine in which the income was supplemented by women's wages, and even in these, with the exception of three colored households where the women partly supported the family by days' work, the money thus gained formed only a small percentage of the income.* On the other hand, the mill offers work at good pay to young men,

* See Appendix I, Tables 2 and 3, p. 201.

and the husband's wage is frequently supplemented by that of the son. Among the native white families, the husband and son in normal times contributed 92.3 per cent of the total income; among the English-speaking Europeans 98.7 per cent.

Among the immigrant families, however, and among all those in which the man's earnings fell within the day labor rate, our budget studies disclosed that another and exceptional source of support was resorted to; namely, payment from lodgers. It is upon the women of the household that this burden falls. In families where the man's wage was normally less than $12 a week, more than half found it necessary to increase their slender income in this way. What this means in congestion and in lower standards of living we shall see in a discussion of the Slavic households.

The third distinctive fact in the Homestead situation in regard to earnings has been the steadiness of employment. Regularity no less than rate of wages determines what a family's annual receipts amount to, and the family adjusts its grade of living more or less closely to this expected income. I was told that from the time of the depression of 1893 up to November 1, 1907, the mills had run almost without a break. Tonnage men who are paid by output of course feel temporary lulls, but if a given department in a mill is not working full time, the day men in that department receive a full day's pay as long as the mill runs at all.

How far income standards which are thus rendered stable by regular work in the Homestead mills have been jeopardized by rate cuts which may or may not be justified by changes in process, but against which the men have no check, and what intense efforts they put forward to increase their speed and keep their weekly earnings up to former levels, are issues of labor administration which are gone into by my colleague, Mr. Fitch.* That most of the men will receive a full fortnight's pay regularly year in and year out, has given a sense of security even in the face of repeated reductions in the rates. It has created a basis for the development of common standards of living which would be impossible where employment was fluctuating.

* Fitch, John A.: The Steel Workers, Chap. XIV.

In Homestead, then, we have a community where half the workmen are day laborers, where families are almost solely dependent on the man's earnings, and where a man's earnings one month are fairly like those of the next. Therefore, if the period covered by the investigation had been a normal one, we could have put opposite each other a family's usual earnings, and what the money went for, as shown by account books, and have drawn direct and simple deductions as to the relation between wages and costs of living for each group. An industrial depression prevented this. The period covered extended from October 1, 1907, to April 1, 1908. Within six weeks after the first budgets were started the trouble began, and by the middle of December the mills were running only about half time, a situation which lasted during the remainder of the investigation. Incidentally, this change brought us special data showing how people met hard times. But, as few families were receiving full wages, many household accounts dropped below what would have been normal for them.

Recognition of this situation called for a special treatment of the budget material as a whole. While the depression, as we have seen, prevented statistical deductions as to how families ordinarily spent their wages, it did not seriously conflict with a main purpose of the economic side of the study. This was to find out what elementary standards of living are possible on an income say of $12 a week in Homestead. To ascertain this, in my major tables I abandoned all reference to normal wages and divided the families according to the amounts they actually expended per week during the period studied, including what was purchased on credit. Rents and the prices of food stuffs did not change during this period, and, with these constant, $12 a week would, in general, buy the same whether the payments were made out of the lowered earnings of a family in slack times, or out of the total wages of a low paid man when the mills were running full. As all accounts were discarded in which there was a discrepancy of five per cent between income and expenditure during the five to eight weeks studied, the entries showed accurately what the families spent for this period, and afforded a basis of fact to correct and strengthen the impressions received in the more general survey of the situation.

43

The study of much larger groups of families carried over more representative periods would be essential for an adequate inter-
pretation of the standards of living in such an industrial town.* But as a simple gauge of the influence of mill town employment upon home life, the items of our budgets,—rent, meals, clothing, help for the housekeeper, and amusements—served to indicate how far earnings will go either for the unskilled immigrant, who seeks a foothold in this country, or for the American, who looks to his work in the steel industry as a permanent basis for a livelihood.†

These budgets, moreover, reflect the character of the working people of Homestead. No less important than the question of how much people spend is the question of what they buy and more important than all, what they want. To learn these things we must catch something of the spirit of their homes, for no account of household expenditure, however detailed, can in itself reveal the struggle people make to attain their ideals. And without knowing these ideals we cannot judge how much the limitations which any system of wages imposes concern society.

TABLE 7.—90 BUDGET FAMILIES.—BY RACIAL AND EXPENDITURE GROUP

Racial Group	Under $12.00	$12.00–$14.99	$15.00–$19.99	$20.00 and over	Total
Slav. . . .	14	5	7	3	29
Eng. Sp. Eur. . .	3	4	3	3	13
Native White . .	4	1	8	12	25
Colored. . . .	11	6	5	1	23
Total . . .	32	16	23	19	90

* The colored group form less than two per cent of the working force in the mill. They are included, therefore, not as numerically significant, but as affording interesting points for comparison with the Slavs.

† For statement as to the methods of inquiry and statistical treatment employed, see Appendix I, p. 187.

TABLE 8.—AVERAGE WEEKLY EXPENDITURES OF 90 BUDGET
FAMILIES IN 1907, AMOUNTS AND PERCENTAGES.—BY CHIEF
ITEMS OF EXPENDITURE AND RACIAL GROUP

Racial Group	Number of Families	Average Expenditure	RENT		FOOD		FUEL		INSURANCE		OTHER	
			Amount	Per cent	Amount	Per cent	Amount	Per cent	Amount	Per cent	Amount	Per cent
Colored . .	23	$12.39	$2.43	19.6	$4.84	39.1	$.82	6.6	$ .92	7.4	$3.41	27.5
Slav. . .	29	13.09	2.00	15.3	5.98	45.7	.38	2.9	.88	6.7	3.86	29.5
Eng. Sp. Eur.	13	16.97	2.91	17.1	7.55	44.5	.45	2.7	1.03	6.1	5.03	29.6
Nat. White .	25	20.47	3.16	15.4	7.44	36.3	.84	4.1	1.21	5.9	7.82	38.2

TABLE 9.—AVERAGE WEEKLY EXPENDITURES OF 90 BUDGET
FAMILIES, AMOUNTS AND PERCENTAGES.—BY CHIEF ITEMS OF
EXPENDITURE AND EXPENDITURE GROUP

Expenditure Group	Number of Families	Average Expenditure	RENT		FOOD		FUEL		INSURANCE		OTHER	
			Amount	Per cent	Amount	Per cent	Amount	Per cent	Amount	Per cent	Amount	Per cent
Under $12.00 .	32	$9.17	$1.88	20.5	$4.16	45.3	$.38	4.1	$ .70	7.6	$2.05	22.3
$12.00–$14.99 .	16	13.32	2.29	17.2	5.86	44.0	.77	5.8	.51	3.8	3.89	29.2
$15.00–$19.99 .	23	17.59	2.73	15.5	7.11	40.4	.66	3.8	1.05	6.0	6.02	34.2
$20.00 and over	19	25.56	3.73	14.5	9.38	36.7	.90	3.5	1.86	7.3	9.68	37.9

TABLE 10.—AVERAGE WEEKLY EXPENDITURES OF 77 HOUSE-RENT-
ING FAMILIES,* AMOUNTS AND PERCENTAGES.—BY CHIEF ITEMS
OF EXPENDITURE AND EXPENDITURE GROUP

Expenditure Group	Number of Families	Average weekly Expenditure	RENT		FOOD		FUEL		INSURANCE		OTHER	
			Amount	Per cent	Amount	Per cent	Amount	Per cent	Amount	Per cent	Amount	Per cent
Under $12.00 .	28	$9.08	$2.15	23.7	$3.81	42.0	$.38	4.2	$ .66	7.3	$2.07	22.9
$12.00–$14.99 .	15	13.23	2.45	18.5	5.64	42.6	.72	5.4	.55	4.2	3.88	29.3
$15.00–$19.99 .	19	17.65	3.31	18.8	7.04	39.9	.61	3.5	1.07	6.0	5.63	31.9
$20.00 and over	15	26.29	4.72	18.0	9.88	37.6	.92	3.5	1.95	7.4	8.81	33.5

* Of the 90 families, 13 owned their dwellings.

CHAPTER IV

RENT IN THE HOUSEHOLD BUDGET

THE type of house available at a given time in any community, whether the tenement of the city or the frame cottage of the country, is largely determined by other factors than individual preference. While in clothes, in food, and in amusements, personal likings play a large part, in housing a certain common standard is accepted to which most people conform. Especially is this true in a growing mill town like Homestead, where in prosperous years there has been a dearth of houses for rent. There is little choice in the kind of dwelling a workingman's family can secure, and yet the house itself is a determining circumstance in shaping the character of the home life.

As in most American towns of the last century's building, the original lay-out of Homestead had little to commend it. Nevertheless, the plan made when the Homestead Bank and Life Insurance Company plotted its first lots has been carried out in the newer parts of Munhall and West Homestead, as well as in the central borough. It is the customary checker-board plan, ill adapted to the gullied hill slopes and triangular flats of a river bend. The streets run parallel from east to west, intersected almost at right angles by those running up and down the hill. The only variation from this general scheme is found in one or two streets in Munhall, which follow the beds of old water courses and have kept the curve of the stream. The lots in Homestead are usually narrow, not more than 20 or 25 feet in width. Originally, there was ample room between the streets for each house to have a good garden in the rear, with plenty of air and freedom, and in the more open parts of the town these gardens are still a source of pleasure. But in other sections they are being built upon and rear houses are multiplying along the alleys which were cut between parallel streets to give access to back doors. In the district nearest the mill, the alleys are

46

paved and are built up almost solid. The houses here, though still only two stories high, cover so large a proportion of the land as to limit the amount of air and light within doors, as well as the space left for the children to play outside. This region is occupied by the Slavs and will be described in a later section.

The hill section, which forms the upper part of all three boroughs, has not suffered to such an extent from the overcrowding of the land, but most of the alleys, still unpaved, are littered with rubbish and lined with outhouses and sheds. Here and there are forlorn and often unsanitary dwellings, hardly more than shanties. Such hill-side conditions as yet tell more against the sightliness of the town than against its healthfulness.

There are in scattered sections attractive residences belonging to business and professional men; but in those parts of Homestead where the working people live, few evidences are to be found of attempts to make dwellings attractive architecturally. They are of that dreary type of small, closely-set frame structure so characteristic of a rapidly growing industrial community. The real estate companies, in their desire for economy, naturally plan their houses on an inexpensive and, as far as possible, uniform scale, and rising land values lead to the use of narrow lots. The common type of house has four rooms, two on a floor, the front door opening directly on the street. The stairway to the second story occupies a narrow hall between the two lower rooms. Some of the houses contain five rooms. In a row of such houses the dining room, back of the "front room," is lighted only by a window on the narrow passageway between houses, and is never reached by direct sunlight. The monotony of street after street is broken only by the bits of lawn and flowers in front. Where there are yards in the rear, they serve as play places for the children, and offer rest and refreshment to the grownups. As the men are usually too tired to enjoy working in them, the women often assume the task of keeping the flowers and grass in order and find it a welcome change from the hot kitchen. One garden, hardly 20 feet square, had along one fence a thick row of violets that the daughter had brought from the woods; a pink "bleeding heart" and several flourishing rose bushes grew beside the house. The square in the center, where grass was being coaxed to grow, was reserved for the drying of clothes. The house contained but five rooms, and with seven children the parents rejoiced in the freshness and quiet of the yard in the evening. The garden pictured on the opposite page, luxuriant with shrubs and flowers and vegetables, formed a fine playground for children, puppies, and Belgian hares.

On the hill the gardens have a substantial aspect. One family utilized an empty lot, and the beans, squashes, and other vegetables raised there so decreased the family's cost of living that they declined to keep an account since they said it would not fairly represent their table expenses. An item of sixty cents for garden seeds in the early spring in another family's budget gave promise of both pleasure and profit. Many of the families also save a good deal by keeping hens. On one visit, hearing a curious noise beneath my chair, I looked down to find a friendly chicken which had come for a feast of crumbs. One woman kept a few hens to provide fresh eggs for her husband's bucket. After his death she found that by selling them she could add a little to a slender income. The gardens too develop neighborliness of spirit, since the women often discuss over the fences their horticultural ambitions.

In view of the unenviable reputation of "company houses" everywhere, it is interesting to note that those owned and rented by the Carnegie Land Company in Munhall are the best houses for the money in the town. Though built in solid rows and wearisomely uniform they are immaculately neat, with squares of lawn and shade trees in front. These houses, which consist of five small rooms, neatly finished, with running water in the house, but with no bathroom, rent for $11 a month. Electric lights are furnished at a cost of $1.50 a month. Another company row contains four-room houses, without lights or running water, which rent for $8.50. Though some families feel a lack of privacy in these unbroken blocks there is always a waiting list. Throughout Munhall, the cottages vary more in design and the lawns are larger than in the other boroughs. Sixteenth Avenue, for instance, is an example of effective, inexpensive house-building.

Bearing these general conditions in mind, the facts in regard to the houses of a few of the budget families will give us a background for the tables to follow. They will suggest how individual

48

Photo by Hine

BACK YARD POSSIBILITIES IN HOMESTEAD—I

Photo by Hine

BACK YARD POSSIBILITIES IN HOMESTEAD—II

and racial preferences modify the general tendency to pay more rent as income increases.

DAVIS.* Colored. Man, wife and four children. Man a hod carrier with irregular work at $3.00 a day. They live in a small dilapidated house, built in the middle of a lot on an alley. Water in yard. Unsewered closets emptied by town on application. Three rooms. $7.50 a month.

CHISMER. Slav. Man, wife, two small children. Man a laborer in mill, $1.65 a day. House on alley, no yard, water from hydrant in court, unflushed toilet. Two rooms. $8.00 a month.

CHECH. Slav. Man, wife, two children and two boarders. Man earns $15 a week in the mill. Water and toilet in yard. Two rooms each about 15 feet square. $8.00 a month.

JONES. American. Man, wife, seven children. Man earns $17 a week in the mill. Small frame house on alley. Practically no yard. Water in house. Toilet in yard. Three rooms. $11 a month.

MCCARTHY. Irish. Man, wife, four children. Man earns $16 a week in mill. Half a double house, unattractive. Small yard. Water and toilet in yard. Four rooms. $12 a month.

BROWN. American. Man, wife, five children. Man earns $15 a week and son $5.00 a week in the mill. Small frame house, very close to mill. Small porch directly on street. Small yard. Running water in house, toilet in yard. Five rooms. $12.50 a month.

SCHMIDT. German-American. Young couple, one child. Man earns $50 a month. Small house in row. No hall. Water from hydrant on porch used by several families. No yard. Three rooms. $13 a month.

KOCIS. Slav. Here twelve years. Man, wife, three children, five boarders. Man earns $10.80 a week. Fairly large yard. Water and closet in yard. Four rooms, one dark. $14 a month.

EVANS. American. Man, wife, one child, lodger. Man earns $3.00 a day. Attractive house. Small porch. Good yard. Toilet and water in house. Four rooms .$15 a month.

LEWIS. Colored. Man, wife, three children, the oldest six. Man earns $2.10 a day in the mill. Rather shabby but comfortable frame house on outskirts of town. A large garden, which they cultivate. Water from pump in yard. Closet not connected with sewer. Five rooms. $16 a month.

* The names used throughout this book are fictitious.

SMITH. American. No children. Man earns $18 a week in mill. Half of double house with only narrow path at side. Toilet and running water in house. Five rooms. $20 a month.

BURNS. Scotch. Man, wife, two sons at work, three children in school. Total income about $30 a week. Frame house, only a narrow path on each side. Small porch directly on street. Good yard behind. Water in house, closet in yard. Six rooms. $24 a month.

Seventy-seven of the 90 budget keepers were tenant families Their expenditures for rent during the period studied are shown in Table 11.

TABLE 11.—AVERAGE AMOUNT OF RENT PER WEEK PAID BY THE 77 HOUSE-RENTING FAMILIES.—BY EXPENDITURE AND RACIAL GROUP

Racial Group	Under $12.00		$12.00–$14.99		$15.00–$19.99		$20.00 and Over		Average of All	
	Number of Families	Average Rent	Number of Families	Average Rent	Number of Families	Average Rent	Number of Families	Average Rent	Number of Families	Average Rent
Colored	11	$2.22	6	$2.37	5	$2.96	1	$2.50	23	$2.43
Slav.	13	1.64	5	2.41	6	2.77	3	2.62	27	2.14
Eng. Sp. Eur.	2	3.38	3	2.50	2	3.75	3	5.35	10	3.78
Nat. White	2	3.85	1	3.00	6	3.99	8	5.56	17	4.65
Total families	28	..	15	..	19	..	15	..	77	..
Average rent	..	$2.15	..	$2.45	..	$3.31	..	$4.72	..	$3.00

With a few exceptions, there is of course in each racial group a general increase in rent according to the amount of income. But in each expenditure class the Slav spends less rent on the average than do the English-speaking Europeans and Americans. In the lowest and the highest groups the expenditure of the other whites is more than double that of the Slavs. The low expenditure for rent among a majority of the Slavic and colored families goes hand in hand with overcrowding and unsanitary tenements, a fact borne out not only by the vivid impression of squalor received by the chance visitor to the courts and alleys in which many of them live, but by a scrutiny of the accommodations which they secure for themselves.* Taking the room as the unit and stating the proposition roughly for all 90 families, in nearly three out of five of the older immigrant families there was but one person to a room. The same was true in four out of five of the native white families, but of only one out of five of the Slavic. Fourteen families out of 17 of those in which there were three persons to the room were Slavs.†

The fact that the Slavs and the colored people come nearest in their expenditures suggests that the housing standard first adopted by the former is very like that of the working Negro.

Turning to the size of the dwelling, 10 out of 13 of the older immigrant stock ‡ lived in houses with four or more rooms, and 22 out of 25 of the native white; moreover, 10 of the latter had houses of six rooms. On the other hand, one-half of the Slavic and colored families lived in one- or two-room houses. It was among these groups in the budget families, and only among these, that such small homes were found. This was a level to which the mill workers who had lived here since before the strike did not go. It was a level still more desperately depressed by overcrowding in the lodging houses of the Slavic courts.

But while thus recognizing that racial standards modify rental expenditures, an economic analysis of these same budgets shows that the determining factor is wages. The two races spending the smallest per cent for rent are those with the lowest incomes. They give too small a margin for the family to consider how desirable a better home would be. As it is, these poorest families put a greater proportion of their expenditures into rent (Table 13) than do any of the others, the percentage being a third higher, 23.7 per cent as against 18.5 per cent, 18.8 per cent, 18 per cent.§

* Four out of five of the native white, and three out of five of other Europeans had running water in the house, as against less than two out of five for colored or Slavs. Only three houses out of 65 occupied by families other than native whites contained indoor toilets, while 12 out of 25 houses occupied by native whites were provided with them.

† Appendix I, Table 5, p. 202.

‡ Appendix I, Table 7, p. 202.

§ These percentages for rent are not widely different from those given by Mr. Chapin in his study of conditions among tenement families in New York City

TABLE 12.—EXPENDITURE FOR RENT OF 77 HOUSE-RENTING FAMI-
LIES. AVERAGE AMOUNT AND PERCENTAGE OF TOTAL EX-
PENDITURE.—BY RACIAL GROUP

Racial Group	Number of Families	Average Weekly Expenditure	Average Expenditure for Rent	Per cent for Rent
Slavs . . .	27	$12.93	$2.14	16.6
Eng. Sp. Eur. .	10	17.90	3.78	21.1
Nat. White .	17	21.72	4.65	21.4
Colored . .	23	12.39	2.43	19.6

TABLE 13.—EXPENDITURE FOR RENT OF 77 HOUSE-RENTING FAMI-
LIES. AVERAGE AMOUNT AND PERCENTAGE OF TOTAL EX-
PENDITURE.—BY EXPENDITURE GROUP

Expenditure Group	Number of Families	Average Weekly Expenditure	Average Expenditure for Rent	Per cent for Rent
Under $12.00 .	28	$ 9.08	$2.15	23.7
$12.00–$14.99 .	15	13.23	2.45	18.5
$15.00–$19.99 .	19	17.65	3.31	18.8
$20.00 and over	15	26.29	4.72	18.0

Rent in the 77 Homestead tenant families rises steadily
(Table 13) from an average of $2.15 per week paid by the laborer
who works for $1.65 per day to the $4.72 per week paid on an
average by the skilled steel worker. How far overcrowding
decreases in proportion to the extra expenditure can be summed
up briefly:* Of the 48 families in the group spending under $15 (in-
cluding the house owners), 26, or over one-half, were living with
two or more persons to the room; of the 42 families spending more
than $15, only 14, or one-third, had two or more persons to the

where families with an income of $500 to $599 spend 25.9 per cent for rent, and
those with an income of $1000 to $1099 spend 18.1 per cent. Chapin, Robert
Coit: The Standard of Living among Workingmen's Families in New York City,
p. 70. (New York, Charities Publication Committee, 1909. Russell Sage Foundation Publication.) The percentages are far in excess of the figures given for normal
families by the U. S. Bureau of Labor which reports 16 per cent for 170 families
with an income of $800 to $900, and only 12 per cent for families with an income
of $750 to $1100. Eighteenth Annual Report of the Commissioner of Labor,
1903.

* Appendix I, Table 6, p. 202.

Photo by Hine

A ONE-ROOM HOUSEHOLD

room; and of the 19 families spending over $20, only five, or one-fourth. Of the 21 budget families who lived in two rooms, over half had less than $12 per week to spend; of the five who lived in one room, none had over that sum.*

These figures do not sustain the oft repeated declaration that people would not live better if they could. With the lowest paid workers spending a larger per cent of their weekly fund for rent than the better-to-do, and with overcrowding nearly absent in the better paid groups, we have tangible indications that overcrowding is ordinarily a result of financial necessity, rather than of either hoarding or spendthrift habits. I am speaking here of the families who rent small houses or let out their rooms, rather than of the lodgers who room with them. When income permits, most families secure room enough to make a genuine home life possible. How long people would maintain this standard in the face of prolonged hard times it is difficult to say. Since the depression of 1908 was recognized as temporary, landlords were lenient and waited for their rents. Residents and real estate men, however, told of many families who moved to smaller tenements, and the unusual sight of "to let" signs among the better houses bore witness to the change. A couple who had considered a $25 five-room house none too spacious, sublet two rooms for $8.00 to another couple who had formerly occupied a three-room $12 tenement. This process, which was going on throughout the town during the months of the depression, shows that rent is an item that is cut down when economy becomes necessary. As it happened, none of the budget families moved during this period, and the expenditures for rent given are those of normal times.

To turn from overcrowding to sanitation, I often found that in a house which had abundance of light and air the water faucet was located on the back porch instead of in the kitchen, and that even when there was running water in the house the only toilet was a privy vault in the back yard. These defects, though due in part to the political inaction which has resulted in a bad water supply and to inadequate housing ordinances, constitute partly an individual problem, involved in the relation of landlord to tenant.

* Appendix I, Table 8, p. 203.

53

How far property owners were in a position to disregard the desires of tenants, is indicated by the fact that when I came to Homestead in the fall of 1907, there were few houses for rent in the whole town. My impression of the general situation was that the under-supply enabled landlords to let unimproved dwellings at profitable rentals without having to put them in good order; and that these sanitary deficiencies were submitted to by many people, not because they did not desire better conditions, but because they were unable to pay the higher rates demanded for improved homes. The average rent per month per room of the houses occupied by the 90 budget families was $3.93. The average rent per month of houses in the courts, where conditions were exceedingly bad, was but $3.63 a room, and that of houses on the hill occupied by the native whites $4.14. The difference between these last two rents, then, for a house of four rooms, was over $2.00 a month.

TABLE 14.—FAMILIES HAVING RUNNING WATER IN THE HOUSE AND INDOOR CLOSETS.—BY WEEKLY RENT

Normal Weekly Rent	Number of Families	Running Water in House	Indoor Closets
Under $2.00 . .	16	3	.
$2.00 to $2.99 . .	34	14	2
$3.00 to $3.99 . .	10	7	1
$4.00 to $4.99 . .	6	3	1
$5.00 to $5.99 . .	7	7	4
$6.00 to $6.99 . .	1	1	..
$7.00 and over . .	3	3	3
Owning homes . .	13	7	4
Total . . .	90	47	15

Sanitary conveniences go (or do not go) with a house as a whole. Only three out of 16 of the families whose rent was less than $2.00 a week had running water in the building; one-third of those who paid less than $3.00 had running water inside; two-thirds of those who paid between $3.00 and $5.00; and all those paying over $5.00. Nine out of 13 of the house-owners, moreover, had running water in their homes. Seven out of 11 of the families paying $5.00 or more had indoor closets, as against four out of 66 paying less than that sum.

Taken together, these facts express fairly the desire of American and English-speaking European families to have houses which in size, sanitation, and conveniences would make a normal and efficient life possible. With the existing prices in Homestead, the amount expended for rent by the households whose budgets ran over $20 a week ($4.72) was none too large for the average family which desired sanitary conveniences and a sufficient number of rooms to insure privacy and the development of the home. The sum paid for rent by those who had less than $12 a week to cover all expenditures ($2.15) did not provide bare sanitary surroundings.

As I passed in and out of the homes I was impressed with the genuine strength of the family ideals manifested in simple and externally unattractive dwellings; for standards of home life depend upon more than rooms and running water. It has often been said that the first evidence of the growth of the social instinct in any family is the desire to have a parlor. In Homestead this ambition has in many cases been attained. Not every family, it is true, can afford one, yet among my English-speaking acquaintances even the six families each of whom lived in three rooms attempted to have at least the semblance of a room devoted to sociability. In one three-room house, where there were seven children, a room which had in it a folding bed, a wardrobe, the carriage where the baby slept in the daytime, and the sewing machine, was referred to with pride as the "front room," a phrase with a significance quite beyond its suggestion of locality.

Much money and interest go toward making this room the center of home life. Here in the evening the family gathers about the soft coal or gas grate, while the mother sews, and one of the older children plays to the father. Such "front rooms" are the scenes of those simple festivities which enliven existence in this town. One mother described happily the evenings with her children: "My boys are so musical and the other fellows come in and we all have such a good sing together, and then Mamie dances the Highland Fling. They offered to pay her to do it in the nickelodeon, but the boys won't let her do it away from home."

The furniture, though sometimes of the green plush variety, often displays simplicity and taste. A center table, a few chairs, a couch, and frequently either an organ or piano complete the furnishings. Usually there are pictures—the family portraits or some colored lithographs—and almost always that constant friend of the family, the brilliantly colored insurance calendar. Pictures of one or two such rooms will show how well the women have succeeded in making them homelike.

In the four-room houses, the family eat in the kitchen. In five-room houses we find an anomaly known as the "dining room." Though a full set of dining room furniture, sideboard, table and dining chairs, are usually in evidence, they are rarely used at meals. The family sewing is frequently done there, the machine standing in the corner by the window; and sometimes, too, the ironing, to escape the heat of the kitchen; but rarely is the room used for breakfast, dinner or supper. One woman said, "My daughter is in High School, and she thought we ought to eat there and said she would wait on the table, but in about a week I noticed she set the table in the kitchen again." Where there is no servant it is much easier to cook and serve in the same room; so the dining room, though finding plenty of use, does not live up to its name.

The kitchen is the important room of the house. Here the mother spends the day, here the family meet for meals and the children come between times for the much sought for "piece." The furnishings usually include a good range, either coal or gas, which most Homestead housewives consider a necessity. As few houses have running water inside, set tubs are rare, but washing machines, which cost about $15, are more often found. The kitchen usually opens on the garden, and in the sections where rear houses have not been built this space provides also a place where the children can play under their mother's eye.

Throughout the part of the town occupied by the English-speaking workmen, we find these evidences of a very real interest in the home. More substantial proof of the instinct of homemaking is shown in the often heroic efforts to buy the house. In view of the number of families who could not pay sufficient rent to secure either rooms enough for comfortable living or sanitary conveniences, it is a striking fact that according to the census

Photo by Hine

A "FRONT ROOM"

Photo by Hine

ROW OF DETACHED WORKINGMEN'S HOUSES IN MUNHALL; MILL STACKS
SHOWING ABOVE HOUSETOPS

figures of 1900, 586 families in Homestead borough, 25.7 per cent of the total number, held title to their homes; and 47.4 per cent of these were free from encumbrance. Personal interviews have corroborated this evidence that mill-town workingmen wish to own their dwellings.

In the budget families, eight out of 25 Americans, three out of 13 of the English-speaking Europeans and two of the 29 Slavs owned their homes, and five others were buying them. While none of these earned normally under $12, not all belonged to the highest wage group. Five had an income of $12 to $14.99, two of $15 to $19.99, and 11 of $20 or over. For the five on the lower income it had been a slow process to buy a home, requiring much self-denial.

TABLE 15.—18 HOUSE-PURCHASERS AMONG 90 BUDGET FAMILIES.
—BY NORMAL WEEKLY INCOME AND BY RACIAL GROUP

Racial Group	Number of Budget Families	Number Purchasing Homes	Families in Which Man Normally Earned			
			Under $12.00	$12.00–$14.99	$15.00–$19.99	$20.00 and over
Slav.	29	3	..	1	1	1
Eng. Sp. Eur. . .	13	5	..	3	1·	1
Nat. White . . .	25	10	..	1	..	9
Colored	23	..	..	..	..	..
Total . . .	90	18*	..	5	2	11

* 13 families owned their houses; 5 were paying instalments.

Ownership is made possible in many cases by the attitude of the real estate companies, which in Homestead prefer building for sale rather than for rent, and which safeguard their clients in such a way that workingmen dare to buy. They have made buying a very simple proposition. The purchaser pays down a small sum, sometimes as low as $150. The company assumes the obligation of paying interest on the mortgage, insurance, taxes, etc., and the buyer pays a monthly instalment large enough to cover this and make a small reduction on the principal. For instance, a neat five-room frame cottage with running water in the kitchen but containing no bathroom, is worth about $2000.* Of this sum the purchaser pays $300 down, and his monthly instalment is $17. Smaller houses can be purchased with instalments correspondingly reduced.

About twenty years ago the Carnegie Steel Company started the plan of permitting their employes to deposit money with the company. At that time also the company commenced making loans to employes to assist them in purchasing homes. It was believed the deposits would be offset by the amount loaned for this purpose, but it did not work out that way, the loans not equalling the deposits. Accordingly, for a number of years the extension of deposits by employes has not been encouraged, although any employe who chooses to do so is permitted to open an account. At the present time only about 1100 employes in the different plants of the company are depositors. Loans up to two-thirds of the value of the property are made to employes to aid them in buying homes. Interest is charged at the rate of 5 per cent per annum plus the state tax.† The principal is pay-

---

* The Homestead Realty Company will mortgage such a house for $1,000, and sell the property on monthly payments, taking a second mortgage for the balance less the money paid down by the purchaser. If the family pays $300 down, this second mortgage would be $700. The company sells on the plan of one dollar per month for each $100 of indebtedness. In this case, therefore, the monthly payment would be $17, half of which would be applied against the indebtedness, and the other half would just cover the six per cent interest on the mortgages. Every six months the company gives credit on the indebtedness, thus reducing the interest charges; it deducts taxes, etc., on the other hand, from the payments made. By this system the second mortgage of $700 would probably be cleared by the monthly payments in six years; in other words, the family would be down to the first mortgage. From this point on, as this is only a 50 per cent mortgage, they are able to shift for themselves without the interference of the company. In view of the fact that good locations in Homestead are very scarce, the manager states that families who have paid in $500 or $600, and then desired to leave town, have always been able to turn their property over at as much, or even more, than they paid for it.

† A point of contrast between the house-building operations in such an American mill town, and those in certain of the European industrial centers, is the fact that on the loaned capital by which the American workman becomes a house-owner, he pays a rate not much if any less than that paid by any small individual borrower. Through the Industrial Insurance Funds of Germany, and grants by the governmental authorities in Great Britain, such building operations can be financed at a much lower rate.

able in monthly instalments. At the present time 165 employes have loans from the company.

Some of the other means adopted to secure a home are illustrated in the story of a delightful Englishman, once a silk weaver but now an engineer in the mill, who lives in Munhall Hollow. The meaning of the word Homestead is all but forgotten by its people, but the story of this man's house building shows much of the spirit of the old settlers. When he wished to build, he had very little money. Mr. Munhall, who was then living, gave him a note to a lumber firm, who sold him $200 worth of lumber on credit. He paid down $24 for the lease of a lot.* Since he did part of the work, the labor cost on his three-room house was only about $40. As soon as these debts were paid, he incurred another for $200 in order to enlarge the kitchen and build a second bedroom over it; then he added a front porch and later a shed in the rear for a storehouse, with a chicken coop beside it. All this was done while there were three children at home, and on the income of an engineer, not over $3.00 a day. Now he and his wife, despite the disadvantage of not having a freehold in the land, take in their comfortable though simple home the pride of the creator as well as of the owner—a feeling rare in these days of huge tenements and "company houses," when men accept whatever can be had for the renting and when long shifts make it difficult for them to put the work of their hands into their homes if they would.

When the house is paid for, the family often takes a genuine pleasure in its improvement. Sometimes it is the addition of a bathroom; sometimes the re-papering in the spring which the busy mother finds time to do; sometimes the building of a washhouse in the yard. To plan and carry out these improvements always means the development of a sense of family life and its common interests. One Italian family had been world wanderers, going from Sicily where the man was a stone mason, to France; from there to South America, to pick coffee on a Brazilian plantation; and at last they had come to America. In each of three places in this country in which they had lived they had secured a

---

* Criticism was made in an earlier chapter (p. 26) of the undesirable features of the leasing system of the John Munhall Estate, which affects between two and three hundred families in the community. In this instance the plan did not work out unhappily.

bit of property. Now, as the man was earning $2.50 a day and two relatives boarded with them, he could buy a four-room house on the outskirts of the town, worth $1500. During the summer, after work hours he built a fence, a hen house, and a cold frame for vegetables, and began to get his ground in shape for a good garden. When winter came he went to work on a basement kitchen so that the first floor could be kept for living rooms. He dug and plastered and ceiled it with matched wood, till it was snug and cozy.

To have a bathroom is a real ambition with the native white families, and some of those who live in the otherwise excellently equipped company houses mentioned the lack of one as a great drawback to their convenience. A number of families who owned their houses had themselves gone to the expense of putting in baths, while others proposed some day to do the same. The woman of the Italian family just referred to, who lives on one of the unsewered streets on the hill, told me eagerly that she expected to have a bath as soon as the town provided water, an indication, in passing, of how the town government often lags behind the ambitions of individual householders.

Much of the burden of buying the home falls on the housewife. She must make the needed economies if the extra money is to be forthcoming; she must see that the sum is ready when the days for payments come. The final value of the effort is shown in the case of one family who bought a house when the sons were at home helping to swell the income. Now when the boys are married and gone, and the father, no longer strong, earns but $2.25 a day, the parents can still live in simple comfort. Another instance was that of a couple from the country who started to buy when they were first married. In the course of five years, on an income of about $2.75 a day, they had purchased a comfortable five-room house. One Friday the young husband made the last payment and on Monday he was killed in the mill, leaving his wife to provide for three children. By renting three rooms for $10 a month and by taking in washing, she hoped, with the money coming from the company and his insurance, to maintain herself.

Granted the obvious advantages in house ownership, why after all does not everybody buy? Some families, it is true, can-

1. FRAME HOUSES. Five rooms and bath.
2. BRICK HOUSES. Four rooms and bath; cemented cellars; yard 40 x 400. $2700 to $2800. Built by Homestead Realty Co.
3. RESIDENCE STREET. Tenanted largely by business and professional men.

not save even $150, nor spare the small extra sums involved in the monthly payments. The study of the budgets of families living on $12 or under a week reveals too small a margin after the necessities of life have been provided for. Some, too, are indifferent; others decide against it after consideration. I was much interested in the different positions taken by two sisters in regard to the wisdom of buying. One, with six children, whose husband makes something over $3.00 a day, said: "I didn't try to buy, because I wanted to give my children everything that was coming to them, and I wouldn't stint them." So, as far as she can, she gives them what the other children in school have; and $3.00 goes but a little way when there are eight to provide for. The other, wiser perhaps, began early to buy her home. She has been married only five years, to a man whose income is about the same as her brother-in-law's, and has two little ones to care for; but already she has made the initial payment on the five-room house which will cost them about $3000. By sub-letting two rooms for $8.00 a month their monthly payments take from their wages only about as much as the regular rent. It will be some years before they have the indebtedness paid off, but they plan to be well on their way toward accomplishing this by the time the children are large enough to need the other rooms.

Considering the number who buy on this plan, there are few foreclosures. Since work in Homestead is steady, loss of income due to lack of employment has not been so serious a menace to house buying as in many communities. The depression of 1907-8, of course, produced unusual conditions, but the real estate companies recognized the importance of keeping the confidence of the community and bore the brunt of the trouble themselves. I was told that of the three mortgages foreclosed in Homestead in 1907, none was on a workingman's home. If a man has shown any disposition to honesty,—and in Homestead it is possible to know people intimately,—the real estate company will allow him, when in a hard place, to suspend all payments except interest on the mortgage. Trustworthy people are therefore fairly safe in starting to buy, so far as normally steady work and the co-operation of the realty company can give security.

The house-buyer, nevertheless, has his hazards, and they are

61

very real ones. The greatest difficulty arises from periodical cuts in wages. In 1908 for example, in mid-winter, I was told that the rate of wages of tonnage men was reduced in some cases 16⅔ per cent. A family which by careful economy out of the wages current in the fall, could make the extra expenditure toward buying a house, might after such a cut find itself in a serious predicament. To keep on with payments would mean cutting down everywhere margins that are already small. As these wage cuts can never be foreseen, they introduce so serious an element of uncertainty that many doubt the wisdom of embarking their entire capital, though small, in such a venture. One family had been saving for some time; then the man was slightly injured in the mill, and $80 of savings went before he was at work again. The family kept on saving, however, and with $300 in the bank was hoping to begin the purchase the following spring, when hard times came and the surplus was again diminished. The woman fearing other catastrophes now hesitated gravely. When a family has put all its savings into a house, death, discharge, or displacement of the man by a machine, may compel a forced sale; a strike or season of hard times, or the removal of a plant from a given town, may leave him in a worse predicament.

Home owning, moreover, lessens the mobility of labor, since when one is partly paid for a man will pull up stakes and seek work elsewhere only under extreme pressure. From the point of view of the company, this is an ever present advantage. For the employe it is a potential disadvantage, especially in a town like Homestead where, since the strike of 1892, the men have had no voice in the matter of wages and no security as to length of employment. Hitherto the disadvantages to the employe house-owners have not been extreme because with the lack of sufficient houses in Homestead it has been easy to realize upon them. In the average mill town, however, house ownership may prove an encumbrance to the workingman who wants to sell his labor in the highest market.

CHAPTER V

TABLE AND DINNER PAIL

D URING my sojournings in Homestead, I found it of little avail to stand knocking at front doors. It was wise to go straight to the back door, which opened into the warm and cheerful kitchen. Here I was sure to find the housekeeper busy preparing for the ever recurring meal, economically her most important task. Not only is food the largest item in the family account, but it is also one which, by thrift and ability, housewives can reduce without lessening the comfort of the family. The "cost of living" is a problem they themselves are studying practically, and many of them took a lively interest in the results of the budget investigation.

In general, the account books revealed a fairly intelligent choice of foods, including a large amount of fruit and green vegetables, chosen apparently to meet the need of men who do very hot work. The following bill of fare for four days is fairly typical of the English-speaking households. The head of the family in this instance earned about $3.00 a day.

Monday
Breakfast: Oat-meal and milk, eggs and bacon, bread, butter, jelly, coffee.
Dinner: Soup, bread, fruit.
Supper: Meat, beans, potatoes, fruit, red beets, pickles.

Tuesday
Breakfast: Chocolate, eggs, bread, butter, and jelly.
Dinner: Spinach, potatoes, pickles, warmed over meat, fruit, bread, butter.
Supper: Meat, sweet potatoes, carrots, beans, tomatoes, tea, bread, butter and fruit.

63

Wednesday

Breakfast: Eggs, corncakes, potatoes, coffee, rhubarb, bread, butter.
Dinner: Soup, bread, butter.
Supper: Lamb stew with dumplings, cucumber, eggplant, beans, corn, coffee, bread and butter, fruit.

Thursday

Breakfast: Eggs, fruit, eggplant, coffee, cakes.
Dinner: Soup, bread and butter, cakes, fruit.
Supper: Fish, potatoes, tomatoes, cucumbers, pie, tea.

When the man does not come home for the noon meal, as in this instance, it is usually a light one for the rest of the household. In another family where they had eggs for breakfast and meat for supper, the children were fed at mid-day on mush and milk with bread and molasses.

In mill-town economics, the dinner pail must be reckoned with as part of the table, and a bill of fare must be read with that in mind. I was struck with the pains often taken with the "mister's" bucket. The women used to carry hot lunches to the mill, but they are not now allowed inside without a pass. Most of the men, as they are not given regular time for eating, snatch a bite between tasks, though some, whose work permits, stop for a leisurely meal. I even heard of men who took steaks to cook on the hot plates about the machines. But they usually rely on the cold meal, and the women take great pains to make it appetizing, especially by adding preserves in a little cup in a corner of the bucket. They try to give the man what he likes the most, apparently half from pity at the cold food and hard work that fall to his lot.

On the other hand, the women do not seem to realize that special care is needed in feeding the children, and generally give them much the same that their elders have. The mothers rarely attempt to check the natural tendency of childhood to be always running in for a bite between meals. The children suffer, too, from the fact that the time for meals is irregular because of the weekly change in the man's hours. One woman told me that the men get a bad habit of eating at odd times in the mill, and with this and meal hours changing every week, expect to eat whenever

Photo by Hine

"Buckets"

An opening in the side-wall of the mill: noon-time

they feel like it. The household naturally picks up the habit with disastrous results both to digestion and housekeeping.

Sunday dinner is the one meal that serves as a time of festivity. Almost every account showed that on Saturday an extra piece of meat, usually a roast, was bought. The men have some leisure on Sunday and sit down with pleasure to a more elaborate dinner. Sometimes the married sons and daughters come home for that meal, and altogether it plays a definite part in the week's pleasure. Unfortunately, however, as the men usually work either Saturday night or Sunday night, they rarely have the whole of Sunday to themselves, with that sense of freedom and let-up which means so much at the end of the week.

Occasionally, especially on holidays, there are family reunions. On Thanksgiving, when the mills run as usual, few preparations are made for the hurried dinner. Christmas, however, is a great day in Homestead. Twice a year, on that day and on July Fourth, the great mill stops. Everyone who can goes home, some to families in Homestead, others to neighboring towns, and there are Christmas trees in many homes. Some of the women who kept budget accounts took care to explain that their unusual expenses in December, both for food and extras, were for Christmas festivities.

Formal guests are infrequent. Where the housewife is also cook, there are difficulties in the way of hospitality, which are accentuated by the irregular meals and the hours of work. People who live simply and eat informally rarely utilize the meal time for guests as do more conventional households. But though rarely a time of festivity, the meal hour is always present in the housewife's mind. When asked for an account of what they spent on food the women usually responded cheerfully, "We spend all we can get." They realized, nevertheless, that economies are possible and necessary if bills are to be met on pay day. For in spite of the reputed high wages among steel workers, the problem Homestead housewives face in trying to provide food and a good home on the man's earnings is no easy one. As we shall see from these budgets, excellent management is required to secure a really adequate food supply with the amount that can be set aside for this purpose.

5

Food stuffs are high in this region. At a hearing before the Pittsburgh Chamber of Commerce in 1906, this fact was partially ascribed to geographical situation and local conditions. Since the river valleys are given over to the production of steel rather than of vegetables, fresh foods must be brought from a distance. This, of course, means added cost, because of freight charges. Some dealers claimed, also, that railroad terminal facilities were totally inadequate, and that fruit and vegetables spoiled while waiting to be unloaded. Moreover, as other local dealers stated, the ease with which money has been made in Pittsburgh has invited high prices.

While comparative statistics as to food prices are usually open to question, those secured by the United States Bureau of Labor may be considered fairly dependable, since the same methods were used in securing the data in different localities. According to the figures in the Bulletin for 1907, the ordinary staple articles were more expensive in Pittsburgh than in any other city of similar size in the country. Pittsburgh slightly outranked even New York, not because its prices were in many cases the very highest, though among the selected articles that was true of lard, molasses, and rice, but because this Pennsylvania city ranked second in the prices paid for the great bulk of the commodities of ordinary consumption,—beans, chuck roast, salt beef, butter, mutton, fresh pork and bacon,—all of them articles entering largely into the workingman's bill of fare.*

All Allegheny County is closely connected with Pittsburgh by suburban trolley lines, and prices in the smaller markets throughout the district are to a great extent uniform. Such comparative data as I gathered, fortified by the experience of the housekeepers I knew, indicated that Homestead prices were practically on the same level with those of Pittsburgh.

Given then a fairly high cost of living, what proportion of the household income goes for food? The answer to this first question to be drawn from the budget material was of necessity

* Bulletin U. S. Bureau of Labor, July, 1907, pp. 175-328. See Appendix I, Table 9, p. 203; also Appendix IX, p, 241. Pittsburgh's excess in the prices of food stuffs is, however, not so great as to render the figures as to cost of living in Homestead inapplicable to workingmen's budgets in many other American industrial districts.

affected by half-time work in the case of many families. Yet with this reservation in mind, the figures which show the comparative expenditures of the different racial and economic groups are interesting; moreover, the expenditures of representative families during weeks when they were working as usual, together with those of families who experienced no slack time, lead me to think that they reflect with fair accuracy the normal proportions in Homestead.

The expenditure for food, though varying widely both in actual amount and in its relation to the total expenditure, is always the largest single item. Among the native whites it constituted 36.3 per cent of the total, and among the Slavs 45.7, this variation, as in the case of rent, being the result of differences in income as well as of differences in racial standards. The percentage for food steadily grows smaller, as the total of all expenditures which a family is in position to make grows larger. Food constituted 45.3 per cent of the total among those who spent less than $12 per week and only 36.7 per cent among families spending $20 or over per week. The percentage in the two intermediate groups, considered jointly (that is, from $12 to $19.99) was 42 (Table 17). These percentages for food expenditure are about the same as those secured in other investigations of costs of living. Mr. Chapin gives the percentage in families with incomes ranging from $600 to $1000 (that is, from $12 to $20 per week) as varying between 44.3 and 45.6 per cent.* According to an investigation made by the Federal Bureau of Labor, 5920 families with incomes from $600 to $1,000 spent from 39.9 to 43.48 per cent.†

It is only proportionately, of course, as shown in percentages, that food expenditures grow smaller as families have more to spend. Actually, families with budgets over $20 per week spent twice as much money for food as families with budgets under $12,— $9.38 per week as against $4.16. The most meagre family expenditure of all was among the colored day laborers earning under

* Chapin, Robert Coit: The Standard of Living among Workingmen's Families in New York City, p. 70. New York, Charities Publication Committee, 1909. Russell Sage Foundation Publication.

† United States Commissioner of Labor, 18th Annual Report, 1903, p. 101

67

TABLE 16.—AVERAGE WEEKLY EXPENDITURE FOR FOOD OF 90 BUDGET FAMILIES AND PER CENT OF TOTAL EXPENDITURE. —BY RACIAL GROUP

Racial Group	Number of Families	Average Weekly Expenditures All Purposes	AVERAGE WEEKLY EXPENDITURE FOR FOOD	
			Amount	Per cent
Slav. . . .	29	$13.09	$5.98	45.7
Eng. Sp. Eur. .	13	16.97	7.55	44.5
Nat. White .	25	20.47	7.44	36.3
Colored . .	23	12.39	4.84	39.1

TABLE 17.—SAME AS TABLE 16.—BY EXPENDITURE GROUP

Expenditure Group	Number of Families	Average Weekly Expenditure All Purposes	AVERAGE WEEKLY EXPENDITURE FOR FOOD	
			Amount	Per cent
Under $12.00 .	32	$ 9.17	$4.16	45.3
$12.00–$14.99 .	16	13.32	5.86	44.0
$15.00–$19.99 .	23	17.59	7.11	40.4
$20.00 and over	19	25.56	9.38	36.7

TABLE 18.—AVERAGE WEEKLY EXPENDITURE FOR FOOD OF 90 BUDGET FAMILIES.—BY RACIAL AND EXPENDITURE GROUP

Racial Group	UNDER $12.00		$12.00 TO $14.99		$15.00 TO $19.99		$20.00 AND OVER		ALL FAMILIES	
	Number of Families	Average Expenditure	Number of Families	Average Expenditure	Number of Families	Average Expenditure	Number of Families	Average Expenditure	Number of Families	Average Expenditure
Slavs . . .	14	$4.48	5	$5.99	7	$8.47	3	$7.12	29	$5.98
Eng. Sp. Eur. .	3	5.93 *	4	6.39 *	3	5.83	3	12.45 *	13	7.55
Nat. White .	4	4.29	1	5.92	8	6.48	12	9.26	25	7.44
Colored . .	11	3.22	6	5.40	5	7.00	1	8.45	23	4.84
Number of families	32	..	16	..	23	..	19	..	90	..
Ave. expenditure	..	$4.16	..	$5.86	..	$7.11	..	$9.38	..	$6.32

* The families in the English-speaking European group were much larger than in the other groups, averaging 7.1 persons per family as against 5.2 in the Slavs, 4.8 in the native white and 3.8 in the colored families. This influenced their total food expenditure in the lower income groups.

$12, who averaged $3.22 per week. The amplest was among English-speaking Europeans who were earning the wages of skilled men and who in dollars and cents spent four times as much for food as the former (Table 18). The food expenditure of Slavs ranged from $4.48 a week for the families under $12 to as high as $7.00 and $8.00 a week; the native whites from $4.29 to over $9.00.*

But all such statements as to average food expenditures for entire households are inaccurate in so far as families differ in size. Professor Atwater† overcomes this difficulty by reducing household expenditures to a per capita basis. In line with his calculations as to the comparative amount of food needed, we have assumed that the average woman eats .8 as much as a man, children over fourteen the same, and children under fourteen, .5 as much.

TABLE 19.—AVERAGE EXPENDITURE FOR FOOD PER MAN PER DAY OF 90 BUDGET FAMILIES.—BY RACIAL AND EXPENDITURE GROUP

Racial Group	Under $12.00		$12.00–$14.99		$15.00–$19.99		$20.00 and over		All Families	
	Number of Families	Average Expenditure	Number of Families	Average Expenditure	Number of Families	Average Expenditure	Number of Families	Average Expenditure	Total Families	Average Expenditure
Slav. . . .	14	$ .25	5	$ .29	7	$.36	3	$ .31	29	$.29
Eng. Sp. Eur. . .	3	.19	4	.19	3	.25	3	.35	13	.24
Nat. White . . .	4	.21	1	.19	8	.28	12	.39	25	.32
Colored . . .	11	.30	6	.24	5	.34	1	.36	23	.30
Total Families . .	32	..	16	..	23	..	19	..	90	..
Average expenditure .	..	$ .26	..	$ .24	..	$ .31	..	$ .37	..	$.29

The per capita food expenditure among our 90 budget families is shown in Table 19 for both racial and expenditure

*The naïve report of the Committee on Trade and Commerce to the Pittsburgh Chamber of Commerce November 18, 1909, estimates that a liberal provision of food for a family of five would in Pittsburgh cost $11.88 a week. See Appendix IX, p. 238.

† Bulletin 21, U. S. Department of Agriculture.

groups. Here, as in the case of other tables in which the 90 families have been cross-classified into racial and economic groups, the subgroups are obviously too small to do more than suggest general tendencies, which commended themselves to me as noteworthy in view of many conversations with housewives.

While the expenditure for food per man per day in each racial group usually increases as expenditures increase, we may note distinctions among them. The native whites and English-speaking Europeans spend in the three lower expenditure groups decidedly less than either Slavs or colored. A reference to Chapter IV will show that with rent this proportion is reversed, the native whites and English-speaking Europeans spending larger amounts for rent in these lower economic groups. That is, their families seem to have a higher standard of housing, which they maintain when the income is low by making sacrifices in other lines. With them, the desire for a good home may outweigh that for more varied and palatable food. The Slavs, on the other hand, who put up with poor housing, will not skimp to a great extent on food.*

My inquiry was concerned, however, less with relative expenditures for food than with the question of how well people could live on the amounts actually spent. The depression did not enter in here as a disturbing factor, as prices in Homestead were unaffected by the hard times. Accurate figures on this point were difficult to secure, but undoubtedly any change would have been immediately noted by the housewives. Many of them expressed their belief that prices kept about as usual.

In a study of a number of household budgets in New York City in 1907, Professor Underhill of Yale estimated that 22 cents per day per man was in general the minimum for which an adequate supply of food could be procured.† This figure was based on a study of the nourishing quality of food measured in calories

---

* See Appendix I, Table 10, p, 204. My Slavic families, moreover, were for the most part smaller in size. They could spend as much as 25 cents per day per man, even in the lowest expenditure group, without making the average outlay for food per family noticeably large.

† "Comparisons between the amounts spent for food by well nourished and poorly nourished families indicate that in general when less than 22 cents per man per day is spent for food, the nourishment derived is insufficient." Report on Nutrition Investigation, Frank P. Underhill, Ph. D., in Chapin, The Standard of Living among Workingmen's Families in New York City, p. 319.

and proteids; the former representing the heat-producing fats and sugars, and the latter the tissue builders—meat, bread, beans, etc. Careful experiments have been made to determine both the amount of each of these elements which given foods contain, and also the amount necessary to keep a man in a condition of physical efficiency. Having before him the actual costs to the housekeeper and the nourishing value of the articles eaten by certain households, Professor Underhill was able to estimate for what sum the ordinary purchaser could secure a sufficient amount of food to maintain a male adult in physical well-being.

By the use of Professor Atwater's ratios as to the relative amount of nutrition needed by men, women and children, such a standard per man per day affords a test of how well the food purchased by a family meets its physical needs.

As we have seen that the Federal Bureau of Labor Report for 1907 rates food prices very nearly the same in New York and in the Pittsburgh district,* and as there were no indications of reductions in the local markets during the weeks of my inquiry, we may accept Professor Underhill's standard of 22 cents a day as fairly applicable to our Homestead budgets of the same year.

Recurring then, with this standard in mind, to a closer scrutiny of actual expenditures for food among English-speaking Europeans and native whites, we find (Table 19) that the average cost of the former was 24 cents per day per grown man, and that of the latter 32 cents. As was to have been anticipated, families with few children and comparatively large incomes spent generously for food (from 28 to 39 cents per man in the higher expenditure groups). But the average for all English-speaking Europeans (24 cents) barely exceeds the amount necessary to supply sufficient nourishment even with wisdom in the choice of food. The average in both racial groups for those spending less than $15 per week fell below that amount.

---

* To apply proportions rigidly, the Pittsburgh district minimum would be 22.9 cents. No attempt was made by the writer to carry on independent experiments in food values as to Homestead dietaries. An analysis was made of the food expenditure of an exceptionally thrifty housekeeper, however. So far as estimates for proteids and calories can be drawn from account books, without weighing the actual food stuffs used, this indicated that even with careful purchasing, less than 22 cents would not provide the standard of nourishment in Homestead.

Altogether, in 21 out of the 90 budget families (Table 20) less than 22 cents per man per day was being spent for food. Low wages, hard times, and large families, all were factors in depressing their consumption below this minimum. Of these families, 14 expended less than $12 a week for all purposes, seven a total of more than that.

TABLE 20.—TWENTY-ONE FAMILIES SPENDING LESS THAN 22 CENTS PER MAN PER DAY FOR FOOD.—BY EXPENDITURE AND RACIAL GROUPS

Expenditure Group	Slavs	English-speaking Europeans	Native White	Colored	Total
Under $12.00 . .	5	2	2	5	14
$12.00–$14.99 . .	..	2	1	1	4
$15.00–$19.99 . .	..	1	2	..	3
$20.00 and over . .	..	..	..	..	..
Total . . .	5	5	5	6	21

In the case of the seven families whose expenditures ranged above $12 per week but whose per capita outlay fell below the minimum of sustenance, size was an important factor. English or American families with nine children (one instance), seven children (two instances), or six (three instances) obviously found it necessary to economize closely on food if the other standards of American life were to be maintained. It may be worth while to note here that I found with all budget families* expenditure for food per person decreasing steadily with the increase in the size of the family. This was true in each expenditure group. For example, among families whose total expenditures were less than $12 per week, those with two to four in the family spent an average of 24 cents per man per day for food while those with five or more in the family averaged but 19 cents. In the $12 to $14.99 group, the per capita sum fell from an average of 29 to 23 cents; in the $15 to $19.99 group, from 41 to 24 cents; and in the group spending $20 or over, from 48 to

* Appendix I, Table 11, p. 204.

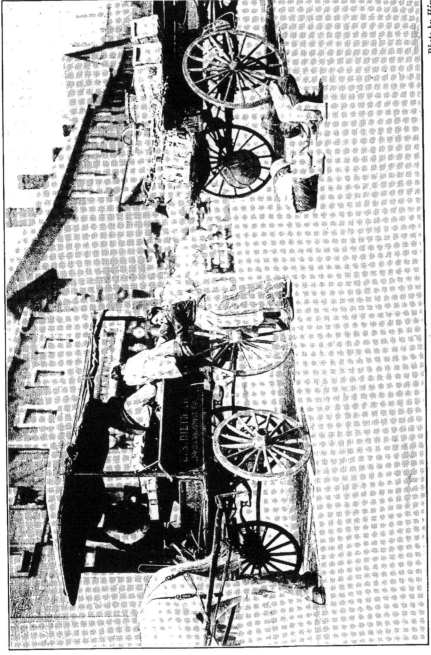

Photo by Hine

THE STREET MARKET

32 cents. This general decrease is in part due to the fact that the housewife can buy more economically for a large family, and also that when the family is small and the sense of economic pressure less heavy she indulges in more costly articles. With respect to the lower expenditure groups, the controlling factor no doubt is that with only a certain fairly definite share of the earnings available for food, that food must be divided among a certain number of mouths.

This will be clearer if we look at the case of 14 families whose expenditures were below $12 a week and who spent less than the minimum standard. On the basis of 22 cents a day per man, a normal family* must spend $5.08 per week on food alone, or 50 per cent of the earnings of a day laborer working the ordinary ten-hour day of the yard laborers in the mill. This is in excess of the percentage which any group studied allowed for food. Unless such a man works overtime or Sunday, or the family supplements the man's earnings by lodgers, lives in a court, or has few or no children (with the Slavs one or all of these factors are often present),† this allowance for food must be cut down if the other items of expenditure are to be met. Among these 14 families, there were some whose income was always at this low margin, as well as some whose weekly expenditures had been depressed by temporary lack of work. The necessity to cut down on food is the same in one case as in the other and as a matter of fact, omitting the Slavs, half of all budget families whose expenditures were below $12 a week, spent less than the sustenance standard for food. Where the family is above the normal in size, this pressure is accentuated.

It is conceivable that a desire to save might lead a family to be niggardly in its food expenditures; though the Slavs, among whom we would first look for such practices, due to their keen desire to lay by money, averaged 25 cents per man per day in the under $12 group. A more extensive study would no doubt have elicited cases where drunkenness, shiftlessness, sickness or other

* Man, wife, three children under 14. See U. S. Bureau of Labor, 18th Annual Report, p. 20.

† Two other alternatives are for women or young children to go out to work— alternatives not present to any extent in Homestead.

immediate causes of small or squandered earnings reduced a family's food expenditures below this standard. A consideration of these tables, however, has shown us unmistakably how near to the line of under-nourishment must be the families of large size or low incomes. More important than that 21 families fell below 22 cents for food, is the fact that, including the Slavs, the average expenditure for food of all our budget families spending from $12 to $14.99 per week was but 24 cents per man a day. That gives a margin of but two cents a day which can only too quickly be lost through a housewife's failure to get the most for her money at market, to select nourishing food, or to secure the nutrient values out of what she puts on the stove. In view of the occurrence of the hard times, these figures should not be taken as an accurate expression of customary food expenditures in Homestead in prosperous years. They do show what Homestead housewives felt it necessary to spend for food when they were economizing.

We must remember, also, that many unskilled housekeepers cannot provide enough nourishment on a minimum outlay requiring wisdom in the choice of food. The sufficiency of food purchased cannot be measured altogether by the amount spent. Perhaps in this expenditure more than in any other there is a chance for women to display their skill, an asset which must be included in the family resources. Two households, undoubtedly extreme types, will serve to illustrate this point.

The first was a Scotch family of seven who had been in this country for about fifteen years. Besides the three younger children in school there were two sons at work, whose wages brought the family income up to $32 a week. The six-room house was none too large to make them all comfortable and enable them to have a pleasant sitting room. As I stepped into the kitchen one frosty morning, I was greeted by the odor of preserves which the wife was making ready to vary the monotony of dinners to be eaten from a "bucket." We fell to discussing methods of economy and she told me many of her thrifty ways; about the pig they would buy as soon as cold weather came, to provide salt pork and ham for the winter; the pickles and preserves she was putting up; the $50 she was saving to buy the winter's supply of dry groceries from the wholesaler's. That this thrift did not amount to parsimony was shown by the good gas range and washing machine in view, and by evidences of ample provision of food. By planning ahead, by extra labor, by wise buying, even luxuries were secured on a food expenditure of only 24 cents per person a day.

The other extreme was shown in the home of a poor, unintelligent woman who had gone to work at the age of eleven, and could neither read nor write. As enough to pay the rent was the only contribution to the family purse made by her husband, a ne'er-do-well, she herself was obliged, by washing and by taking a lodger, to provide money for food and clothes. This money, which averaged $4.50 a week, was very irregular, as the lodger was frequently out of work. With a wayward boy in school and a sickly baby at home, she had but little time and thought to give to housekeeping. Food was bought daily by the five and ten cents' worth,—pork chops, cheap preserves at ten cents a jar, two quarts of potatoes, a loaf of bread, etc.—a pitiable record viewed either from the standpoint of the children's health or of the pocket-book. The least nutritious food was bought in the most expensive way, because of ignorance and of a small and uncertain income. The items of her expenditures (at 25 cents per day) were deficient in the elements which provide heat and energy to the body, and lacking in the foods which replace worn-out cells. The sample week's account from each of these budgets on page 76 shows the contrast in their methods of buying.

Usually the housekeeper buys a large order of supplies on Saturday and supplements it during the week with additional purchases of meat, vegetables and other foods. Among Homestead women no subject provokes discussion more readily than economy in buying. Some claim that the chief evil of Homestead life is an extravagance fostered by the ease with which families buy on credit. As the accounts run for two weeks and are settled on "pay Friday," the family never catches up. A number of women expressed their conviction that when prices of articles like butter and eggs are not constant, the grocers are inclined to overcharge a little for goods on credit. Moreover, it is much easier to be extravagant when no cash is paid out and the price is simply jotted down in the "book." A woman who tried this method once, found it so expensive that at the end of two weeks she threw the book into the stove and would never use one again.

75

TABLE 21.—ITEMIZED ACCOUNT OF FOOD EXPENDITURES FOR ONE WEEK BY A THRIFTY HOUSEKEEPER

Saturday

Milk	.08
49 lbs. flour	1.75
Bananas	.15
Grapes	.25
Cabbage	.25

Monday

Milk	.08
2½ lbs. beef	.30
Steak	.30
Pie	.12

Tuesday

Milk	.08
Tea	.60
Cheese	.36
2 doz. eggs	.60
Coffee	.25
Candy	.10
Grapes	.10

Wednesday

Milk	.08

Friday

16 lbs. ham	$2.00
Spices	.10
Vanilla	.10
Milk	.08

TABLE 22.—ITEMIZED ACCOUNT OF FOOD EXPENDITURES FOR ONE WEEK BY A POOR HOUSE-KEEPER

Saturday

Bread	$ .05
Jelly	.10
Coal	.10
Pork (3 lbs.)	.50
½ pk. potatoes	.15
Cabbage	.12
2 lbs. sugar	.11
½ lb. prunes	.05
Can corn	.10
2 loaves bread	.10
½ doz. eggs	.14
Cooking apples	.10
½ lb. butter	.18
1 lb. cheese	.20

Monday

Lima beans	.10

Tuesday

2 lbs. boiling beef	.25
Can peas	.10
Can syrup	.10
½ doz. fig cakes	.06
Baking powder	.05
½ pk. potatoes	.15
Bread	.05
Pork chops	.15

Wednesday

Boiling Beef	.15
Barley	.05
½ doz. pickles	.05
Bread	.05

Thursday

Can molasses	.10
1 doz. rolls	.10
Pudding	.10
2 lbs. sugar	.11
Turnips	.10
Tea ¼ lb.	.15
½ doz. doughnuts	.05

Friday

Pie	.10
Sausage	.10
Can corn	.10
Bread	.05
Jelly	.10

Women expressed varied opinions upon the economy of buying in Pittsburgh. There were those who believed that even when prices were slightly lower in the city, the saving was more than counterbalanced by the time and carfare expended in the trip. Some housekeepers also claimed that low priced goods purchased from wholesale houses in town were of so poor a quality that it was not economy to buy them. Then, too, the women felt that loyalty to Homestead demanded that they purchase in their own town as far as possible. So, though on Saturday afternoon the cars are filled with women carrying baskets home from Pittsburgh markets, the larger part of the purchases are made in Homestead. Hucksters, who come out each morning with goods from the Pittsburgh commission houses, sell fruit and vegetables. Though some of these men undoubtedly give poor quality and short measure, the older housekeepers usually find a trustworthy one and become regular patrons.

Many women show a genuine pride in their skill in buying and in utilizing different cuts of meat. One woman assured me that it was no economy for her to buy pieces which contained bones, gristle and fat, since her family would not eat them. If instead of buying such cuts at 10 cents a pound she paid 15 for solid meat, her money really went further. I shall not soon forget the enthusiasm with which one young wife described a special potato meat pie, her husband's favorite dish, which she made from the ends of steak too tough to use in any other way. These women are anxious not only to practice economies, but to conceal them by good choosing and skilful cooking.

When sickness or lack of work reduces wages temporarily, the amount available for food is lessened. During the depression I was surprised to see how quickly certain housewives rose to the emergency in their determination that the family should feel this change as little as possible. Sometimes this meant a serious cutting down of the amount essential to physical well-being; at other times economies were accomplished by foregoing luxuries and by the purchase of simpler but more nutritious food. Here is an interesting budget, the two accounts having been kept by the same woman, one in December, when the man was working steadily; the other later in the winter when, having lost his regular

77

employment, he took laborers' work at little more than half his former pay. While the cost in the second account dropped noticeably, a rough calculation indicates that the nutrient value remained almost the same. This was accomplished, at least in part, by doing without meat and with less fruit, both expensive in proportion to nutrition.

TABLE 23.—TWO WEEKLY FOOD BUDGETS OF A THRIFTY FAMILY

Article	(1) Account When Man Worked on Full Pay		(2) Account When Man Worked on Half Pay	
	Cost	Pounds	Cost	Pounds
Meat . . .	$1.81	12.1	$0.75	5.7
Beans. . .	.06	.5	.06	.7
Milk . . .	.11	2.7	.30	10.0
Cheese . .	.12	.6	.06	.3
Butter . .	.21	1.2	.35	1.3
Eggs . . .	.17	.8	.28	2.6
Flour. . .	.14	2.3	.42	10.3
Bread. . .	.47	5.5	.31	3.3
Potatoes . .	.21	12.0	..	..
Turnips, etc. .	.05	2.2	.10	3.6
Green veg. .	..	..	..	..
Canned veg. .	.25	2.5	.11	1.3
Fruit . . .	.62	20.3	.40	12.0
Sugar. . .	.31	7.1	.28	9.3
Sundries . .	.58	..	.42	..
Total . .	$5.11	69.8	$3.84	60.4

Such economy is usually instinctive rather than the result of special knowledge or interest in food values. Both in good times and bad times this woman failed to give her family sufficient of the tissue builders. The housewives expressed some scorn of the theoretical aspects of the problem as taught in the cooking classes of the Schwab Manual Training School, feeling that practical experience was of more value than any theory. As the girls who attended the cooking classes were many of them only in the grammar grades, they probably did not make clear at home the everyday applications of theories expressed in unfamiliar terms. Proteids and calories seem to bear so little relation to pork and beans.

The four prize housekeepers I knew were daughters of Pennsylvania farmers. They had learned as country girls how to work, how to provide, and how to economize, and how at the same time to create a real home atmosphere. Girls, on the other hand, who had worked in factories or been clerks, lacked the practical training necessary to help them solve the problems awaiting the young wife of a wage-earner. To my surprise also I found that in some instances domestic service was a no more satisfactory preparation for housekeeping. I remember a kitchen where all was wretched, the children unwashed, the woman untidy, the room unswept. Though the man earned $3.20 a day, his wife, trained as a servant in a wealthy home, had learned extravagant ways and realized helplessly that she could not "get caught up" with her bills, manage her home efficiently, or train her children. "He doesn't see," she said, "why it is though he earns twice what he did when he married me, we are still behind, and he doesn't even carry any insurance."

The task of solving these problems demands, as already suggested, no mean degree of patience, of practical skill, of intelligence and interest. We demand that the worker save, and forget that this often can be accomplished only by constant, intelligent watchfulness on the part of the wife, or by doing without some of the essentials of a normal, healthful life.

The marvelous success of some women should not blind us to the fact that they are exceptional housekeepers. After watching the busy lives and the problems of these women, I came to believe that the woman who can keep her home healthful and attractive on $15 or less a week has in her elements of genius. Many a woman who can keep house fairly well on an income that does not require close economy would find herself, I am sure, sadly at a loss to maintain a satisfying table on 25 cents a day per man—the level upon which, in a period of hard times, my "under $15" budget housekeepers managed their expenditures for table and dinner pail. If these per diem tests are indicative, this would allow little more than enough to maintain the physical efficiency of a workingman's household even with the most skilful expenditure; a margin of only 15 cents a day to make good any lack of skill, or to provide a leeway for the purchase of appetizing trifles. A round of food chosen solely for its value in proteids and calories would be an undue tax on the housekeeper's brain. Only skilled housekeepers can set a table that is both nourishing and appetizing for such a sum.

Buying nourishing food at a small cost is not a task completed once for all. These are three-times-a-day problems. Even the most skilful fail at times to buy wisely, and what is to be anticipated for those whose large families make such heavy demands on them that they are unable to find the time to plan and provide ahead of the need; those with an uncertain income; those especially who are just incapable and unintelligent? If vigilance is relaxed or if some disaster lessens income, the food supply is bound to fall below what is essential.

CHAPTER VI

OTHER EXPENDITURES: THE BUDGET AS A WHOLE

THE vital problem which in normal times confronts these homemakers is not provision against physical destitution. With the wages given in the steel mills, that may safely be assumed for the families of the English-speaking workers. The question is whether when they have met their rent and food bills there is money enough left to provide for the other vital needs of mind and body.

The answer to this question was partly revealed by a study of the detailed items of expenditure from which the accompanying tables were drawn. Once the food and rent account had been paid, the margin for other family expenditures, during the period studied, ranged from $3.14 a week in the group spending under $12, to $12.45 among those spending over $20. This margin increases proportionately, as well as actually, with increased income; for while only a little over one-third of the expenditures of families spending under $12 goes for other needs than food and shelter, the proportion in the higher groups approaches one-half of the total outlay. At every level, this increasing margin must be distributed among three main spheres of expenditures: (1) for other home and personal needs, such as fuel, clothing, furniture, service and minor housekeeping items, through which, no less than through rent and food, the family expresses its household standards; (2) sundry outlays for social purposes such as education, recreation, religion and the like, through which the family shares in the community life; and (3) savings and insurance through which the family provides for old age or for such emergencies as sickness, accident and unemployment.

Since the margin is often not large enough to provide equally for all these ends, each family reveals something of its inherent character by the choices it makes. One family chooses present pleasures as against the comfort of owning a house; one mother music lessons as against pretty clothes for the children. In each sphere some items are regarded as essentials, and others as non-essentials.

As between expenditures in these three directions then, not only the contents of pay envelopes, but the individual preferences of families within the various expenditure groups, play an important part. I shall not attempt to discuss the relative expenditures for such purposes, complicated as they were by the occurrence of the hard times,* but rather to suggest to the reader some things which influence the decisions made by a family, and indicate how far incomes at the different levels may permit of rational expenditures one week after another in all these directions.

The tables and general discussion will mean more if the facts concerning the expenditures of a few families are first noted, bringing out some of the distinctive items which fall into individual budgets:

STONE. A colored family of five, the man a teamster earning $12 a week, had an average weekly expenditure of $12.24 during the time the account was kept. Rent, $2.00; food, $6.23; coal, $1.45; washing materials, $ .09; insurance, $ .39; church, $ .10; tobacco, $. 08; medicine, $1.09; sundries, $ .86.

STEARNS. An English family of five who own their house had an average weekly expenditure of $12.03. Food, $6.49; fuel, $ .80; clothing, $ .09; repairing house, $3.58; insurance, $ .39; medicine, $ .19; sundries, $ .59.

AHEARN. An American family of five who own their house, had an average weekly expenditure of $14.68. Food, $9.27; clothing, $3.29; fuel, $1.50; washing material, $ .06; kitchen utensils, $ .20; sundries, $ .26.

---

* For instance, furniture and clothing are not representative items in a four weeks' study of a family's spendings; still less are they so during hard times. The extent of savings represented by house-buying on the instalment plan is extremely difficult to get at. The small expenditure for tobacco and liquor in these budgets is to be accounted for, at least in part, by the fact that men did not tell at home what they had purchased. It is to be remembered that in these tables the basis for classification is weekly expenditure, not normal or actual earnings. The women usually hesitated to ask the man about his spending money, and as in the days of slack work they did not know just what he earned it was difficult to learn of such personal items.

ROTH. Young American couple with one child, had an average weekly expenditure of $16.96. Rent, $3.33; food, $6.19; clothing, $5.30; furniture, $ .17; household expenses, $ .26; insurance, $1.00; sundries, $ .69.

STILLMAN. Man, wife and two children; Scotch; had an average weekly expenditure of $18.63. Payment on house, $5.00; food, $5.19; fuel, $ .83; clothing, $1.00; furniture, $ .87; household expenses, $ .87; insurance, $2.65; tobacco, $ .53; medicine, $ .52; sundries, $2.05.

LESTER. Family of eight, had an average weekly expenditure of $21.09. Rent, $2.21; food, $8.02; fuel, $ .45; clothing, $5.37; furniture, $1.44; household expenses, $ .60; insurance, $ .34; tobacco, $ .29; medicine, $ .75; sundries, $1.56.

WHITE. American family of five, the man dead but two sons support the family. They own their house. Their average weekly expenditure was $21. Food, $8.56; fuel, $1.00; clothing, $ .39; household expenses, $ .22; furniture, $2.75; insurance, $2.55; newspapers, music lessons, etc., $1.81; church, $ .27; recreation, $ .14; medicine, $ .90; sundries, $1.15.

BYRNES. American couple living in an attractive house with bath. Their average weekly expenditure was $22.57. Rent, $5.00; food, $9.22; gas, $3.42; furniture, $ .80; insurance, $1.02; medicine, $2.50; sundries, $ .59.

HOWE. An Irish-American family of five owning their house. Their average weekly expenditure was $30. Food, $14.04; fuel, $2.47; clothing, $1.62; washing, $ .31; furniture, $5.57; insurance, $ .66; education, $ .30; spending money, $ .96; tobacco, $ .34; dentist, $1.25; bank, $2.50; sundries, $ .10.

The following paragraph gives the total expenditures for four weeks for everything but food and rent of a family of seven whose average weekly income was $16.38.

Oil, $ .40; coal, $5.20; interest instalments on furniture, $2.00; lamp wick, $ .06; shovel, $ .10; basin, $ .15; brush, $ .05; soap, $ .30; stove and shoe blacking, $ .16; paint, $ .50; broom, $ .35; stockings, $ .35; shoes mended, $1.55; gloves, $ .10; hat, $ .10; underwear, $ .40; shoes, $1.40; thread, $ .06; ribbon, $ .28; candy, $ .15; carfare, $ .20; insurance, $1.10; medicine, $ .10; church, $ .08; "flowers for the dead," $ .60; spending money for children, $ .36; for boy at work, $1.00; for man, $4.50. Total for the month, $21.54.   This gives an average for everything above food and shelter of $5.38 a week.

TABLE 24.—AVERAGE WEEKLY EXPENDITURE OF 90 BUDGET FAMILIES FOR VARIOUS ITEMS.—BY EXPENDITURE GROUP

Expenditure Group	Number of Families	Average Weekly Expenditure	Rent	Food	Fuel	Clothing	Furniture	Minor Household Expenses	Insurance	Tobacco	Liquor	Medicine	Sundries
Under $12.00 .	32	$9.17	$1.88	$4.16	$.38	$.94	$.09	$.15	$.70	$.07	$.20	$.10	$.50
$12.00–$14.99 .	16	13.32	2.29	5.86	.77	1.57	.20	.23	.51	.05	.14	.47	1.23
$15.00–$19.99 .	23	17.59	2.73	7.11	.66	2.10	.36	.58	1.05	.05	.63	.48	1.83
$20.00 and over .	19	25.56	3.73	9.38	.90	3.36	.80	.66	1.86	.08	.11	.58	4.09

TABLE 25.—RATIO OF WEEKLY EXPENDITURES FOR VARIOUS ITEMS BETWEEN DIFFERENT EXPENDITURE GROUPS

Expenditure Group	Total Expenditure	Rent	Food	Fuel	Clothing	Furniture	Minor Household Expenses	Insurance	Tobacco	Liquor	Medicine	Sundries
Under $12.00 .	100	100	100	100	100	100	100	100	100	100	100	100
$12.00–$14.99 .	145	122	141	203	167	222	153	73	71	70	470	246
$15.00–$19.99 .	192	145	171	174	223	400	387	150	71	315	480	366
$20.00 and over.	278	198	225	237	357	889	440	266	114	55	570	818

A glance at Tables 24 and 25 indicates how different items respond to changes in available income.   Expenditures for food, rent, fuel, and insurance increase less rapidly than do total expenditures, while clothing, furniture, minor housekeeping expenses, medicine, and sundries, increase more rapidly.   This suggests the main distinction made by these people as to what they consider necessities and what luxuries.   There is a limit below which necessities will not be cut down even when economy is necessary; the more essential the item, therefore, the smaller is its rate of increase as more income becomes available.

Undue economy, may result in the lowering of more than

Photo by Hine

Where Some of the Surplus Goes

purely physical standards. It may also interfere with the development of social standards. We are all imitators, and the inability to have what others have, even when the absence of the thing is not in itself a privation, reacts on the individual life by lessening the sense of self-respect and social standing. For example, to turn to our first group of marginal expenditures, the development of home life depends in part on having furniture enough. The front room to be used must be cozy. Fresh curtains, a couch, and an occasional carpet are household effects which must be currently reckoned with. To secure these, the instalment dealer is often resorted to. The majority of the people often buy on the instalment plan though in conversation they usually admit that it is an extravagant method. As one thrifty housewife said, "I must have new curtains this spring, and I haven't the money." There seems to be in the main little difference in the financial standing of the families buying on cash and on instalment. It is in fact more often from those with small incomes that you hear the emphatic statement, "I won't buy anything unless I have cash for it." It is largely a question of thrift and the will power to wait for things till the money is in hand. While the most frequent purchases are such expensive articles as pianos, sewing machines and couches, with some families everything even to blankets, curtains, and clothes are bought in this way. Some married people even start their housekeeping on this basis, though the more thrifty among them put off the wedding day till the money is ready. One young couple began life in a three-room tenement, equipped with pretentious furniture for which they had paid cash. The woman showed me the "mahogany" bed set, elaborately carved, the dining room furniture and a good kitchen range, which she assured me were purchased at reasonable prices for cash, the two sets costing respectively $136 and $60. The bride, who is very proud of them, feels that they justify the delay in marriage. As she is only seventeen now, one can quite agree with her. There is little danger that people whose work is as steady as is usual in Homestead, will be unable to keep up payments, and I learned of no instances where furniture was taken for failure to pay. However, the decision to buy a new piece of furniture is often a matter for grave consideration, and an unattractive home may be a sign, not of indifference, but of actual inability to pay for anything beyond the merest necessities.

Again, if the need for economy in fuel is too insistent, front rooms are left unheated, and bedrooms have no stoves. While the picture often conjured up of the whole family gathered about the kitchen table in the evening is delightful ,the custom has some drawbacks. It is hard to do "home work" when the baby cries; it is harder still to do one's courting under the family eye; it is hardest of all to develop mentally or spiritually when solitude is impossible. While these disadvantages result from overcrowding, we must remember that an economy in fuel also which makes some of the rooms useless during the winter months has the same results.

The same desire for social sanction which finds expression in the ambition to have a well furnished parlor affects the expenditures for clothes. The woman referred to earlier who did not save because she wanted her children to dress as well as others exemplifies the strength of this desire. Providing clothes is an ever present task to many women, especially to those with growing daughters. One woman who had a home to keep on $2.00 a day achieved remarkable results in economical and attractive attire by buying remnants at bargain sales and making them herself into tasteful dresses. She was rewarded by the pleasure given to her three girls,—yet the strain of overwork in the long run wore her out, mind and body. It is not fair to look only at results and not count the cost, to say that because women can keep attractive homes on low wages we are justified in expecting them to do so, unless we know what may be the physical and mental outcome of their struggle.

Some leeway in household purchases is a definite help to overburdened housewives. For example, under minor housekeeping expenses is included not only the item of kitchen utensils, washing materials, etc., but also of personal service. To pay for sewing is possible only in rare instances, so clothes are either made at home or bought ready-made. Except in families having an income of over $20, the washing is rarely done out, unless there is sickness. Housework may be materially lightened by the use of gas instead of coal, and in Homestead, with its supply of natural gas, the relative cost is not great,—only thirty cents a thousand cubic feet. But even with care its use for baking, washing and ironing, as well as heating, makes the bills grow, and an income of $12 a week does not permit a gas bill of $2.50 a month,—that of one careful housekeeper,—nor the purchase of gas ranges. Again, $15 washing machines, which families with larger incomes frequently have, serve to lighten the tedious task of keeping clothes clean in a smoky mill town. Incidentally, they make it possible for the man to help, since not uncommonly "the mister" when working at night "turns the machine" before going to bed in the morning. In one family the husband had attached it to the hydrant so that the water served as motive power and turned the machine while the woman attended to her other duties,—a great advance over the back-breaking washboard. These four items, then, of fuel, furniture, clothing and housekeeping expenses, represent specifically the financial problems the woman must meet. To reduce them is her special economy, and freedom to increase them relieves her in part of that monotonous and constant struggle to make the home attractive on the man's earnings.

One interesting point in Table 25 (page 84), is that expenses incurred for health (which may well be grouped with these other home expenditures) count as a luxury to be indulged in only with increasing income. When, for instance, a child is ill, the state of the pocket-book, no less than the seriousness of the disease, determines whether the doctor shall be called. Tonics for the rundown in spring time are dispensed with in a laborer's home. Perhaps the tendency in this direction that is most serious in its results, is the custom of relying upon midwives in confinement. While this is more frequent among the foreigners (the abuses associated with it will be referred to in Chapter XI), many English-speaking women call in midwives because their fees are much smaller and because they help in the housework. There are no visiting nurses in Homestead whose assistance can be secured for an hour or so.

Under "Sundries" (Table 24) are grouped not only miscellaneous items which fall under no other head, but those that might be called the social expenses of the household; those which enable it to bear its part in the community life,—expenses for church, education, newspapers, and recreation of all sorts. Two accounts taken at random will illustrate the variety of needs to be met by this allowance. In one colored family where the man earns $2.10 a day the expenditure of $1.65 a week was as follows: Candy, $ .05; toys, $ .20; garden seeds, $ .11; carfare, $ .12; postage, $ .01; school, $ .30; church, $1.00. In another family where there are six children, and the income was about $3.00 a day, the expense for sundries for a week was but $ .70: Candy, $ .09; carfare, $ .20; lunches away from home, $ .14; shoe polish, etc., $ .08; bird seed, $ .02; repairing wringer, $ .12; amusements, $ .05.

Fortunately public school education is not a direct expense to the household in this country, but outlays for newspapers, books and, in Homestead, membership in the Carnegie Club are to be included. Many people take one of the two local papers which, though they contain the more important general news, are largely devoted to town matters, including a good deal of neighborhood gossip. The second-rate stories and anecdotes on the inside pages form a substitute for cheap magazines. These papers, while possibly financially independent are, as far as I could see, over-loyal to that industry which has created the town's prosperity and are lamentably weak as exponents of the real sentiments of the workers. The dues of $2.00 a year in the Carnegie Club, entitling one to membership in all classes, are within the reach of almost all, and probably do not deter many from joining. Library books are free and good current magazines, including those treating of the manufacture of iron and steel, are in the library. The members of the family, therefore, may have books to read, even if they cannot buy them for the home. Whatever education the town offers is practically free to all.

A second expense included in sundries is that for church support. In a recent book entitled Christianity and the Social Crisis,* the author reminds us that modern industrial conditions have made it practically impossible to obey the old command that a tenth of the income should be devoted to the church.

* Rauschenbusch, Walter: Christianity and the Social Crisis. New York, The Macmillan Company, 1908.

Photo by Hine

EIGHTH AVENUE AT NIGHT, HOMESTEAD

Photo by Hine

A NICKELODEON AUDIENCE IN HOMESTEAD

If only these narrow margins remain for amusements, education, church and sundries, obviously a tenth for church is quite out of the question. One reason, Mr. Rauschenbusch claims, why the church has lost its hold on working people, is because they cannot afford their share in its maintenance. In the cities this burden is sometimes assumed by the members of wealthy churches who support mission chapels, but in Homestead there is no such group to depend upon if the working people cannot themselves support the churches. The family whose item for sundries included $1.00 for church was an enthusiastic and pious colored family, but except among this race and among the Slavs the contributions for church were pitifully small, rarely more than a few cents for Sunday school. Upon examining the budgets one realizes why church suppers and other similar methods of raising money under the guise of amusements are frequently necessary.

Under sundries come all purely recreational expenditures. In another chapter are described some of the opportunities for play and festivity which are open to Homestead people. When we note that during the period studied, the families whose budgets ran between $12 and $15 a week allowed themselves on the average but $1.23 for all sundries, we see how small an amount can be free at this and lower levels for what could be called amusements. Ten cents a week for the nickelodeon or for candy, a car ride to the country once in a while,—these are the possibilities which seem open to mothers and children depending on a day laborer's pay.

Thus far we have considered the costs of shelter, food, clothing, and other ordinary charges for maintaining a home, together with some few further expenditures growing out of the family's relation to the world about it. Its plans for the future next concern us. This is my third category under marginal expenditures, and includes provision for the contingencies of death, sickness, and lack of work. The problems these may present to the household are readily illustrated.

The Petersons, an American family of five had, with genuine thrift, saved enough to buy their own home and also had started a bank account. The man was a skilled workman and earned over $20 a week. A long illness brought them to dependence on their savings and the sick benefits from two lodges. For two months their accounts were kept, when their expenditures had fallen from $20 to $9.35 a week. These weeks averaged as follows: Food, $4.38; fuel, $ .40; clothing, $1.41; furniture, $ .08; housekeeping expenses, $ .20; insurance, $1.20; tobacco, $ .13; medicine, $ .60; sundries, $ .95.

The Webers's income dropped off with the hard times. This thrifty German household had a comfortable four-room house with running water for which they paid $15 a month. The man was a skilled worker in the mill who earned ordinarily $4.00 a day. For four weeks, however, in which they kept account for me, his earnings amounted in all to but $35, and this had to suffice for a family of six. They had to let part of the rent remain unpaid and with this credit added in, their total weekly expenditures averaged $10.48 or $1.49 a day. Some relatives who were less pinched helped with food, which accounts for the extremely low table expenditure. Their expenses were as follows: Rent, $3.75; food, $2.94; clothing, $ .27; housekeeping expenses, $ .06; insurance, $2.52; tobacco, $ .15; liquor, $ .20; sundries, $ .59.

These figures will give some hint of the drastic way in which a temporary emergency cuts down a wage-earner's income and cuts out of a family's expenditures all but the most essential items. With the customary regularity of work in the mill, however, anxiety for the future in Homestead usually focuses itself on the possible sickness or death of the breadwinner. The usual way in which working people prepare for these two emergencies is by insurance. It is noticeable that the tendency of the insurance item in the budgets is to increase less rapidly than total expenditures (Table 25, page 84); this form of provision for the future, therefore, is counted a necessity in Homestead. Both fraternal and regular insurance are carried. Of the men in the budget families 57.8 per cent held memberships in lodges; 43.3 per cent had policies in regular companies;* 11 men held two policies, 10

* The social features of lodge membership, to be discussed later, undoubtedly create a preference for insurance in fraternal orders rather than in commercial companies; but cheaper rates are also partly responsible for the larger percentage insuring in the former. The question which, of course, arises as to whether these low rates are consistent with safety is too large to discuss here. The people themselves have usually unbounded faith in their reliability, though I was told of at least one order which had failed.

TABLE 26.—NUMBER OF PERSONS INSURED IN 90 BUDGET FAMILIES AND PER CENT OF FAMILIES CARRYING INSURANCE.*—BY EXPENDITURE GROUP

Expenditure Group	Total Families	COMPANIES		LODGES		Number of Families having Insurance	Per cent of Families having Insurance
		Men Insured	Others Insured	Men in Lodges	Others in Lodges		
Under $12.00 .	32	12	20	15	10	26	81.3
$12.00–$14.99 .	16	8	9	8	12	14	87.5
$15.00–$19.99 .	23	10	16	18	11	22	95.7
$20.00 and over .	19	9	17	11	14	15	79.0
Total . .	90	39 (43.3%)	62	52 (57.8%)	47	77	85.5

TABLE 27.—NUMBER OF PERSONS IN 90 BUDGET FAMILIES INSURED IN REGULAR COMPANIES AND LODGES.—BY RACIAL GROUP

Racial Group	Total Families	NUMBER OF MEN HOLDING ONE OR MORE POLICIES, OR UNINSURED							Total Families Carrying Insurance	Per cent Families Carrying Insurance	NUMBER INSURED IN COMPANIES		NUMBER INSURED IN LODGES		Number not Paying at Time of Investigation
		Uninsured	One Policy	Two Policies	Three Policies	Four Policies	Five Policies	Others Insured Where Man not Insured			Men	Others	Men	Others	
Slav . . .	29	2	25	2	..	..	..	..	27	93.1	2	6	25	15	3
Eng. sp. Eur. .	13	4	1	3	5	..	..	..	9	69.2	8	17	8	17	..
Nat. white .	25	5	10	3	3	2	2	0	20	80.0	13	20	14	8	..
Colored . .	23	2	12	3	2	..	..	4	21	91.3	16	19	5	7	..
Total . .	90	13	48	11	10	2	2	4	77	85.6	39	62	52	47	3

* It was difficult to secure accurate statements as to the amount of the policies since, in some instances, industrial insurance and lodge insurance vary with the length of time a policy has been running. Often the families themselves did not know the exact amount. No attempt has been made, therefore, to classify insurance by the amount of the policies.

three, two four, and two five. The two groups overlap, so that altogether 85.6 per cent of the budget families carried insurance in one form or another. In no expenditure group did the percentage fall below 80.

Among these families the amount expended for insurance, as well as the proportionate number insuring, increases with income until the group spending over $20 per week is reached. The lower percentage in the latter group may indicate that the families are better able to rely on savings, and find insurance less essential for burial and sickness expenses. Most of the policies held in this group called for materially larger death benefits. It is of interest to note that the two nationalities in which the largest proportion of families carried some form of insurance were the Slavs and the colored. Most of the Slavs carried insurance in lodges rather than in the commercial companies. Some reasons for this we shall see in our later discussion of the Slavic community life.

One reason why workingmen's families feel so keenly the need of insuring can be shown by the roll of accidents reported in the Homestead paper for three typical months, January, February, and March, 1907.* Fifty-two men were injured during that period in the Homestead mill, and 13 others who lived in Homestead at the time of the accident, were injured in mills of the United States Steel Corporation outside of Homestead. Of this total of 65, seven died. Of the remaining 58, 30, or a little over half, suffered such injuries as crushed feet, lacerated hands, sprained ankles,—injuries for the most part that laid them up for at least a week or two. But there were more serious accidents—three men had a leg or an arm broken, two had an arm amputated,

---

* In May, 1908, a central committee was appointed by the United States Steel Corporation to co-ordinate and improve the work of eliminating preventable accidents on the part of constituent companies. The Carnegie Steel Company had been one of the most active in this field in the year preceding. The Company's inspector stated in the spring of 1908 that in seven months he had made two thousand recommendations for increasing the safety of men. During the past two years there has been a systematic development of this work. It is but fairly begun, however, and aside from preventable accidents, there are many which are inevitable because of the nature of the work. For a further discussion of the causes and results of accidents in the steel industry, see Work-Accidents and the Law, by Crystal Eastman, a companion volume in the series of the Pittsburgh Survey.

ten were wounded about the face and head, the eyes of four were hurt, eight received internal injuries, and one was paralyzed. The accompanying clippings show minor injuries reported in the Homestead papers for two weeks when the plant was working only part time. They further illustrate how constantly the men are confronted with danger.

Along with other employes of the Carnegie Steel Company—in Duquesne, Braddock and elsewhere—the men in the Homestead mills have benefited by the Carnegie Relief Fund of $4,000,000 given in trust in 1901, "to provide for the employes of the Carnegie Company . . . injured in its service and for those dependent upon such employes as are killed." This gift was made by Andrew Carnegie at the

Andy Pasios had his right hand lacerated while at work in the mill yesterday morning.

F Taylor, of Bellwood, had his right foot injured while at work in the blacksmith department at the steel works yesterday

John Kristoff, of Whitaker, had his right wrist sprained while at work in the 140 inch mill yesterday.

HOT METAL FELL IN WATER AND EXPLODED

Last evening at 5 o'clock an engine hauling hot metal from the mixing house to open hearth No. 2, sideswiped a yard engine near the 48 inch mill. The impact of the collision tilted the ladle and some of the liquid steel spilled in a pool of water along the track, exploding with loud report, causing a large number of mill workers to rush to the scene. No one was injured, but several had a narrow escape from the flying metal.

Joseph Novic, of Ravine street, is suffering from contused wounds of the left wrist, received while at work in the 23 inch mill yesterday.

TWO MEN INJURED BY CHAIN BREAKING

Two men were injured by a chain breaking in the 32 inch mill last evening. John Joseph, of Whitaker Way, was cut about the head and body, and John Hoan cut on the head and neck. Both were given medical attention and sent home.

John Joseph of Whitaker Way, Munhall, is suffering from contused wounds on the shoulder and neck received while at work in the 32 inch mill last evening.

Frank Stein had a finger on his right hand lacerated while at work in the mill last evening.

Michael Kane, of Eighteenth avenue, had his right hand hurt while at work in the mill yesterday

John Evans a steel worker who resides near Franklin school house, had his left hand lacerated while at work in the 140 inch mill yesterday

FOREMAN INJURED AT STEEL WORKS

W. N. Crawford, a foreman in the 123 inch mill, met with a painful accident this morning. While walking through the mill he fell in a hole and sustained a contusion of the hip and head. After his injuries were dressed by the company physician he was able to go to his home on Ninth avenue, Munhall.

John Doyle, of Eleventh avenue extension, is suffering from contused wounds of the back, received while at work in the mill yesterday.

FRACTURED HIS ARM. Peter Morris, a well known citizen of 1256 Ravine street, was a victim of a painful accident yesterday afternoon at 3 o'clock, while at work in the steel works. He was adjusting a pipe in the 35 inch mill in the boiler house, when he lost his balance and fell from a platform to the ground below with sufficient force to fracture his left arm. He was taken to the office of the company physicians, where he received medical attention and was later removed to Mercy hospital.

Thomas Salisbury, of Whitaker Way, who was injured in the mill some time ago, is improving slowly. Bernard Wood will entertain the Excelsior class of which he is a member at his home on next Friday evening.

time of the organization of the United States Steel Corporation, a "first use of surplus wealth upon retiring from business, as an acknowledgment of the debt which I owe to the workmen who have contributed so greatly to my success." The fund was not intended as a substitute for compensation on the part of the company. It was intended, to quote Mr. Carnegie, "to go still further and give to the injured, or employes who were needy in old age, some provision against want as long as needed, or until young children can become self-supporting."* Under this fund the sum of $500 has been paid to the widow of each workman killed, with $100 additional for every child under sixteen. To the family of a single man killed, $500 has been paid wherever it has been shown that he was a regular contributor to the support of the family. When damage suits have been brought against the company, these benefits have been withheld, but only until the cases were decided. The original plan provided benefits also for all injuries causing disability for more than two weeks, but these proved more numerous than the fund could deal with, and beginning in 1905, benefits have been paid from the fund only in cases where the injuries resulted in disability lasting more than one year, and in such cases benefits have been paid only until the injured man could get work. Thus, if a man who had lost a leg secured a job as watchman, his benefits ceased. In 1907, the fund paid employes in the Homestead works $11,398 (38 cases) in death benefits, $2,583 (7 cases) in accident benefits, and $4,756 (36 cases) in pension allowances. Thirty families who received death benefits, six who received accident benefits, and 21 who received pension allowances, were still resident in Homestead.

The Carnegie Relief Fund has been the most notable voluntary provision against the hazards of work covering any group of employes in the Pittsburgh District. Its importance is shown by the fact that in the case of 42 married men killed in the Carnegie Company's employ in Allegheny County in twelve months in 1906-7, the company paid less than $500 in 35 instances (about the treatment customary among the employers of the district). With the Carnegie Relief benefits added, $500, or over, was re-

* See Appendix XI, p. 245.

ceived by 31 out of the 42.* But as three-quarters of the cases, even with this addition, received less than $1000, it is clear that the bulk of the burden of lost income still fell upon the families of the killed workmen.

In injury cases, as stated, aid has been available from the fund only when disability lasted for more than a year. The company has frequently paid the hospital bills† and sometimes made a donation, but in a great majority of these cases, even those that have meant six or nine months of idleness, the families could not count on any stated assistance.‡ For household expenses

*TABLE A.—COMPENSATION PAID BY CARNEGIE STEEL COMPANY TO WIDOWS OF 42 EMPLOYES KILLED IN ALLEGHENY CO., PENNSYLVANIA, JULY 1, 1906, TO JUNE 30, 1907

Number of Families	Amount Paid
10	0
17	$ 100 or less
8	$ 101 to $ 500
3	$ 501 to $1000
2	$1001 to $2000
2	Over $2000

TABLE B.—COMPENSATION RECEIVED BY 42 WIDOWS ENTERED IN TABLE A, PLUS CARNEGIE RELIEF BENEFITS

Number of Families	Amount Received
1	0
5	$ 100 or less
5	$ 101 to $ 500
20	$ 501 to $1000
8	$1001 to $2000
3	Over $2000

From Eastman: Work-Accidents and the Law, pp. 160–161.

† A Homestead Hospital was organized in 1907 but the movement received no encouragement from the Carnegie Company. In addition to contributions from residents and organizations in the town, it received a state appropriation from the legislature. It suffers from the handicap of any small hospital, that with a small number of cases it cannot secure the best appliances or the services of specialists. Within the last two years the Carnegie Steel Company has put up, near the mill, a one-story emergency hospital with an operating room and two or three beds. Here cases can be treated that require only immediate attention or that are not in condition to be carried to the West Pennsylvania Hospital in Pittsburgh.

‡ In April, 1910, announcements were made of sweeping changes establishing a stated system of relief. The $4,000,000 of the Carnegie Relief Fund has been united with an $8,000,000 fund set aside by the United States Steel Corporation and will be used to provide pensions for superannuated workmen. Distinct from this the Corporation announced a plan for the relief of injured workmen and the resident families of those killed in work-accidents (for details see Appendix XII, p. 249) which provides far more adequately for these emergencies. The amounts given, however, do not make up for the income loss entailed by death or permanent injury. They afford a systematic scheme of relief from want due directly to industrial causes, but insurance must remain an important item in the family budget, as a safeguard against natural causes of death, and also if a family's standard of living is to be maintained subsequent to serious or fatal accident to the breadwinner.

during such periods they have had to depend on savings, the help of friends, or on sick benefits. Therefore, for protection to their families against death and injuries they have turned to insurance. One woman told of a serious accident her husband suffered in the mill in the first year of her married life. He was unable to work for three months and during that time the $12.50 a week he received from three benefit orders supported the family. "My baby came then," she added feelingly, "and if it had not been for that money, I could not have bought clothes for her." The frequent accidents, moreover, have tended to keep insurance rates high in Homestead so far as the men are concerned. Not long ago one of the largest industrial insurance companies, the Prudential, made a first-hand investigation of work hazards in steel mills in order to put its policy rates on a sound footing. With the exception of superintendents and office men, it no longer accepts steel workers as first-class risks.*

Among the budget groups the average weekly insurance payments ranged from $ .70 to $1.86. To put in concrete form what such weekly insurance expenditure means in actual benefits for the family, we find in the Home Guards, for example, that a weekly premium of $ .35 for a man whose occupation puts him in an intermediate grade, allows a sick or accident benefit of $13.50 for 16 weeks, a compensation of $525 for the loss of two eyes or two limbs, with benefits for lesser accidents in proportion, and a death benefit of $150. In the Modern Woodmen or the Royal Arcanum a premium of about $ .15 a week provides a death benefit of $1000. That is, for $ .50 a week a family can partially safeguard itself against the loss from sickness or death of the man, while if there are a wife and three children in the family an additional $ .25 to $ .40 is necessary, to provide even for their funeral expenses. So nearly one dollar a week is required to make modest provision† against these contingencies,—a large

---

* See Appendix X, p. 243. Another insurance company which has 3800 industrial policy holders in Homestead states that it makes no extra charge because of the occupation.

† Compare the English workmen's compensation act which provides that in case of death the family shall receive the equivalent of three years' wages. This for a man earning $12 a week would equal $1872; for a man earning $15 a week, $2340.

proportion of a wage of $12 or $15 a week. Only those families whose expenditures averaged $17.59 per week felt that they could spend as much as that.

It is significant that with the exception of three Slavs, all the families continued their insurance payments during the period of depression. One woman told me that her husband could not afford to keep up his membership in his lodge though they continued to carry their company insurance, but I heard of no English-speaking people who discontinued payments entirely. Saving in any other form during this time was an impossibility, but families even when drawing money from the bank kept up their insurance.

The marked absence of savings in these budgets was, of course, inevitable during such a period of slack work. As the mills had hardly shut down at all for fifteen years, the need for saving for periods of idleness had not been an ever present one to the minds of the people. But the thriving business done by the four savings banks in Homestead in ordinary times indicates that there is popular sentiment in support of this form of thrift. Four from which figures were secured had on September 1, 1907, total deposits amounting to $2,179,624. I was unable to secure definite data as to the number of budget families having bank accounts, since this was one point on which I found people reticent. At least ten of those whom slack work threw out of employment, drew on savings funds. The amounts spent in purchase of homes, which were discussed in a previous chapter, are of course another form of savings. Thirteen budget families owned homes and five were buying them under mortgage.

There was no evidence, however, of any such wide-spread provision through savings for old age, non-employment, high school education, or other use, as there was for sickness, injury or death. For all these latter contingencies provision may be made through insurance policies or lodge memberships; such provision for the future is deemed a necessity; and however inadequate in amount, it is practically universal in all grades and groups. But however strong the desire for money savings may be, it appears that with only a small margin above the sum deemed necessary for essentials, most families in the lower wage groups must face a choice between some present comforts and

7

enjoyments and the peace of mind which a bank account gives. Yet in Homestead, as elsewhere, the advantages of such a margin of ready money are only too apparent. No individual family income keeps always at its maximum; sick benefits do not equal wages; cuts in rates are declared without warning, and occasionally comes a time like the winter of 1907–8 when the whole town has to face the problems that arise when the mills are running only part time. Not only were men out of work, but lodgers were unable to pay their rent. Families who had had washing done out or a woman come in to clean retrenched by doing this work themselves. The entire town, therefore, was affected by the partial shutdown of its one industry.

A number of the budget families suffered from this temporary decrease of income. To meet it, expenditures in many households were cut to the quick, money that had been saved was taken from the bank, and food was purchased on credit. In one family, for instance, two accounts were kept; one when the man was working full time, the other when his pay was reduced by half. The contrast shows that the reduction fell heavily on kitchen expenses (which means an increase in the woman's work), on recreation, and on sundries.

TABLE 28.—EXPENDITURES OF A FAMILY FOR ONE WEEK IN 1907 (NORMAL TIMES) AND IN 1908 (TIME OF DEPRESSION)

Year	Total Expenditure	Food	Fuel	Clothing	Housekeeping Expenses	Service	Furniture	Instalment on Home	Insurance	Papers	Recreation	Medicine	Sundries
1907 (Man working full time)	$18.79	$5.19	$.82	$1.00	$.17	$2.43	$.92	$5.00	$.53	$.19	$.67	$.51	$1.36
1908 (Man working half time)	10.63	3.85	.73	1.00	.01	..	..	4.02	.11	..	.11	.49	.31

One woman said, "I believe in cutting things according to my cloth. What we can't afford to pay for now, we won't have." In another family the usual income of $19 a week was temporarily reduced to $9.10, an additional $4.72 being obtained on credit. This $4.72 was the entire amount spent for food for a family of eleven. During this period, however, they expended weekly $2.80 for insurance, $2.00 a week for the man's spending money and carfare (they lived in a suburb), $2.75 for rent, $ .32 for tobacco, $ .82 for gas. Aside from these regular weekly items their total sundry expenditure for the month consisted of coal hod and fender, $1.10; a lantern, $ .25; candy, $ .05; a child's coat, $1.98; a pair of stockings, $ .10; matches, soap, blueing, etc., $ .65.

Apart from economies in all lines, the chief dependence of these families in supplementing the man's lessened earnings was credit. Forty-six families were depending upon it for either food or rent.

TABLE 29.—BUDGET FAMILIES WHOSE INCOME INCLUDED MONEY DRAWN FROM THE BANK OR GOODS SECURED ON CREDIT.— BY EXPENDITURE AND RACIAL GROUP

Income Group	SLAV		ENG. SP. EUR.		NAT. WHITE		COLORED	
	Credit	Bank	Credit	Bank	Credit	Bank	Credit	Bank
Under $12.00	9	2	3	..	3	0	5	..
$12.00–$14.99	3	0	3	..	1	..	3	..
$15.00–$19.99	3	2	1	1	3	1	3	..
$20.00 and over	2	2	0	0	4	2	0	..
Total	17	6	7	1	11	3	11	..

The conditions of town life probably enabled people to resort to credit more than would have been the case in a larger city. Since the entire town is dependent on the steel industry, the men could not find other work in Homestead and were unwilling to take the uncertain chance of obtaining it elsewhere in a dull season. There was, moreover, the recurring probability that the mills would soon resume their normal output. Nor could the women find employment. On the other hand, both landlords and grocers knew their customers personally and therefore granted credit freely to the trustworthy. They felt that the confidence thus created would help their trade when better times came. Grocers particularly taxed their credit to the utmost, saying that they would trust their regular customers as long as the wholesalers would trust them.

The amounts actually purchased in this way make one realize how appallingly behindhand wage-earning families get during long-continued hard times. For example, the 32 families with an income of less than $12 a week secured an average credit per family of $1.09 a week for food; those with $12 to $14, $1.45; those with $15 to $19, $ .87, those receiving $20 and over, $ .78. The native whites bought an average of only $ .27 worth on credit, but the Slavs bought an average of $1.57; the English-speaking Europeans, $1.34; the colored, $1.01. As the depression lasted for more than a year, months would have to elapse before the families could wipe out their accumulated indebtedness. One woman in May, 1908, told me that she already had a bill of $75, with prosperous times still a long way off.

In these emergencies, neighbors quietly helped each other; but a local relief committee found that few of the older residents would come to them for assistance, however unostentatiously given.

It was then by means of household economies and by going into debt, that the majority of families, whose men were wholly or partly out of work, met the hard times which came to Homestead. But we must recognize that these economies often meant physical hardship and that the accumulated credit was to be a burden which it would take months to wipe out; that spent savings put off for a long time the buying of the house and that children perhaps had to give up another year in school.

The question of how far the present should be sacrificed in order to guard against future emergencies is raised sharply by such a period of hard times. That savings are eaten up and families thrust into debt by long periods of slack work are facts bound up in the general problems of industrial prosperity and depression.* But that after fifteen years of almost steady work,

* The United States Steel Corporation stood out strongly against a general reduction in wages in the industry during the depression. In January, 1908, the Carnegie Steel Company, however, reduced rates in most of the skilled departments at Homestead. The plate mill men, for example, received reductions of from 3 to 22 per cent.

so many families, especially in the lower earnings group, should be so unprepared to weather the hard times, raises questions both as to the sufficiency of the normal wages and as to the foresight of the wage-earners.

What, we may well ask, do savings cost the family of a wage-earner who earns less than $3.00 a day? Are they readily possible without discomfort or meagreness of living, or do they come out of a food supply none too large to furnish adequate nourishment? Do they come out of what should go for the amusements essential alike to mind and body?

Only an exhaustive study of great numbers of budgets could answer these questions with any finality. The decision in individual cases between present pleasures and provision for the future seems to be partly due to experience and partly to temperament. One woman told me the story of the early experiences of hard poverty she and her husband had endured as children. She was the child of a widow employed in a factory, and he was one of a big family on a farm where all had worked early and late. And now though he is on tonnage rates they save nothing. Aside from her husband's heavy insurance, their money goes for present pleasures and comforts, with a conscious enjoyment possible only to those who have had to do without. With no children to make the future a problem, they have definitely chosen the pleasures of the passing moment. An occasional trip to the theatre, plenty of good clothes, company for meals,—the money goes fast enough. In marked contrast is the expenditure of an American family of five who have the same income. Their house is smaller, and their festivities are less numerous; besides carrying heavy insurance, they are saving to buy a home, and at the same time are giving the daughter music lessons. Their average weekly expenditure was as follows: Rent, $2.54; food, $8.60; clothing, $2.24; furniture, $ .84; household expenses, $ .19; insurance, $3.02; education, $ .65; church, $ .28; recreation, $ .23; tobacco, $ .11; medicine, $ .29; sundries, $ .43. During the period the account was kept, their savings did not average half a dollar a week.

Interesting as they are, however, such individual cases offer little more than a glimpse of the personal equations involved. The average expenditures in the various groups are more representative as indications and enable us to state the problem with more accuracy. For we have now reached a point where we can recapitulate our 90 budgets, and see more clearly what they indicate as to the round of possible expenditures open to average households run at each of the expenditure levels.

In the lowest expenditure group of budget families, the average weekly outlay was $9.17, and the averages for the items were:

Rent. $1.88	Insurance. . . .$ .70
Food. 4.16	Tobacco 07
Fuel 38	Liquor 20
Clothing 94	Medicine 10
Furniture. 09	Other expenses . . .50*
Household expenses . .15	

We have certain standards of physical necessities by which to test what may be secured for given amounts. For example, rent at $1.88 a week is less than $8.00 a month. In the Slavic district I found that $8.00 was the cost of the two-room tenements without improvements, facing on courts. Of the budget families in this group only about a third had running water in the house, and in two-thirds of these homes there were two or more persons to the room. This certainly is below the minimum standard of comfort or health even for a laborer's family.

In the chapter on food expenditures, we found that 22 cents per man per day is the minimum for which a skilful housekeeper can provide food sufficient to maintain physical wellbeing. Thirteen out of 32 families in this group were actually spending less than the minimum of 22 cents. For the average family in the group, the expenditure of $4.16 a week furnished just this amount. For families of normal size, however,—father, mother and three children under fourteen,—this weekly expenditure would allow but 18 cents per man per day.

These average allowances for food and shelter are inadequate for normal standards. They include no excess from which the sum available for the remaining items might be increased.

* See Table 24, p. 84. For expenditures of 28 house-renting families in this expenditure group, see Table 10, page 45. The situation would not be materially altered if we had taken the average expenditures of the house renters as a basis for our discussion.

On the Outskirts: Munhall Hollow and its smoke-blighted trees in June

Photos by Hine

In the Crowded Section: Three families share the house and seven the yard

WHERE RENTS ARE CHEAP

Yet as we analyze the $3.11 a week remaining after food and rent have been secured, we find it obviously inadequate to provide wholesome living. The needs of the future are recognized in an elemental way in the 70 cents a week for insurance. For 50 cents a week, as we have seen, the man could through fraternal orders secure a death benefit of $1000 and four months' sick benefit yearly, leaving only 20 cents a week toward burial insurance for his wife and children.

According to the estimate made by Mr. Chapin in New York, $100 a year is the smallest amount that will supply sufficient clothing for a family. Here clothing expenditure for the weeks studied was less than half this sum. Yet even so, there would remain only $1.50 a week to cover all family expenditures for fuel, furniture, recreation and liquor, for support of the church, for newspapers and magazines, to say nothing of savings for sickness or hard times. We find then that the average expenditure of this lowest group of families, $9.17, could not supply in Homestead a "living" for a family in its simplest meanings. The objection may be made that as many of these families were, at the time of the study, living on less than their ordinary wages, these figures (though they are to be deplored as a level to which the family of a workman may be depressed even in hard times) do not represent household conditions in normal years. The average weekly expenditure for these families, however, was but 10 cents a day less than the prevailing wages of Homestead laborers in 1907-8,—$ .16½ an hour for a ten-hour day, or $9.90 for a six-day week.* Under the section on Slavs (page 140) the analysis of the actual expenditures of a group of laborers getting an average of $10 per week, during the period studied, offers further indications that these earnings do not constitute a "living wage" for a family. They were the nominal earnings of the great bulk of unskilled immigrants employed in the mills in the "good times" of 1907.

In the next expenditure group (ranging from $12 to $14.99) the average expenditure was $13.32 (Table 24, page 84). Though

---

* If we apply the same percentages for the different items to this total of $9.90, we find that the expenditures for food would be $4.48 (or 19½ cents per day per man), for rent $2.03 (which would secure a two-room tenement without improvements) and a margin for other items of $3.39 as against $3.12—differences too small to invalidate the conclusions reached.

the problem of supplying the physical necessities may be less pressing, we find no adequate margin above them for other expenditures. The $2.29 a week spent for rent would provide three rooms, but without sanitary conveniences. For a family of five this is very close quarters; more than one-half of the families in this group averaged two or more persons to the room. Besides the danger to health, especially in time of sickness, such small and crowded apartments permit no opportunity for privacy or for social gatherings in the home. Food at an average of $5.86 a week for the family of five persons gives an expenditure of 24 cents per man per day. This, as we have seen, at best allows little leeway for a large family or an incompetent housewife. In fact, four of the families in this group spent less than 22 cents. A margin of $5.17 is thus left for clothing, furniture, insurance, minor household expenses, fuel, liquor and sundries. While budgets covering a period of less than two months are not a sound basis for any conclusions as to these expenditures, the items as we find them are at least indicative of the ways in which the margin above food and shelter may be proportioned. Clothing at $1.57 a week, on Mr. Chapin's estimate, would still not provide the absolute essentials. With $10 a year one could buy little furniture, except such as would replace linen, carpets, and curtains, and an occasional article to meet the needs of growing families. The families studied here averaged less for insurance than did the lower expenditure group, with its preponderance of Slavs. Similarly the other headings show no easy chance for economy as a means of increasing the amount free for sundries; yet reference to the account of the families on page 88 shows that the $1.23 a week remaining would be eaten up so quickly by small necessities that little would be left for savings or recreation. The items are a fair indication of what it is possible for a workingman to provide for his family out of $2.25 a day. The impression to be gathered from a review of them is unmistakably that of a sub-normal household.

The next group ($15–$19.99), which had an average expenditure of $17.59 (corresponding roughly to earnings at $3.00 a day for six days a week), shows a marked increase in these household items. Rent at $2.73 would provide a small detached four-room house. But it falls far short of the sum which we estimated would secure sanitary conveniences and a sufficient number of rooms to insure privacy and the development of the home. Nine out of the 23 families in this group were still without running water, and nine of the families had two or more persons per room. The rise in expenditure for food to $7.11 a week, or 31 cents per man per day, gives a fair margin, though three families, in two of which there were seven children each, dropped again below the 22 cent limit. Here a balance of $7.75 is available for the rest of the budget. The expense for clothing is slightly above the cost Mr. Chapin estimates as essential, and that for furniture about doubles the $10 per year of the previous group. Insurance is also increased to the point where it would secure the modest provision noted on page 96, though it still fails to provide at all reasonably against the lost income due to the breadwinner's death. The gain in sundries, which have risen to $1.83 a week, marks our first noteworthy leeway in expenditure; it is still too small, as we have seen, to enable the average family to lay by any appreciable savings and at the same time permit itself recreations essential alike to mind and body.

The group spending over $20 a week had an average expenditure of $25.56 a week, or above $4.00 a day. Rent at $3.73 a week or $16 a month provides a detached four-room house without a bathroom. A house with a bathroom can hardly be rented for less than $20 or $22 a month. Food at $ .37 per man per day is plainly ample to supply necessities, and yet one or two accounts where this amount was spent showed no actual extravagances, if measured by our American standards. The expenditure for clothing for this period is the equivalent of $175 a year, for furniture $42. The amount for sundries, $4.09, is more than double what the previous group had to spend for these items.

We find, that is, so far as this group of 90 family budgets can show us and at the range of prices current in Homestead, that only when earnings are $15 a week, or more, can we confidently look for a reasonable margin above the requisite expenditures for necessities. It is only in the group spending more than $20 that we find that the average family has reached a point where, without being spendthrift of the future and without undue pinching in other directions, they can spend enough to satisfy

105

what we should recognize as the reasonable ambitions of an American who puts his life into his work. The household problem for the great number of English-speaking workmen in Homestead whose earnings fall between these two figures, is that of proportioning earnings so that, with the children fed and housed in such a fashion as to maintain physical well-being, the wife may gain some leisure from household cares, they may all have some share in the pleasures and responsibilities of the community, and may make such provision for future emergencies as their own experience and that of their neighbors show to be essential. Failure to attain the ideal should not be considered prima facie evidence of the unfitness of the family to meet its problems.

For Homestead has its ideals,—ideals of a genuine home life for the family, if possible in a home of its own, where there shall be sufficient leisure and attractive enough surroundings to make it the center for happy lives; ideals of such security as in time of sickness or misfortune shall enable the home to care for its own. With the wages offered by the industry many of the workers can attain these ideals, if at all, only by unremitting work and inexorable compromises. We find housekeepers facing cheerfully the problem of providing wholesome and attractive food, that shall at the same time be economical, three times a day; giving up even five-cent treats at the nickelodeon to save for a house. We find them failing often, failing through ignorance or indifference, but also succeeding against heavy odds. To the onlooker it is a brave fight, the braver that it is so full of deadly monotony, a fight the weapons of which are pots and pans and bargain sales. In its outcome, however, is bound up the happiness and efficiency of the next generation.

Photo by Hine

Spontaneous Recreation Center, Homestead, 1907

CHAPTER VII

OF HUMAN RELATIONSHIPS

THERE are other and more subtle factors in living together than rooms or meals. The place in the budget of the home, amusements, church going, and lodge insurance were discussed in the last chapter. They are also significant as expressions of human relationships, and in their activity and organized forms reveal the character of the people as no account-book footings can reveal it. The relations of parents to each other, to their neighbors, and to their children, affect the development of household life among the people.

Yet even these relations are in a measure determined by outside forces. Industrial conditions, for example, determine the type of family life. In the families here, the women almost never go out to work—a marked contrast to cotton mill towns, for instance, where wives and daughters seek employment almost as a matter of course. This dependence on the men's wages is due not primarily to any theory as to woman's sphere, but to the simple fact that the one industry cannot use the work of women and children. Moreover, in this town where there are no marked differences in financial status and by far the larger number of housewives do all their own work, there is not much opportunity to obtain any form of domestic service by the day. Women apparently think it wiser to save money by good housekeeping than to earn a little more and neglect the home. This feeling, combined with the difficulty in securing work, has developed the type of family in which the man's wages constitute almost the entire income.

Among the English-speaking and native white budget families* only two women went out to do day's work. There were four

* Appendix I, Table 3, p. 201.

of these families who took lodgers, but since the women were either widows who had no other means of income, or women who had no children, the presence of lodgers interfered very little with the household life. As these families averaged only 1.2 persons to a room their homes were not seriously overcrowded. For the most part the women, relieved from the task of increasing the income, use their time and interest to good purpose in developing in their households a distinctive quality of homelikeness.

The men are inclined to trust all financial matters to their wives. It is the custom in Homestead for the workman to turn over his wages to his wife on pay day and to ask no questions as to what it goes for. He reserves a share for spending money; otherwise his part of the family problem is to earn and hers to spend. When the man was at home and I suggested to him that they keep accounts for this investigation he usually referred the matter genially to the wife, saying, "Oh, she's the one that knows where the money goes. If she wants to help you out she can."

Though the men show in general a frank appreciation of home comforts, they do not always realize all the work behind them. One wife said, "The only time 'the mister' notices anything about the house is when I wash the curtains." But many chance remarks showed that the women realize the importance of keeping the home attractive. One woman compared her husband, who stayed at home evenings unless they went to "the show" together, with the man next door who was always going off to Pittsburgh "on a lark." Her explanation of the difference was simply, "I always put on a clean dress and do my hair before he comes home, and have the kitchen tidy so he will enjoy staying. But she never tidies up a bit." Her kitchen was spotless, with a bright geranium in the window; that of her neighbor was hot and mussy and the children were noisy. No wonder the husband did not care to stay at home; but in a small house with washing and cooking to do, with babies to look out for, it is often hard for the housekeeper to have time or energy, after the children are home from school and the dinner cooked, to stop and make herself presentable. That so many women do this is a proof of their energy and genuine ability.

Supper time in Homestead will always be associated in my

mind with one family whom I knew. When the men began to come from the mill in the evening the mother with a fresh apron on and the two children in clean dresses came out on the front porch. The children sat on the lowest step until the father was in sight, and long before I could recognize him were off down the street, the older one to carry his bucket, the little one to take possession of his hand. After supper he smoked contentedly with a child on each knee and talked with his wife of the day's doings. That hour of rest was bought at the price of a busy day for her; she swept off porch and walk, she washed almost daily to keep the dresses clean, she had dinner all cooked before he came. A woman must be a good manager and have the courage to appear cheerful when tired, if she is to make the evening at home happy.

The thoughtful women are especially conscious that part of the responsibility for keeping the men away from the saloons belongs to them. The heat and thirst due to mill work, combined with the lack of other amusements, make the brightness and festivity of bar-rooms very appealing, and intemperance is consequently a serious evil in the town. The wives feel that they must help to overcome this temptation. One woman told me that she had been brought up to consider it wrong to play cards. She feared, however, that if she refused to have them in the house, her husband who was fond of playing would be tempted to go to the back rooms of the saloons for his entertainment. So, putting aside her scruples, she planned informal gatherings to play in the evenings. To her the drink evil was the more serious. There are many, however, to whom these real homes are not possible. There rises to my mind, in contrast, a two-room tenement down in the grimy corner where the mill joins the town. Here a woman was trying to support four little children by sewing and washing. Her husband had died after eight years of semi-invalidism resulting from an accident in the mill. With his small wages they had not been able to save, and as the injury had occurred so long ago she was not eligible for a benefit from the Carnegie Relief Fund. The kitchen was small and hot and the younger children noisy, and the not unnatural consequence was that the oldest girl drifted to the streets, mixed with a gay crowd, and eventually became a charge of the Juvenile Court. The girl was not bad at heart, and had there been a cheerful home where her friends could come, the end might have been different.

That home life has a strong hold and is a social force in keeping pure what we call the moral life of the town, is shown by the infrequency of immorality among these English-speaking families. There are instances, to be sure, of unfaithfulness among married people, and there are those who love to retail these bits of gossip. But even the way in which they are told reveals how strongly the general sentiment of the town condemns such moral laxity. It is very rare to hear of girls going wrong. These townspeople watch their daughters jealously, and make every effort to have the home the center of life so that the dangers almost inevitably attendant on public dances and skating rinks may not touch the girls of the family. I found it part of many a mother's problem to create such a household atmosphere that the children should find their happiness in the home rather than seek it in the doubtful amusements the town offers. They planned, for instance, to give the children music lessons so that in the evening they might enjoy such gayeties together. In one or two homes the children had learned to play on different instruments and had an embryo orchestra. These quiet family gatherings are apparently the source of much pleasure.

However amusing to the chance reader a small local paper may be, it furnishes some pretty reliable data as to the happenings in a town. The columns of the Homestead papers describe a round of birthday festivities and surprise parties for grown-ups as well as children, and we are assured each time that "the evening was a most enjoyable one." Music and refreshments, cards and other games furnish the usual entertainment.

Where the mother is tactful and wise, the lack of amusement outside the home may have no serious results. But all women are not geniuses in making their homes happy; some make the effort and fail, others never try, with disastrous results. And unfortunately, when this attraction fails, as often happens when the mother does not welcome the surprise party or when the father resents having the children noisy in the evening, there is little in the community to take its place. Practically the only public

Photo by Hine

Saloon Corner, Saturday Night

amusements in Homestead, during my stay there, were the nickelodeons and skating rinks. Six of the former, all but one on Eighth Avenue, sent out their penetrating music all the evening and most of the afternoon. There was one ten-cent vaudeville house, but the others charge five cents for a show consisting of songs, moving pictures, etc., which lasts fifteen minutes or so.

The part these shows play in the life of the community is really surprising. Not only were no other theatrical performances given in Homestead, but even those in Pittsburgh, because of the time and expense involved in getting there, were often out of the reach of workingmen and their families. The writer, when living in Homestead, found few things in Pittsburgh worth the long trolley ride, forty-five minutes each way. Many people, therefore, find in the nickelodeons their only relaxation. Men on their way home from work stop for a few minutes to see something of life outside the alternation of mill and home; the shopper rests while she enjoys the music, poor though it be, and the children are always begging for five cents to go to the nickelodeon. In the evening the family often go together for a little treat. On a Saturday afternoon visit to a nickelodeon, which advertised that it admitted two children on one ticket, I was surprised to find a large proportion of men in the audience. In many ways this form of amusement is desirable. What it ordinarily offers does not educate but does give pleasure. While occasionally serious subjects are represented, as for example pictures of the life of Christ given in Easter week, the performance usually consists of song and dance and moving pictures, all of a mediocre type. Still, for five cents the nickelodeon offers fifteen minutes' relaxation, and a glimpse of other sides of life, making the same appeal, after all, that theatre and novel do. As the nickelodeon seems to have met a real need in the mill towns, one must wish that it might offer them a better quality of entertainment.* Many who go because they can afford

* In New York City a board of censorship passes upon the films, and this has eliminated any tendency to bid for trade by showing degrading subjects. In the absence of such a censorship, the probation officers of the Allegheny County Juvenile Court have protested against pictures exhibited in some of the nickelodeons in Pittsburgh and neighboring towns. Without supervision some of them become ill favored resorts.

nothing expensive would appreciate something better, even at a slightly higher price.

The other popular amusement was the skating rink, of which there were three or four in Homestead.* "A marriage on skates" (apparently a bona-fide one, announced for ten days), masked balls, races, moonlight skating parties, all cleverly advertised, attracted the young people. While the two large rinks were fairly well conducted, some of the smaller ones were attended by a rough crowd. To a certain extent the danger felt in regard to public dances, bringing together young people some of whom were of doubtful character, applied also to the rink, and mothers often refused to allow their daughters to go, unless it was with "our own crowd."

But some diversion young people must have, nor are their elders exempt from this need.† Surely with none is the necessity for stimulus and variety of interest greater than with the men who turn daily from twelve hours in the din of the huge mills to home, supper, a smoke and bed.

I have already noted that in this community of 25,000 there are over 50 saloons and other drinking places, ranging from "speak-easies" to the conventional bar-rooms with plate glass and bright lights. It was no part of my study to investigate the ownership or police surveillance of these establishments, the profits gathered in on pay nights, or the intoxication which, as we have seen, the courts prove so ineffectual in controlling. As places of relaxation, they fill a need not otherwise supplied. The Carnegie Library has a gymnasium and clubs, but, except for the saloons and the club rooms of one or two fraternal orders, there are no free and easy lounging places for refreshment and friendly intercourse. The Slavs bring much of the liquor they buy home and drink it sociably there, many of them being heavy drinkers. The budgets gave no basis for a conclusion that English-speaking Homestead men are hard drinkers. My inquiries naturally lay among men

---

* During the hard times of 1908 these were closed and have not been reopened.

† The Public Recreation Centers of Chicago, with their dance halls and club rooms, to which all ages resort, in which the young people are safeguarded in ways which do not dampen the ardor of their good times, suggest the sort of non-commercial pleasure places which the mill towns need.

Photo by Hine

The Lights of Kennywood Park

with families rather than among the unattached ones, who are the constant tipplers in all towns. In the homes on the hill streets I heard almost no complaints that men were drunkards, though many men undoubtedly, in good times, spent money that way that was needed for the household budget. An old resident said that among the older stock he could name perhaps a half dozen men known as drunkards in the town. With hot work to whet thirst, and with the natural rebellion of human nature against the tension of long hours, the liquor interests have exploited the needs of the adults for recreation and refreshment. It is true that they have not really met that need, and have exploited the opportunities they offer; but it is equally true that the need is met in no other way.

Outside of home festivities and the meagre or commercialized public provisions, the chief dependence for sociability is on the lodges, churches and other voluntary organizations.

In Homestead, as in other working communities, we find benefit organizations playing a prominent part. In one day's paper, 50 meetings of fraternal orders were scheduled for one week. Facts were secured concerning 23 out of a total of perhaps half a hundred lodges. The 23 had a membership in 1907 of 3663; of these 3400 were men. Almost all the organizations include both social and benefit features. The Order of Elks, which has no regular benefits and is a purely social organization, nevertheless gives generous assistance to members in distress. On the other hand the fraternal insurance orders, such as the Protected Home Circle and the Royal Arcanum, are important, not only because they help provide for the future, but because they provoke social intercourse in ways which help make this form of insurance popular.

The lodges seek to arouse the sense of fraternity and common interest which otherwise finds little stimulus in the town. The following paragraphs from the prospectus of the Modern Woodmen reveal this purpose:

> While the beneficial (or insurance) department of the Modern Woodmen Society is admirable—is, indeed, as over $1,200,000,000 of insurance in force proves, of vital importance to the man of family—yet Woodcraft's fraternal feature is in reality the basal stone of the Society's existence.

8   113

The world needs more genuine fraternity. There is a power of comfort in brotherly sympathy extended in time of distress. The kindly visit and solicitude of a Neighbor for one lying on a bed of sickness is appreciated. The aid freely extended to our families when we are so unfortunate as not to be able to help them ourselves is truly fraternal— Christ-like. None of us are so strong or so fortunately situated that there may not come a dark hour, when we will require assistance and sympathy. It is comforting to know that in such an hour we need not appeal for Charity, but we may command the kindly ministrations of our fraternal brothers—our "Neighbors" of the Modern Woodmen of America. They solemnly obligate themselves to extend such aid and you will receive it if you stand in need.

But in addition to this general sense of brotherliness, the lodges supply some of the good fun which Homestead craves. Besides the regular meetings, they have summer outings at Kennywood Park and elsewhere, dances and card parties in the winter, whereby they raise money for some charitable purpose, for the lodge expenses or, as a special benefit, for some member who is in peculiar distress. These ends do not lessen the real enjoyment in the festivity itself, though they form, of course, an extra tax. Even the business meetings are a source of pleasure, and help develop a spirit of neighborliness.

To the women especially, whose duties keep them at home, the lodge offers almost their only chance to meet other people and get for a few minutes into a different atmosphere from that of household tasks. Some housekeepers are firmly opposed to lodges on the ground that as they take time they must result in neglect of the home. This was also the opinion of a man whose wife had announced that she could see no objection to woman suffrage, since women could learn how to vote by going to meetings. "Well," he retorted feelingly, "if you went to any more I don't know when I should get anything to eat." Another woman who belonged to four lodges and attended on an average two meetings every week considered them the pleasantest part of life, while her attractive home indicated that they did not interfere with her household duties. On the whole, the lodge meetings afford a genuine pleasure while they make no serious break in the routine of household tasks. Those fraternal insurance orders which include in their membership both men and women serve also as a center of common family interest.

The meetings, however, are probably of most value to the men, since Homestead has comparatively few other organizations to bring men together. There are no unions to give a sense of common interest, and the political organizations are largely dominated by a few gangs. The lodges form really the only clubs. The most successful one in the town is the Odd Fellows with a membership of about one thousand, mostly steel workers, and a building of its own. It is probably the most influential organization in Homestead. As the dues are not large and the sick benefits are comparatively generous, many can afford to join.

The associations not only arouse fraternal interest in fellow members, but also offer at times the means of expressing sympathy with those outside their membership. During 1908, for example, many of the orders gave entertainments, to raise money either for the hospital which was being built in Homestead or for the committee which cared for those in need during the industrial depression. As I went into one woman's kitchen one day, she showed me a half bushel basket full of fine, large potatoes scrubbed clean and ready for baking, which she told me with a good deal of pride and evident pleasure were her share in a supper her lodge was giving for the benefit of the hospital. "My husband," she explained, "isn't in a dangerous place in the mill, but I am glad to help even if most of the injured are Hunkies." Again, in December of 1907, within forty-eight hours after the mine explosion at Monongah, West Virginia, one Homestead lodge had voted a contribution for those left destitute. This ready sympathy for suffering and desire to help often find their only expression through the joint effort of these societies.

Social needs are further met by the churches, which in Homestead, as is usual in a town, play a more important rôle in the community than they do in a large city. While church affairs and suppers may not be the best ways to raise money, they offer good times. "Ten cent socials," for instance, provide a jolly evening for the young folks; chicken and waffle suppers, advertised often during the winter, proved to be pleasant, homelike affairs.

The churches also provide a real though limited intellectual stimulus. One has a large men's club at whose meetings speakers talk on subjects of current interest. In another church a club of young men and women has regular debates on sociological subjects. The church in such ways becomes a center for broadening the life of its members by other than purely spiritual interests.

The mill-town lodges and churches, though each must work out its own salvation, are more or less closely affiliated with larger organizations. It is interesting to see what purely local societies the town has developed. There are the usual number of women's clubs, with various objects, from embroidery to civics. The most prominent and enterprising is the Homestead Woman's Club, of whose work in conducting a playground and attempting to secure a kindergarten I shall speak later. These women's clubs which have formed a union, with a joint meeting yearly, are centers of interest in the lives of their members. The members are, however, largely wives of business and professional men or of those in responsible positions in the mill.*

The young men have formed numerous athletic clubs, some informal, some with professional teams. During the winter, basket ball games, both professional and amateur, are very popular. "The 3rd Ave. team plays the 5th Ave. team" and similar notices in the Homestead papers show that local rivalry and athletic zeal go hand in hand. The Homestead "Americans" have won championship matches all over the Eastern states. The players are, of course, usually young men. The older men and those whose work is hard prefer watching. Women when questioned as to the man's spending money often said, "Well, he goes to a basket ball game most every Saturday and that's thirty-five cents." It is perhaps needless to say that in summer baseball is to the front. There are the usual matches between local teams, and a "Business Men's League" conducts a series of games at Homestead Park after business hours. The standing of the various teams, which include doctors, grocers, steel workers, etc., arouses a good deal of interest. The boys, of course, have innumerable small clubs, and not infrequently on warm spring days

*See Appendix XIII, p. 264 ff., for a list of the clubs and their objects.

Photo by Hine

CARNEGIE LIBRARY, MUNHALL

ORCHESTRA; CARNEGIE LIBRARY

BAND STAND

O en air concerts are given here in the summer b the Carne ie Li rar Band

passers-by are called upon to buy undrinkable lemonade to help supply the uniforms.

While the clubs connected with the Carnegie Library are not, in a sense, of spontaneous growth, they may nevertheless be referred to here, since their particular form is largely a matter of popular demand. The library, it should be said in passing, touches the town's life at several points, and I have several times had occasion to refer to it. To give a more complete picture of its activities, and of the spirit of the librarian in charge, his annual report is published in Appendix XIII. There is an excellent gymnasium open to all on payment of $2.00 a year. This includes gymnasium, swimming pool, bowling alleys, fencing, etc., with good instruction. It was very popular with the young men. Men engaged in either clerical or professional work were found more often than those doing manual labor in the mill. Many of the latter (as seems natural to any one who has visited the mills) say they are too tired after their hours of heavy work. Consequently, they miss entirely the all-round development of gymnasium work and the mutual stimulus and refreshment of playing games together. For the boys, the "gym" offers both fun and good training.

The library also has had a series of paid entertainments, conducted by a lecture bureau which offers illustrated lectures, monologues, humorous readings, etc., at a low price. These were held in the auditorium of the library, but were only fairly well attended and later were abandoned. In addition the club has good musical classes, a band, an orchestra and chorus, each of which gives at least one free concert a year. The boys play well and this work undoubtedly helps to raise the standard of music in the homes.

Aside from the lecture course there was almost no entertainment in Homestead the year of my inquiry that could be called cultural. The amusements in the main were the simple festivities of home and lodge and church, narrow in their round. Lacking the stimulus that comes from bringing a community into contact with new ideas or new people, they yet helped to keep life sane and wholesome.

CHAPTER VIII

THE CHILDREN OF HOMESTEAD

THROUGH children, more than through insurance, or savings, or even through home owning, does a workman's household lay claim upon the future. Here both the oldest instincts and new half-formulated ambitions find expression. They have asserted themselves even in a town where the men have submitted to exclusion from all control over their work, and where as we have seen they have failed to master the town's government as a whole. Here the community has set before itself what it feels to be high standards.

The working people of Homestead when talking of their children show a distinct recognition of the value of education and home training, as compared with the immediate money value of wages. English-speaking parents, at least, do not hurry their children to work the day they are fourteen years of age. Of the 17 boys between fourteen and twenty-one, in the English-speaking families from whom budgets were secured, 15 were at work; but of 16 girls, four were still at school and 12 were at home helping their mothers. This last figure is a striking one in view of the fact that in at least five of these families the man was earning less than $15 a week; yet even under such circumstances the parents did not seek to increase their income by sending the girls to work. A typical case is that of a girl of 18, the eldest of six children, in a family with an income of $14 a week. It was assumed to be her place to help her mother, rather than to supplement the father's wages. While the number of families studied is, of course, not large enough to warrant sweeping conclusions, their attitude in this matter corresponded with general impressions I received in visiting a much wider circle.

In contrast to their general political indifference, the voters

Photo by Hine

In Carnegie's Footsteps

have insisted on efficiency in the one branch of borough government which specifically affects their children, and are proud of having a "good school board" and of having created a public sentiment which makes the best men in the town willing to accept this office. The board included in 1907–8 three physicians, four men in the steel works, including a steel inspector, two lawyers, and several business men. Though this board has not adopted all the modern improvements in school equipment, it has, through its straightforward efforts to provide good service, secured the co-operation of the people. So far, school facilities have kept pace with the rapid growth of the town and there has been a seat for every child.

The Second Ward school, one of the older buildings visited, was neither well constructed nor fireproof. The first grade room had 34 double seats, or 68 children for one teacher—an excessive number. Drinking water was brought in buckets from a well in the yard; the toilets were cemented privy vaults flushed only by waste water from the yard and by rain water from the roof, except in dry seasons when the flushing was done by a hose.* Heat was provided by sheet-iron incased coal stoves situated in the rooms, and there was no system of ventilation.

In contrast to this old school, changes in the newer buildings show that the board is adopting progressive standards. For example, the Fifth Ward school, the newest, is semi-fireproof and has excellent lighting arrangements,—six windows in each of the rooms,—the light in all cases coming from the back and left of the pupils. It has no double desks, and in two rooms the desks are graded in size. The heating is by hot air generated by steam. The building, a two-story one with no fire-escapes, had, however, a wooden stairway in the center hall, and a fire drill was introduced only after public sentiment had been aroused by the Collingwood School fire in Cleveland in which several hundred children were killed. Graduated desks are still urgently needed, since the presence in the same school of both native-born children and newly arrived immigrants results in unusual variations in size among pupils in the same grade. With more facilities for bathing and especially with better toilets, the schools also could

* Sanitary porcelain closets were installed in 1908.

serve to educate public opinion to demand better sanitary standards in the homes.

The principal school in Munhall is a more up-to-date structure than those of Homestead,* being fireproof and built with iron stairways and sufficient exits. The toilets are within the building, the lighting is sufficient and the heating system modern. It contains an assembly hall, though this was used only for school purposes. The mothers' meetings and little entertainments in the kindergarten, and the literary exercises held once a week to which the mothers were invited, served to arouse interest and bring the women in touch with the teachers. This school is beginning to have a real influence in the life of the borough. It is, however, situated on the hill in the most prosperous part of the town. The schools in neighborhoods where such work would be more essential are not so equipped.

An outsider, unless an expert, can hardly judge whether methods of instruction are of a high order or the work of the teachers efficient. The residents themselves believe that they are, and take genuine pride in every advance in standards. The authorities have been less ready to develop the social uses of the school plants. It is perhaps not surprising that a conservative town has not introduced such new features as school nurses and medical inspection of school children. Parents who are so eager to secure benefits for their children would undoubtedly welcome such work were its value made known to them. Superintendent T. M. Norris of the Homestead schools has expressed himself as in favor of school nurses in the Second Ward. So far there has been no effective demand for them, nor has Homestead had the example of such a public system in the Pittsburgh schools. There has been less excuse for the belatedness in providing school playgrounds. In the Second Ward, where a play center has been most needed, the school has a large yard. Though this would have made a good playground it was used for games the year of my residence in Homestead only during the fifteen-minute recess twice a day. As the school is on the main street only two blocks from the mill,

* Up to 1910 the Homestead High School has been conducted in a part of one of the grammar buildings. Plans are now under way for building a High School to cost $125,000. This will have baths, a gymnasium, an assembly hall, etc.

The Brook in Munhall Hollow

Now to all intents an open drain. Its toleration is a crime against health and childhood

the yard proved an attractive spot for loungers and was on that account closed out of school hours. While paid supervision in such a location is undoubtedly necessary, the difficulty or expense in providing it should not have remained an insurmountable obstacle where a place to play was so sadly needed. The children who attend this school live at the foot of the hill in crowded courts, in which there is little room for games, and a long climb is necessary to reach the vacant lots back of the town.

Clipping from the Homestead *Messenger* which was an interesting bit of evidence of the need for recreation grounds.

BOYS CLAIM THEIR RIGHTS ARE BEING INTERERFED WITH

For two years the Woman's Club of Homestead used this school yard for a vacation school. They employed teachers to conduct a kitchen garden and sewing classes, and provided swings and sand boxes for amusement. Each afternoon club members helped with the work and they seem to have made it a success. Some felt, however, that the children who came were not from families who really needed this stimulus, and since

The boys of Homestead are sore at the burgess and members of the police froce, who they accuse of interfering with their rights as free born Young Americans. Last night a committee of six, representing the First and Second wards called at the Daily Messenger office and left the following which they hope will receive careful consideration at the hands of the chief executive of the borough.

"The boys of Homestead want to know why they cannot play basketball on the street, and they want to know what they can do.

"Burgess please answer in Mondays' Messenger."

the women could not secure an appropriation from the school board, and had difficulty in raising the necessary funds, they finally gave up the work. This was unfortunate; for not only was the vacation school needed by the pupils, but it also was a way in which the intelligent women of the town could come into personal contact with the problems of their Second Ward neighbors.*

* In the summer of 1909, a vacation school and playground were maintained for six weeks in this Second Ward school yard. A Playground Association was organized with which the National Vacation Bible School Committee of New York co-operated, providing the play director. A similar playground was carried on by the Homestead people in 1910.

This same club—the most wide-awake body in the town—tried also to persuade the school board to start public kindergartens. The members canvassed the town to see how many mothers would send their children to a free kindergarten, how many if a fee were charged, and how many with no children of kindergarten age would contribute toward its support. They demonstrated by this inquiry that mothers would welcome the addition of kindergartens to the school system. But when the request to introduce them into the public schools was presented to the school board by a member who favored the project, it was refused. The reason offered was that the board could not afford the money necessary to maintain the ten kindergartens Homestead needs. Nor did the authorities recognize their practical value. It was even said by one member of the board that the women merely wanted to be relieved of the care of the children so they would be free to "go gadding."

A similar failure to comprehend the difficulties in giving proper training in the home and the need for providing it elsewhere, might have put off for a long time the introduction of domestic science and manual training. As it was, Mr. Charles M. Schwab, who was once superintendent of the Homestead works, gave the town a well equipped manual training school in which the children from all the schools, parochial as well as public, receive a half day's instruction a week while attending the sixth, seventh and eighth grades and the High School. The girls have cooking and sewing classes in alternate years and the boys classes in sloyd, wood and metal turning. Some of the girls do very creditable work, drafting patterns and making shirtwaist suits in their last year. In the cooking class they study the theory of food values, and have practical cooking lessons besides. The instruction in sewing the mothers generally approve. One woman who had been a clerk in a store before her marriage expressed her regret that she had never been taught at home to sew. When clothing must be provided for a family of six it is a distinct handicap to be able to make only aprons and other simple things. This woman was therefore appreciative of what her daughter learned in school. Other mothers who themselves taught their girls to sew did not consider the instruction so important, yet with all their other cares they were glad to have this help.

In regard to the value of the cooking classes, opinions differed. When you turn from the large, spotless kitchen in the school, with its equipment of modern ranges and elaborate cooking utensils, to the humble kitchen in the home of a laborer, with a second-hand coal stove and only a few kettles, or even to the modest kitchens of the more well-to-do families, you understand why some girls find it difficult to translate into everyday usefulness the lessons of the school. Moreover, too often the emphasis of the lessons is on the preparation of fancy dishes, instead of on how to make cheap cuts both digestible and palatable; and yet, if girls learn new things which they can make at home, they take an increased interest in housekeeping. One girl insisted that her father get her some waffle irons. The family was so pleased with her first experiment that they now count upon having waffles every Sunday morning for breakfast. The girl's pride in providing the treat of the week undoubtedly helped to develop in her a real enthusiasm for homemaking.

The school stimulates a similar interest among the boys by giving them a share in furnishing the home; for many of the articles made, especially in the wood-working classes, become their property.

This Schwab school, which is supported by the public taxes, and is carried on under the direction of the superintendent of schools, rounds out the town's system of elementary education. In its maintenance and standards it is a public recognition of the need for manual training in an industrial community, and in its work a distinctly progressive spirit among the people is feeling its way.

In these needs the adults, especially among the immigrants, share. Evening schools or educational centers would be valuable to Homestead and welcomed. The plant of the Schwab Manual Training School could be used in providing courses in domestic science for housekeepers, and a number of the older women would appreciate courses in domestic arts. Young men and boys would undoubtedly take advantage of night courses, both technical and literary. These wants are met in some measure by the Carnegie

Library, which, besides amusements, provides many opportunities for study. Unfortunately, a class feeling seems to have developed with respect to the library. The clerical and managerial force of mill employes make free use of its privileges, but some of the unskilled workmen expressed a doubt as to whether they are really welcome. This is not, however, due to the attitude of the directors, which is cordial to all comers. Nearly 200 students were enrolled in the educational classes during 1908 besides those in the musical clubs. Until 1908 attempts to teach English to foreigners had not succeeded, but in that year there was a class of 25.

The fact that the library is on the high ground in Munhall discourages its use by men tired by a day's work. If classes and reading rooms could be opened in the school buildings in more accessible sections of the borough of Homestead, there would, I think, be an increased attendance. The development of the library clubs has been such as should serve to stimulate the school department to a further use of its own plant, rather than to encourage the belief that the library meets all the cultural needs of the community.

One exceptional opportunity for technical training, within reach of Homestead, is offered by the courses at the Carnegie Technical School in Pittsburgh. That this privilege is not unappreciated is shown by the fact that in 1907–8 six boys from Homestead were taking the regular all-day course, and 17 boys the evening courses. I knew of one boy of seventeen employed in the mill who was attending the regular evening course, hoping eventually to become an electrician. His work gave him some leisure time in which he could study, and when he was on night turn a friend managed to do the first hour's work for him so that he could continue his course. As the Institute is at least half an hour's ride from Homestead, it required some will power and enthusiasm to take this trip after a ten or twelve hours' day in the mill.*

* Arrangements are now made between the Carnegie Technical Schools and the Carnegie Steel Company (and other employers), by which a young employe who wants to attend the night courses is put on working shifts which will not break into his classes.

Draughting Room

Carpenter Shop

SCHWAB MANUAL TRAINING SCHOOL

The girls, too, can secure training in domestic science, millinery, dressmaking, etc., in the girls' department of this school—the Margaret Morison Carnegie School.

Among the English-speaking people the daughters rarely go out to service, though many of their mothers have done so. Nor are they inclined to work in the Homestead stores, where, I was told, the Homestead girls receive a lower rate of wages than do those from out-of-town—never above $5.00 a week. They prefer the change and excitement of the Pittsburgh stores, where they can get more pay, though hardly enough at first to counterbalance carfare. A number were employed in the great Westinghouse Electric Works across the river; but the distance, the conditions under which some of the work is done, the speeding and low pay, and the doubtful reputation of some of the employes among Homestead mothers made them consider this employment undesirable. A few girls took commercial courses either in the Homestead High School or in business colleges in Pittsburgh; the extra expense of the latter was considered to be justified by the fact that the colleges assured positions on graduation. As one woman said of her young daughter, "We are poor, and we must consider how she can get to work soonest." The morning train carries a company of such office workers into the city.

But the proportion is small, and in contrast to the prevailing custom of industrial communities, in New England, for instance, the continuance of this reservoir of woman's labor, largely untapped by commercial interests, is a matter of note. Undoubtedly home instincts and standards would not keep all the girls from work were a factory to be opened which would have use for them even at low pay. That they have so far largely remained at home has resulted in positive advantages. One may question whether the family would not be better off to have the additional earnings. But to the daughter who helps with the housekeeping, this household training is valuable. Its importance is shown by the fact that the most capable housekeepers I came upon, with the greatest capacity for making a small income go a long way, had been girls who by working at home had learned methods of economy.

The mill makes it possible for the sons to work and live in

Homestead and thus, before marriage, to develop the economic unity of their father's family. It is significant that among the budget families having a total income of $20 or over, 29 per cent of the income of English-speaking Europeans, and 11 per cent of that of native white families was contributed by the sons. Some of these boys of nineteen or twenty earned as much as their fathers. The period before they leave home is, therefore, the high-water mark of financial prosperity for the family. During this time a home can sometimes be bought. I visited one such where the whole atmosphere was one of comfort. Though the man himself earned very moderate wages, two sons had grown up at home, and during the period when they added to the family income the house and its furnishings (which included plush furniture and a music box!) had been purchased. The boys are married now, but their parents, in a way, are reaping the harvest of those fruitful years.

The parents' ambitions for their sons are, as a rule, very simple; usually to follow in their fathers' footsteps, getting from the practical work in the mill a training for future success. There is a fascination about the mill against which even unwilling mothers find themselves helpless to contend. One woman, whose husband had been a mill worker all his life and two of whose sons had worked up to responsible positions, had had her fill of the terror of accidents which haunts many a Homestead woman. So she wished her third boy to do something else, and secured a place for him in a large department store. His wages seemed small compared with those received by his brothers, there was little prospect of promotion, and so he was soon hard at work in the mill. The fact that the best paid men, such as rollers and heaters, have worked up to these jobs through experience has increased the natural tendency to put sons directly into the mill rather than to give them a technical training. While occasionally a boy wishes to go to college, the general attitude of the community is one of scorn rather than of respect for academic education. There is a general belief that the college trained man, with all his theory, is less expert than the man who has learned the industry through work with his hands. As few men with technical training are at the start familiar with the processes of steel mak-

Schwab Manual Training School
Machine Room

ing, the value of their theoretical knowledge cannot overcome the prejudice created among the men by their early blunders.

Whatever its disadvantages the mill usually gives a boy a chance to earn a fair livelihood for a single man as a semi-skilled workman. Some want what are known as pencil jobs, weighing and marking steel, where the work is light and apparently considered more gentlemanly, though the pay is lower and the chances of mastering the business are less. The parents often accede to this desire. Others begin at regular boy's work, as messengers or door openers.* Promotion is rapid in the beginning, and sometimes by the time a boy is eighteen he has already attained his maximum wage. One woman who regretted that her boy had not learned a trade, said that he was unwilling to go through a long period of apprenticeship as a mechanic, when at certain mill jobs he could earn good pay at once. Another woman told me that her brother early acquired dissipated habits because he earned man's wages while he still had a boy's lack of responsibility and self-control.

The sons may work a little further up than their fathers; a man told me with pride that his son, who was a foreman, had secured for him a job in the mill, and a mother was eager to relate how her boy had taught the new assistant superintendent the way to do his work. Only rarely, however, do they secure an education that fits them for an entirely different kind of labor.

The mothers, too, expect that their daughters will eventually marry mill workers. Yet they desire for their children greater ease and culture than they themselves have enjoyed. One woman told me very sweetly of her efforts to teach her children better manners than she had ever learned. She bought a book on etiquette and was assiduously trying to instruct them in the little acts of courtesy which to many of us are a matter

---

* Mr. Norris, superintendent of the Homestead schools, spoke of the care with which the mill superintendents refuse to employ any boy under fourteen, and forbid boys under sixteen to work in dangerous places. Yet in 1906-7 "A boy was killed in the Homestead Steel Works at 1.30 in the morning. He was a 'pull-up,' fifteen years old, who had worked eight hours out of a thirteen-hour night turn. He had a few minutes to rest, and went back of the furnace to lie down in a wheelbarrow. He fell asleep and was struck and killed by the extending arm of a ladle which the crane-man was bringing back to the pit." Eastman, Work-Accidents and the Law, p. 88.

of course. She explained her own embarrassment in attempting to set an example to the children, which she did with the self-consciousness that comes to grownups. "If I do get up from the table, I make myself say 'Excuse me,' but it is awful hard. I never learned very much, but I do want my children to be different,'—and the courtesy of the child who had opened the door for me demonstrated her success.

In this home, as in many another, the plans of the parents centered about the development of the children, rather than about any change in their own economic status. We must remember that in the steel industry fortunes have been piled up by individual men who started in as water boys, and couple with it the fact that in Homestead there is no longer any method by which the men can collectively raise the general level of wages. It is but natural then that a family's hopes should be bound up very largely in its individual fortunes, and if these hopes are unfulfilled through the father, that they should be centered in the sons. Yet in so far as my observations as to the future of the children are not conclusive, they reflect the vagueness of outlook of the people themselves.

For dynamic changes are affecting the town's growth, and the lives of the people composing it. It would be difficult to prophesy how far the children of the present steel workers will man the mills of the next generation; there is another stream of recruits coming in which as time goes on may more and more dispute with the native born and the sons of the old immigrant stock for place in the ranks of the semi-skilled and skilled. We must recognize the part the Slavs are to play. They today make up a full half of the working force of the plant. They already affect every phase of the town's life, as newcomers in the ranks of industry, as aliens from East Europe, and (the great majority of them) as day laborers at 16½ cents an hour, whose earnings fall below what we have seen to be a living wage for a family.

That the members of this economic group in Homestead are largely of one race, and this a different one from the men in ranks above them, gives a distinctive character to the situation, and warrants its treatment in a separate section. It is a situation common to an important group of the major industries in America today.

Drawn by Joseph Stella

SLAV: CALLING

PART III
THE SLAV AS A HOMESTEADER

CHAPTER IX

THE SLAVS

FROM the cinder path beside one of the railroads that crosses the level part of Homestead, you enter an alley, bordered on one side by stables and on the other by a row of shabby two-story frame houses. The doors of the houses are closed, but dishpans and old clothes decorating their exterior mark them as inhabited. Turning from the alley through a narrow passageway you find yourself in a small court, on three sides of which are smoke-grimed houses, and on the fourth, low stables. The open space teems with life and movement. Children, dogs and hens make it lively under foot; overhead long lines of flapping clothes must be dodged. A group of women stand gossiping in one corner, awaiting their turn at the pump,—which is one of the two sources of water supply for the 20 families who live here. Another woman dumps the contents of her washtubs upon the paved ground, and the greasy, soapy water runs into an open drain a few feet from the pump. In the center a circular wooden building with ten compartments opening into one vault, flushed only by this waste water, constitutes the toilet accommodations for over one hundred people. Twenty-seven children find in this crowded brick-paved space their only playground; for the 63 rooms in the houses about the court shelter a group of 20 families, Polish, Slavic and Hungarian, Jewish and Negro. The men are unskilled workers in the mills.

This court is one of many such in Homestead; one of hundreds of similar courts in the mill towns of the Ohio valley. The conditions produced by the incoming of these alien workers form one of the unsolved problems of the steel district.

Two elements in the old country feed the population of these crowded sections: the ambitious young men, with no ties, unless to aged parents; and the men with wives, sometimes with children, who come over here to make a better home for them. They are all stimulated by the successes of their friends, who perhaps have returned with savings that seem fortunes. Often these people mortgage their all for the passage money and if they fail here no place is left to which they can go back. From quiet villages they come to this smoky town; from labor in the open fields to heavy work in the yards and thundering sheds of the mill.

As employment is steady and the workman's needs are simple, the wages seem large. The newcomer if a single man finds groups of his fellow workers living in close quarters—three or four in a room—who are enjoying life and saving money at the same time. So he too begins to save, and presently, if he has a family at home, sends for them to join him. If he is single, he sends for his sweetheart or marries some girl of his race, whom he meets in the mill-town courts of an evening or at church or at one of the lodge dances. If she has been at service here, she too will likely have a small account in the bank. Then, as the family grows and expenses increase, they resort to the old expedient and begin themselves to take boarders. Children come and grow up. The man's wage does not increase; as he is a "Hunkie" the chances are that he will remain a laborer. Most of these men come intending some day to go back with a thousand dollars—men of property. But even if they return once to the old country, they often turn again to America; growing attached to the new world, they become permanent residents.

An occasional family, when the man gets into tonnage work or when the children reach earning age and add their wages to the common fund, achieves a long desired happiness; they move to a separate house in the suburbs, perhaps even to one of their own. But to many the crowded court with its isolation from the rest of the community continues to be America.

While there were no definite figures available as to the number of these foreigners in Homestead in 1907–8, two Slavs intimately acquainted with the foreign colony estimated that there were between 6000 and 7000. When the mills were running full in October, 1907, 3603 Slavic men were at work there, forming 53.2 per cent of the total number of employes.* As 1092 of these were single men, the estimate as to the total Slavic population is prob-

*Table 3, p. 13.

Photo by Hine

SLAVIC COURT

Showing Typical Toilet and Water Supply, also a few of the Boarders in these houses.

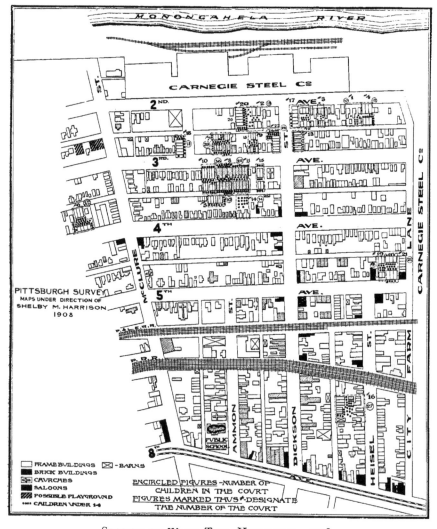

SECTION OF WARD TWO, HOMESTEAD, 1908

Showing location of 22 courts studied; number of children under 14 in each; location of churches and saloons; absence of playgrounds

ably fairly accurate. The rapid increase in numbers is shown by the fact that while there were no Slavic churches in the town in 1896, there are now Polish, Slovak, and Lithuanian Roman Catholic churches, a Slovak Greek Catholic church, a Hungarian Reformed church, and one or two Slavic Protestant missions. These churches hold property the value of which is estimated at $400,000.

Numerous national distinctions divide this body of immigrants as a whole, but of these the English-speaking community is in large measure ignorant; to the rest of the town they are all just "Hunkies." Of the Slavs employed in the mill in 1907, 51.7 per cent were Slovaks, 15 per cent Magyar, 10.2 per cent Roumanian, 9.6 per cent Russian, 6 per cent Polish, 3.6 per cent Lithuanian, 3.9 per cent miscellaneous.* Between some of these groups, such as Slovaks and Hungarians, Poles and Russians, feuds dating back many centuries still provoke quarrels in this new-world town. The crowded courts bring them into close and sometimes irritating contact, and as yet there have been few amalgamating forces to counteract the old hatreds. Rather the segmentation of churches and lodges, due to differences in language, tend to keep alive these old antagonisms.

In spite, however, of these national conflicts the Slavs are of similar temperament. Like the Irish who preceded them here, they are in most instances in their own country the ruled rather than the dominant race, and the majority come from agricultural countries, where money is scarce, where living conditions are of the poorest, where hard work in the open air has developed rugged strength. With them they bring the standards of village life, reflecting its crude sanitation (counterbalanced in the old environment by the unlimited supply of fresh air), its bare existence and its low levels of comfort.

The mode of living which we find among the Slavs is in a measure due to a conflict between the nature of community life and industry in America, and the customs and conditions that prevail under a different civilization. In some measure, at least, wages, housing conditions, opportunities for relaxation, conform

---

* For convenience in this book, as already noted, Magyars, Letts, etc., are spoken of as Slavs. Though not of the blood, they come from the same general district in mid-Europe and are part of the same wave of immigration.

to the "standards of living" of the influential group in a town,
—in Homestead, the standards of the native whites. The forces
of imitation and self-respect make it easier for a native to
achieve these standards, but the newcomers must live under conditions which are not determined by their kind. Moreover, the
ambition of most in coming to this country is financial, or largely
so; and the determination to get ahead, even at risk of immediate
health and happiness, accentuates the problems which their presence creates. They come, then, with this background of meagre
surroundings, but with a vision of future riches. They come as
prospectors come, ready for any hardships that may help them
reach their goal, and with the passive endurance that has been
characteristic of their race. Those early dreams of money to be
picked up in the streets of the new world are bygones no doubt,
but these Slavic adventurers bring with them, nevertheless, the
expectation of returning some day men of wealth,—wealth made
up of savings from American pay.

Their labor is the heaviest and roughest in the mill,—
handling steel billets and bars, loading trains, working in cinder
pits; labor that demands mostly strength but demands that in
large measure. They work usually under the direction of an
English-speaking foreman whose orders they often fail to understand. Accidents are frequent, promotions rare. In 202 families in the courts studied, 88 per cent of the men belonged to the
unskilled group, a proportion roughly true for the mill as a whole.*
Only 2.2 per cent of the Slavs in the mill are skilled (Table 6, p.
40). Some of the men about the furnaces thus work up by slow
degrees to be skilled or at least semi-skilled, but in the main,
the Slavs have as yet small prospect of advancement.† Of the 21
budget families whose men were earning laborer's wages, five had
been here from five to nine years, two from ten to fourteen years,
and four had been here fifteen years or over. If the rank and file

---

*The somewhat higher average of skill among the Slavic budget families
is due to the fact that representative units from each of the economic groups
were selected; also that the investigator belonged to one of the oldest Slavic
families and her acquaintance included many of the most prosperous.

† The sons occasionally enter occupations outside the steel mills which they
think more desirable. Two were reported to be drivers for livery stables and one a
roofer. But these young men did not earn much more than their fathers.

are to satisfy their ambitions they must do it on less than $2.00 a day, or leave Homestead.

Moreover, the Slavs find their work quickly affected by an industrial depression. During the winter of 1907 they were the first to be laid off. Many returned to Austria-Hungary; many could not go. In a group of 295 Bulgarians only 115 had work, while among 212 Russians, 131 were unemployed. The stories of these months of idleness and privation were pathetic. Remittances to wives and old people in Europe dropped off, bank deposits lessened, and goods were purchased on credit till future wages were heavily mortgaged. As Americans were sometimes given laboring work formerly done by Slavs, the latter bore more than their share of a burden that seriously affected the whole community. The company's policy of caring for its skilled workmen by giving them labor that would normally have been done by the unskilled, was in certain ways estimable; but it made the winter a desperate one for such of the unskilled foreigners as could not return to their own country.

The steel industry, then, requires these strong men to do its heaviest labor, pays them its lowest wage, with little prospect of advancement and with the chance that they will be first to suffer if work grows slack. What for its part does the town offer? The section where the Slavs live is in itself gloomy. The level ground in the Second Ward cut off from the river by the mill and from the country by the steep hill behind, forms a pocket where the smoke settles heavily. There are oases in these wards, sections of street with yards and trees, but for the most part here on the original site of the town, garden plots as well as alleys have been utilized on which to build small frame houses till the blocks are all but covered. While these houses are sometimes built in haphazard fashion, they usually surround such a court as that described at the outset of this chapter. For our cinder path led us directly to the heart of the crowding and the sanitary evils of the steel town.

To determine the extent of such congestion, with the help of the Slavic member of my staff I made a study of 21 courts in the Second Ward, shown on the plan opposite page 134, where yards, toilets and water supply are used in common. In these courts lived 239 families,* 102 of whom took lodgers. Fifty-one families, including sometimes four or five people, lived in one-room tenements. One-half the families used their kitchens as sleeping rooms. Only three houses had running water inside, and in at least three instances over 110 people were dependent on one yard hydrant for water.

Each court is shut in between the houses facing the street and a similar row facing the alley at the rear which cuts the block in half. A narrow passage serves as an outlet. Some of the houses are four or six-story buildings, but more than half in the courts studied were but two stories high with four rooms each.† This type usually shelters two families each; one family living in the room opening upon the street and the upstairs room above it; the other, in the two rooms looking into the court.

In summer, to give some through ventilation to the stifling rooms, doors leading to the stairway between the front and rear rooms are left open. As the families are often kin this opportunity for friendly intercourse is not unwelcome. Indeed, the cheerful gossip about the hydrant that enlivens wash day, like the card playing in the court on a summer evening, suggests the neighborliness of village days. Nothing in the surroundings, however, bears out the suggestion. Accumulations of rubbish and broken brick pavements render the courts as a whole untidy and unwholesome. Some of the houses have small porches that might give a sense of homelikeness, but for the most part they are bare and dingy. As the houses are built close to the street with only this busy court behind, the tenant can scarcely have that bit of garden so dear to the heart of former country dwellers. Only here and there a little bed of lettuce with its note of delicate green or the vivid red of a geranium blossom brightens the monotony. Dreary as is the exterior, however, the evils to the dwellers in the court lie deeper; in the inadequate water supply, in meagre toilet facilities, and in overcrowding.

The deficiency in the water supply is serious. In the 21 courts,

* Of these, 168 were Slovaks, 22 Hungarians, 16 Russians, 10 Poles and 23 Slavs of other origins.

† Only four had more than six rooms.

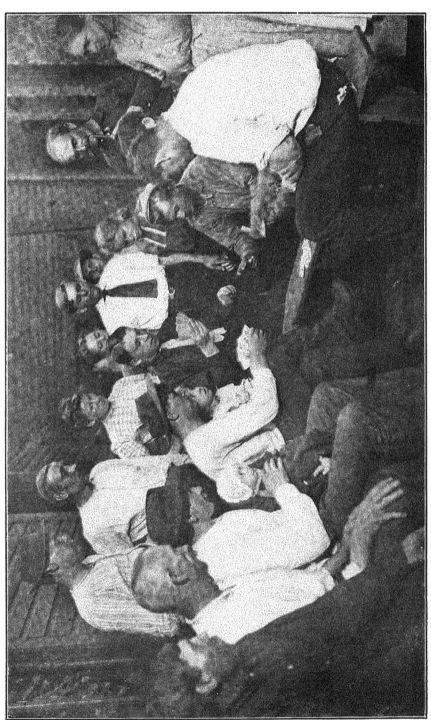

Photo by Hine

Summer Evening in a Court

only three families, as stated, had running water in their homes. In no court were fewer than five families using one yard hydrant or pump, while in exceptional instances it was the sole supply of as many as twenty. As waste-water pipes were also lacking in the houses, the heavy tubs of water had to be carried out as well as in, and this in a smoky town where a double amount of washing and cleaning is necessary. When the weather permitted, the heavy washes were done in the yard. The pavement of a populous court covered with tubs, wringers, clothes baskets, and pools of soapy water, is a poor playground for children.

The toilet accommodations, while possibly more adequate than the water supply, are a menace to health in consequence of the lack of running water. There was not one indoor closet in any of these courts. The streets of Homestead all have sewers, and by a borough ordinance even the outside vaults must be connected with them. These are, however, ordinarily flushed only by the waste water which flows directly into them from the yards. When conditions become unbearable, the tenants wash the vaults out with a hose attached to the hydrant. As long as the closets remain in the yards, it is difficult to introduce a system of flushing because of the danger that the pipes will freeze in winter. The vaults are usually in the center of the court only a few yards from the kitchen doors, and create from the point of view either of sanitation or decency, an intolerable condition. While occasionally three or four families must use one compartment, usually only two families do so. But even this means frequently that the closets are not locked and that no one has a special sense of responsibility for their condition; in consequence they are often filthy.

The Slavic courts of Homestead typify the conditions which result when an industrial district is invaded by hundreds of unskilled immigrant laborers, largely single men, largely country people, who want a place to sleep for the least possible cash. Most of the petty local landlords who provide these quarters care nothing for the condition of their places and regard the wages of these transients as fair spoils.

CHAPTER X

LIFE AT $1.65 A DAY

TO sum up the situation, then, we find a group of slow, hard-working country people, ambitious to attain prosperity, coming in large numbers in response to the demand of the mills for strong, unskilled labor. The mill offers them its lowest wage; the community meets them with indifference; the landlords exploit their helplessness. There is no reason for surprise, then, that the inability of these people to understand or cope with the adverse conditions which await them results in much unwholesome living.

Let us turn from general facts and consider, in the first place, how the economic problem of life can be worked out on $1.65 a day.

With the single men the problem is of course a simple one. Many care little how they live so long as they live cheaply. One of the lodging houses which I visited during the depression consisted of two rooms one above the other, each measuring perhaps 12 by 20 feet. In the kitchen was the wife of the boarding boss getting dinner,—some sort of hot apple cake and a stew of the cheapest cuts of meats. Along one side of the room was an oilcloth-covered table with a plank bench on each side; above it a rack holding a long row of handleless white cups and a shelf with tin knives and forks. Near the up-to-date range, the only piece of real furniture in the room, hung the "buckets" in which all mill men carry their noon or midnight meals. A crowd of men were lounging cheerfully about, talking, smoking and enjoying life, making the most of the leisure enforced by the shut-down in the mill. In the room above, double iron bedsteads were set close together and on them comfortables were neatly laid. In these two rooms, besides the "boarding boss," a stalwart Bulgarian, his wife and two babies, lived 20 men.

The "boarding boss" runs the house and the men pay $3.00 a month for a place to sleep, for having their clothes washed and their food cooked. In addition an account is kept of the food purchased and the total is divided among the men on pay day. The housewife also purchases and cooks any special food a man orders; beef, pork, lamb, each with a tag of some sort labeling the order, will all be fried together. A separate statement for each boarder is kept of these expenses. Such an account for a group of men in a small Slavic household may prove of interest. The family (which consisted of a man, his wife, his brother, three children aged eleven, eight, and one, and four boarders), occupied a house of four rooms, one of them dark, for which they paid a rent of $14. The man, though he had been in this country about twenty-one years, still earned only $10.80 a week with which to meet the needs of a growing family. One-half the cost of the food was paid by the boarders including the brother, and amounted for each man to about $1.06 a week. The expenditures for the week for the whole family of seven adults and three children were as follows:

```
Vegetables.                        .$ 1.06
Fruit .                             .  .56
Milk, eggs, etc. .                  . 1.98
Sugar .                             . .49
Sundries                            . .76
Meat .                             . 5.78
                                    ─────
    Total .                        .$10.63
```

The following table made up from the account book shows the men's individual likings as expressed in the "extras" they ordered:

TABLE 30.—FOOD PURCHASED ON SPECIAL ORDER FOR BOARDERS DURING MONTH ACCOUNT WAS KEPT

Article	Pambay	Baker	Droby	Pilich	Timke
Beef	..	$ .87	..	$1.20	$ .48
Pork	$3.71	.92	$2.14	3.04	2.30
Veal	..	.90	..	..	..
Eggs	..	..	..	.10	.05
Milk	..	.21	.90	..	..
Cheese	.10	.19	..	.09	.05
Fruit	.15	.25	..	..	..
Total	$3.96	$3.34	$3.04	$4.43	$2.88

The average expense for each man, including his share of the general sum, together with the amount spent individually, was about $8.02 a month. Adding $3.00 a month for room and washing, the total expense to each was about $11 a month. In prosperous times these men make regularly $9.90, which may be increased when they work more than 10 hours a day, and on Sunday, to as high as $12 a week.* It is obvious, therefore, that if the fixed expenditure of these single men is about $3.00 a week, a large margin remains over and above clothes either for saving or indulgence. They can thus send for wife and children, fulfill their duties to aged parents, live high according to their lights, or make provision for their own future.

While this program is an economical one, it by no means furnishes to this group of homeless foreigners a normal life. Though some expect to return and others to send for their families when they have made their fortunes, all for the time being are in a strange country with neither the pleasures nor the restraints of home life. As in all barracks life, drunkenness and immorality are common.

But while 50.5 per cent of the Slavs employed in the mill are single, the remainder have families to support, usually on this same wage. How does this other half live? Let us take the average expenditures of ten Slavic budget families (without boarders) earning less than $12 a week, whose total average expenditure was $10.03 a week, 13 cents above the usual day laborer's wage of $9.90. The figures are as follows:

Food .	.	.	.	.$4.64	Tobacco .	.	.$ .07
Rent .	.	.	.	. 1.62	Liquor .	.	. .55
Fuel .	.	.	.	.27	Medicine .	.	. ..
Clothing .	.	.	. 1.57	Furniture .	.	. ..
Other housekeeping ex-					Insurance .	.	. .77
penses .	.	.	. .13	Other .	.	. .41

We may consider the distribution of expenditure in this group as fairly representative of the amount of money that the majority of the Slavs can count upon unless they work overtime or increase their income by taking lodgers. The $1.62 a week for rent provides only a one or two-room tenement, two rooms in one

* While men engaged in the processes in steel mills work 12 hours, the nominal day of yard laborers is 10 hours.

Photo by Hine

Wash-day in a Homestead Court

of the undesirable houses costing $8.00 a month. This is plainly too low a housing standard for any family. With an average expenditure in this group of $4.64 a week, the cost of food for the average family would equal 20 cents a day per grown man, two cents a day less than Professor Underhill's estimate for essentials, five cents a day less than the general run of Homestead housekeepers got along on in hard times. As the Slavic accounts were not kept in sufficient detail it is difficult to show the food value of their provisions, but the statement of the average expenditure of one family, including a man, his wife and three children, twelve, three years, and nine months old, may give a suggestion as to the kind of food purchased. This family was dependent on the man's earnings of $9.90 a week.

TABLE 31.—FOOD EXPENDITURES OF A SLAVIC FAMILY FOR ONE WEEK

Article	Cost
Bread	.$ .75
Bakers' food	.03
Meat	1.46
Flour	.26
Potatoes	.25
Other vegetables	.09
Dried beans	.06
Eggs	.24
Milk	.11
Butter	.38
Cheese	.05
Fresh fruit	.13
Sugar	.14
Tea	.08
Coffee	.76
Sundries	.40
Total	.$5.19
Average a day	.74
Average a day per grown man	.23

While the sum expended was slightly more than 22 cents, a rough calculation indicated that the nutritive value of the food was a little below the requisite amount. In all probability these Slavic women are not skilful buyers,—the accounts consist of a rather monotonous alternation of "bread, meat—bread, meat" that does not promise an inspiring diet. As many of the wives are burdened by the extra work involved in taking lodgers, and as the men do heavy work and are hearty eaters, they choose food that is quick to prepare, and that satisfies appetite with the least effort rather than at the lowest cost. This probably accounts for the preference for meat in place of vegetables which would not otherwise be expected in country-bred people.

The expenditure for clothing among the ten families considered was below what Mr. Chapin estimated was essential in New York, though it formed a slightly larger percentage than in American families in the same income group. No money was expended for furniture; a fact borne out by the utter barrenness of the two-room homes of many of the laborers. With the exception of insurance, the value of which as we shall see is fully appreciated, and the comparatively high expenditure for liquor, these figures surely indicate that life measured in terms of possessions is at a low ebb among these Slavic laborers. There was but $ .41 left for amusements, for church, for education. And what had become of the margin which was to make possible the attainment of that old-country ambition, a bit of property or a bank account? Some other means must be found to achieve these ends.

What that device is we saw in our study of the 21 Slavic courts, when we found that 102 families out of 239 took lodgers.* The income from this source is no mean item. Of the 102 families, three-quarters received from lodgers a sum at least the equivalent of the rent, while a fifth received twice the amount of the rent or more. If we compare the income from lodgers with the man's wages, we find that in over half it added 25 per cent or more to the family's earnings. A glance at the sources of income of the budget families suggests that among the Slavs themselves the

---

*The ways by which families increase their income in order to get ahead are indicated by these notes of the Slavic investigator in regard to families which had bought homes.

"John C———. Woman goes out cleaning and cooking. By doing this she has been able to add her earnings to her husband's so as to pay for the property they now own."

"The mother took boarders till too old. Now the daughter does not prove to be a good housekeeper" (perhaps because this was poor training for the future).

"Mrs. Y. since her marriage has gone out to work by the day, and then done washings in the evenings—she also has a boarder who pays $18 a month. But she no longer goes out to work since they have paid for their home."

wages of an unskilled laborer are considered insufficient to support a family, even according to the standards of the Second Ward.*

Single men, then, who must find homes, and families with small wages who want to save, together give rise to the lodging and boarding system of the Slavic courts. The outcome is over-crowding. Of the 102 families taking lodgers, 62 had four lodgers or less; 33 from five to nine lodgers; seven from 10 to 15 lodgers.

TABLE 32.—TWO HUNDRED AND THIRTY-NINE SLAVIC FAMILIES IN 21 COURTS.—BY NUMBER, NATIONALITY† AND NUMBER OF LODGERS

Nationality of Lodgers	Total Families	Families Having no Lodgers	FAMILIES HAVING LODGERS			
			1–4	5–9	10–15	Total
Slovak . . .	168	107	44	16	1	61
Pole	10	7	3	..	..	3
Hungarian . . .	22	11	4	6	1	11
Russian . . .	16	..	6	5	5	16
Croatian . . .	6	..	2	4	..	6
Lithuanian . . .	4	2	2	..	..	2
Others. . . .	13	10	1	2	..	3
Total . . .	239	137	62	33	7	102

Even among the families that did not take lodgers, half averaged over two persons to the room. Of those who did take lodgers, all but 15 suffered this same degree of overcrowding. Forty-three lived three to the room, 31 four, seven five, and six more than five to the room. It is in itself a proof of the meagre standards of home life, that of the 102 families who took lodgers, 71 lived in two-room tenements, where obviously there were no superfluous rooms to be rented and where this economy

* Appendix I, Tables 2 and 3, p. 201

† As 70 per cent of the families living in these courts were Slovaks, with the remainder scattered among many different Slavic races, it is perhaps fruitless to attempt any conclusions as to racial distinctions in the matter of overcrowding. But in the accompanying table it is to be noted that among the Russians not only were there no families without lodgers, but that they had also the largest number of families with over ten lodgers.

involved the overcrowding of space already inadequate. Of the 71 families in two-room tenements, 55 had three or more persons to the room, 27 had four or more persons, and 8 had five or more.

TABLE 33.—NUMBER OF PERSONS PER ROOM IN THE 21 COURTS IN FAMILIES WHICH TOOK LODGERS COMPARED WITH THE NUMBER IN FAMILIES WHICH DID NOT TAKE LODGERS, JANUARY, 1908

Total Families	Families Having an Average per Room of					
	1 Person	2 Persons	3 Persons	4 Persons	5 Persons	More than 5
With lodgers, 102 . .	6	9	43	31	7	6
Without lodgers, 137. .	19	49	52	13	2	2
Totals	25	58	95	44	9	8

This study was made in 1908 and the extent of overcrowding was far less than during the previous summer, since with the business depression of 1908 hundreds of men, especially those without families, had returned to the old country.

We have now fairly complete before us the picture of the household establishment in which the family of the Slavic immigrant takes up life in Homestead. Wages at 16½ cents an hour and the lodger as a means for supplementing them, are its chief factors. Taking lodgers is not giving a home to a friend from the old country nor letting an extra room; it is a deliberate business venture on the part of a family to increase the inadequate income from the man's earnings. This thrifty measure may seem to the reader a wise means of solving the problem. It is only as he comes to know the actual effects on home life that he realizes the iniquity of a system which makes this necessary to attain the altogether natural ambition to own a home or save a thousand dollars,—or even for a husband to have his wife and children about him.

We have yet to see what life at this level means as a basis for rearing children, as affording human recreations, and as a foothold for getting on in the world.

Photo by Hine

INTO AMERICA THROUGH THE SECOND WARD OF HOMESTEAD

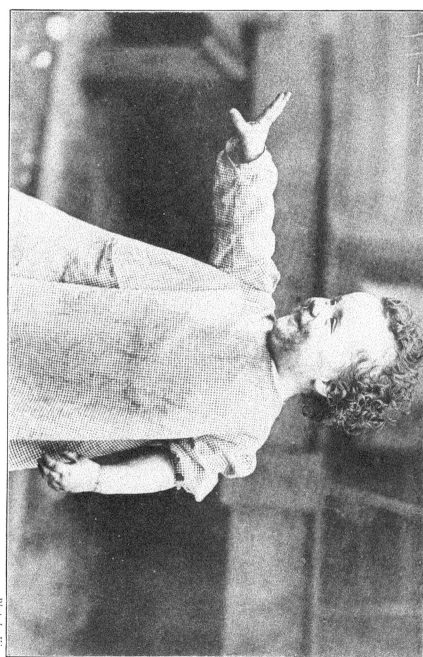

When Meadows Have Grown Too Many Smokestacks

Photo by Hine

CHAPTER XI

FAMILY LIFE OF THE SLAVS

ONE morning I entered a two-room tenement. The kitchen, perhaps 15 by 12 feet, was steaming with vapor from a big washtub set on a chair in the middle of the room. The mother was trying to wash and at the same time to keep the older of her two babies from tumbling into the tub full of scalding water that was standing on the floor. On one side of the room was a huge puffy bed, with one feather tick to sleep on and another for covering; near the window stood a sewing machine; in the corner, an organ,—all these, besides the inevitable cook stove upon which in the place of honor was simmering the evening's soup. Upstairs in the second room were one boarder and the man of the house asleep. Two more boarders were at work, but at night would be home to sleep in the bed from which the others would get up. Picture if you will what a week or a season means to a mother in such a home, the overwork, the brief respite from toil—to be increased afterward—when the babies come?

Yet it is even more disastrous to the children both in health and character. In the courts studied, out of 102 families who took lodgers, 72 had children; of these, 25 families had two, 10 had three, and seven had four. There were 138 youngsters in all. A comparison of births and deaths of children under two, shown in the tables on the following page, shows that among the Slavs one child under two years of age dies to every three children born; among the English-speaking Europeans, one dies to every seven born; among the native whites and colored, one to every five. In the crowded Second Ward, taking all races, one child under two dies to every three born,—compared with one to every four in the First Ward, one to every five in the Fifth, one to every eight in the Third, and one to every seven in the Fourth.

TABLE 34.—NUMBER OF BIRTHS IN EACH WARD IN HOMESTEAD FOR 1907.—BY RACIAL GROUP

| Racial Group | WARD | | | | | Total |
	1	2	3	4	5	
Slav	23	338	34	5	16	416
Eng. sp. Eur.	17	41	23	19	27	127
Native White and Colored . .	39	37	55	27	55	213
Total	79	416	112	51	98	756

TABLE 35.—NUMBER OF DEATHS OF CHILDREN UNDER TWO YEARS OF AGE IN EACH WARD IN HOMESTEAD FOR 1907.—BY RACIAL GROUP

| Racial Group | WARD | | | | | Total |
	1	2	3	4	5	
Slav	5	113	6	3	6	133
Eng. sp. Eur.	2	9	2	1	4	18
Native White and Colored . .	12	10	6	3	9	40
Total	19	132	14	7	19	191

TABLE 36.—RATIO OF BIRTHS IN EACH WARD IN HOMESTEAD IN 1907 TO DEATHS OF CHILDREN UNDER TWO IN THE SAME WARD.—BY RACIAL GROUP

| Racial Group | WARD | | | | | Total |
	1	2	3	4	5	
Slav	4.6	3.0	5.7	1.7	2.7	3.1
Eng. sp. Eur.	8 5	4.6	11.5	19.0	6.8	7.0
Native White and Colored . .	3.3	3.7	9.2	9.0	6.1	5.3
Proportions between total number of births and deaths under two in each ward	4.2	3.2	8.0	7.3	5.2	4.0

Against many of these deaths was the physician's entry "malnutrition due to poor food and overcrowding"; that is, the mother too poor, too busy, and too ignorant to prepare food properly, rooms over-tenanted, and courts too confined to give the fresh air essential for the physical development of children. A priest told me he believed that the taking of lodgers caused the appalling death rate among the babies in his parish. Neither preaching nor pointing out to women personally the folly of the economy had sufficed to check the habit.

Not only is the mother too busy to give much time to her babies, but she also suffers from overwork during pregnancy and from lack of proper care afterward. Housework must be done, boarders must be fed, and most women work until the day of confinement. In accordance with their home customs, almost all of them employ midwives and call a doctor only in an emergency. I was told by a local physician that nearly half of the births in Homestead, the large proportion of them among the Slavic people, were attended by midwives. These women, who charge $5.00 or $10, include in their services the care of both woman and child for several days, and thus perform the services of trained nurse as well as doctor. While of the 21 midwives registered in Homestead, five or six have diplomas from schools of midwifery abroad, most of them are ignorant and are careless about cleanliness. In a paper before the Allegheny County Medical Society, Dr. Purman, a local physician, reported numerous instances where both mother and child had suffered serious injury from the ignorance of these women.

The necessity for mothers to be up and at work within three or four days adds to the harm. In at least 10 of the 29 Slavic families visited, special reference was made by the Slavic investigator to the ill health of the mother due to overwork and to lack of proper care during confinement. The strength to bear much doubtless comes to these women from years of work in the fields, but the change to the hot kitchens where their work is now done undoubtedly entails a strain which not only injures them but lessens the vitality of the children. This weakened condition at birth combines with the inadequate food and insufficient air and the neglect which comes through over-burdening the mother to produce the appalling infant death rate in these courts.

Yet sometimes as you watch the stunted, sickly looking children, you wonder if the real tragedy does not lie rather in the miserable future in store for the babies who live, many of them with undervitalized systems which may make them victims either of disease or of the dissipation that often fastens upon weak wills and weak bodies.

Keeping lodgers ruins the training as well as the health of the children. The overworked mother has neither time nor patience for wise discipline. As the men who work on night turns must sleep during the day, crying babies must not be allowed to disturb this uneasy rest. All this adds to the mother's weary irritation and makes it harder to maintain any sort of uniform control. This failure of intelligent discipline was noticeable in most of the families I visited, where cuffs and sharp words were the usual form of correction. One of the Protestant missions which tried through mothers' meetings to give the women some suggestions as to child training, found them too busy to come. Fortunately, however, the children who attend the public schools receive some training. This the parents value. A teacher in the Second Ward school said that while she had a great deal of trouble in teaching the Slavic children obedience, she at least found the parents willing to uphold her in whatever action she took.

Even more serious is the injury to the moral tone of the Slavic community caused by the crowding together of single men and families. In only four instances in the courts studied were lodgers found in families where there were girls over fourteen, but even younger children learn evil quickly from the free-spoken men. With the husband at work on the night shift the situation is aggravated, and reports are current of gross immorality on the part of some women who keep lodgers; two or three actual instances came to my knowledge from unquestioned sources. Since half the families in the courts studied used the kitchen as a sleeping room, there was close mingling of lodgers and family among them. This becomes intolerable when families living in but two rooms take lodgers. This was true, as we have seen, in 71 instances. Even when extreme crowding does not exist, family and lodgers often all sleep in the kitchen, the only warm room, in winter.

Certainly there is little to quicken mental and spiritual

148

Photo by Hine

OUT OF WORK

Homestead Court, Spring of 1908

Photo by Hine

OUT OF WORK

Homestead Court, Spring of 1908

development in these crowded tenements where there is neither privacy nor even that degree of silence necessary for reading. We agree in the abstract that the individual needs room for growth, yet complain of the stunted mental stature of these people who have the meagre development of seedlings grown in a mass.

Moreover, families who live in narrow quarters have no room for festive gatherings. In the evening a group often gathers around the stove gossiping of home days, playing cards, drinking, and playing simple musical instruments. On the Saturday after pay day the household usually clubs together to buy a case of beer which it drinks at home. These ordinarily jovial gatherings are sometimes interrupted by fights and the police have to be called in. One officer who had been on the force for nine years said that these men were generally good-natured and easy-going, and in all his experience he had never arrested a sober "Hunkie"; it was when they were drunk that the trouble began. The punishment usually inflicted for disorderly conduct in Homestead, a small fine, has little deterrent effect among the Slavs. It is indeed currently said that some are proud of having a large fine imposed, as they feel that it indicates increased importance. Usually, however, they gather without disturbance simply to chat and drink, to pass the hours after the day's work.

The women have few opportunities for relaxation. Sometimes they gossip around the pump or at the butcher's, but washing, ironing, cleaning, sewing and cooking for the boarders leave little time for visiting. The young people perhaps suffer most from the lack of home festivities. A two-room house has no place for games or "parties," or even for courting; there is not even space enough, to say nothing of privacy. So young folks are driven to the streets for their gayety. Almost the only time when the house is really the scene of festivity is when those primal events, birth, and marriage, and death, bring together both the old-time friends and the new neighbors.

On most of these occasions, whether weddings, christenings or funerals, joy and grief and religious ceremony are alike forgotten in a riotous good time. The weddings are the gayest affairs in the life of the community. After the morning service at the

149

church, all return home if the house is big enough, and if not, they go to a hall, and there the dancing begins. Each man pays what he can, usually a dollar, for the privilege of dancing with the bride, and the money—their form of a wedding present—helps furnish the home for the young couple. At one wedding during the winter $75 was thus received, but the girl by evening felt that she had earned the money. In the afternoon the drinking begins and by midnight the revel is at its height. The neighborhood considers a family under obligation to provide these festivities. I was told of one pathetic instance where a woman, as she was very ill, did not invite any one to her baby's christening. Her offended neighbors refused to visit her, but when she died they were ready enough to come to the funeral and share in the drinking.

Some old-world customs, too, are maintained which seem strangely at variance with new-world conditions. All summer over the doors and windows are seen dried, smoke begrimed branches from which the faded leaves hang disconsolately. These decorations are part of a joyous religious festival in the spring time similar to those that added merriment to the village life at home. At Eastertide they keep up an old custom, said to date from pagan days. On Monday the men go about with willow branches and switch the women until they make them a present, while on the following day the women retaliate by throwing water on the men.

In other superficial habits of life they show themselves eager to adopt American customs. This tendency is clearly—sometimes humorously—exemplified in the quickness with which they adopt our style of clothing. The men on Sunday can often be differentiated from the American workmen only by the unmistakable Slavic type of face. Even in their own homes the women quickly adopt the machine-made cotton wrapper and on Sunday the streets blossom with cheap ready-made adornments. I was fairly startled by one apparition in a gay pink hat, crude blue skirt, and green silk waist that no grass in Homestead could hope to vie with, all products of a department store, which evidently gave the wearer a proud sense of being dressed like other Americans. As I stood Easter Sunday watching the kneeling women, the mass of vivid colors showed how easily they copy the less desirable habits of their native born sisters. If opportunity offered they would doubtless be as ready to pick up our customs in other more essential matters.

Lack of intercourse, however, hinders. The Slavs must keep up their own festivities the more because they cannot join in the amusements of the rest of the community. To the better class of entertainments they are not welcomed, and to others the difference in speech is still a barrier. Obviously the theatre, and even in a measure the nickelodeons, are uninteresting to those who cannot understand the language. Thus cut off from what little normal amusement Homestead offers, they cling to the few festivities their limited opportunities make possible.

In summer there are of course more chances for recreation; trolley rides and picnics in the park make a welcome variety from the heat of the courts. The following statements, taken from the notes of the Slavic woman who assisted in making the investigation, tell the story simply:

—They do not go to amusements of any kind on account of being so poor and feel so badly after they have finished their day's work.

—Husband and wife go to the lodge dances, which they enjoy very much. Wife goes to the five cent theatres, to the parks in the summer and for trolley rides. Is fond of all kinds of amusements and goes when they can afford it.

—The family have no amusements at all outside of their own home, simply because they cannot afford it. They would like to be able to go to some places of amusement, if they could. Spend their Sundays at home in a pleasant way. The mother and children go to church every Saturday evening to say the rosary, which is one of their chief pleasures.

Starting in with such a household as that described at the opening of this chapter, how far do any of these Slavic families succeed in working out ideals they have set for themselves?

If we turn from the crowded courts with their two-room tenements to the homes of some who have attained their ambitions, we find conditions that show an inherent capacity for advancement in the race. As an illustration, note the change in type in two houses, the homes of families from the same place in the old country, the one newcomers, the other among the "oldest inhabitants" of the Slavic community. The first family live in a one-room tenement, where even though the furniture includes only absolute necessities, it is hard to keep all the crowded belongings in order. On wash-day morning the disorder is increased. Nevertheless, the home is kept as neat as the circumstances permit, and the bright pictures on the wall are proof of a desire to make it attractive. As the man earns only $9.90 a week, they must keep their rent low if bills are to be paid and anything laid by for the future. In the other picture, the "front room" with its leather-covered furniture is in a five-room house which the family owns. The sacred pictures with their vivid coloring relieve the severity of the room while they also reveal the religious note in Slavic life, for if happiness is to stay with the family, the priest must come

TABLE 37.—AVERAGE WEEKLY EXPENDITURE OF 29 SLAVIC BUDGET FAMILIES

Expenditure Group	Number of Families	Average Weekly Expenditure	Rent	Food	Fuel	Clothing	Furniture	Household Expenses	Insurance	Tobacco	Liquor	Medicine	Other
Under $12.00	14	$ 8.98	$1.53	$4.48	$.23	$1.24	$.01	$.13	$.60	$.05	$.42	..	$ .31
$12.00–$14.99	5	13.42	2.41	5.99	.76	1.67	.08	.34	.40	.05	.43	$.25	1.04
$15.00–$19.99	7	17.47	2.38	8.47	.56	1.80	.05	.39	.77	.05	1.26	.18	1.55
$20.00 and over	.. 3	21.55	2.62	7.12	.07	3.11	..	.56	3.22	.05	.37	.48	3.95
Average	29	$13.09	$2.00	$5.98	$.38	$1.64	$.03	$.27	$.84	$.05	$.62	$.14	$1.11

yearly to "bless the home." This family after many years in America has, by hard work and thrift, succeeded in obtaining a real home.

Turning from this visible evidence of the way in which an individual Slavic family has prospered, we find in the mill census that the number of skilled, and therefore highly paid members of the race, are few. Of the 3603 Slavs in the mill in 1907, 459 were ranked as semi-skilled, 80 as skilled. The Slovaks from Austro-Hungary are the most numerous of the race in Homestead, and

Close Quarters.   One Room and Three in the Family   *Photo by Hine*
A CONTRAST—I

Photo by Hine

Parlor, Well-to-do Slavic Family 20 Years in America
A CONTRAST—II

were the first of this stock to come here. Among them we find proportionately a slightly larger number of semi-skilled workers.*

We have seen that of the budget Slavs still earning laborers' wages, a third had been here over ten years; it is apparent, however, that individuals are slowly making their way into skilled work—a movement which, as the older English-speaking men drop out, is probably bound to increase. In the 29 immigrant families keeping budgets all of the men who earned $12 or more a week had been here over five years. It is interesting to note that some had come here when they were very young, eleven, fifteen, sixteen, or seventeen years old; for example, a tonnage worker had been here ten years; a man at one of the furnaces earning $3.50 a day, seventeen years, and a machinist who earned about the same amount, eighteen years. Even with the higher wages, their families continue to make sacrifices to secure the desired property more rapidly. A helper at one of the open-hearth furnaces, who had been here for seven years, was earning $2.50 to $3.00 a day. The husband and wife still took in two boarders, so that with their two children there were six people in a two-room house, which was but scantily furnished. They had a bank account of at least $400. Another Slav, the head of a family of three, had been here ten years and was working on tonnage, in good times earning about $6.00 a day. They, too, lived in a two-room house, but it was neat and from their standpoint probably seemed large enough as they had no lodger. They had purchased the farm in the old country and besides had a $500 bank account. Again, take a family of six. The father, still only about thirty years old, had been here for over fifteen years. Out of his wages—about $3.50 a day at fairly skilled work in the mill—he was buying a small house with a garden. He was naturalized and the family stood as a fair type of our new citizens. They took no lodgers, but the limitations imposed by such thrift as they practiced are illustrated by the notes on this household made by my interpreter. Herself a Slav, their circumstances were a matter of no special interest, and she therefore wrote her notes with no attempt to add "local color" such as a person of another race

*They formed 51.7 per cent of all the Slavs in the mill in 1907, 60.1 per cent of the semi-skilled Slavs, and 56.2 per cent of the skilled Slavs.

would have put into them. To her the statement was simply one of facts:

Conditions of Work:
> The man works on day and night shifts alternately.

Home:
> They don't own their own home, on which there is a mortgage. The man gives all his earnings to his wife and when he needs any spending money, he asks for it.

Furniture:
> They live in two rooms comfortably furnished, one a living room and the other a bed room. They have a sewing machine on which the mother does the sewing for her family. Does her washing by hand.

Clothes:
> They wear plain clothing. The woman does all her own mending with care. The father buys ready-made clothing. They have a change of clothing for Sundays, of a fairly good quality.

Food:
> They buy their food at grocery stores; don't get all at one store. They live principally on vegetable diet, not using much fruit. The man works hard and they are obliged to have good substantial food. The family eat their evening meal together.

Woman's Work:
> The woman does her own work at home, but does not earn anything outside, her time all being taken up with caring for her family.

Lodges:
> The man belongs to St. Stephen's Lodge, and his wife belongs to St. Catherine's, both church lodges. They attend one meeting every month unless something to prevent. When not able to go, they send in their dues. The man gets $5.00 a week sick benefits, also a death benefit of $1000 to his family after his decease. His dues are $2.00 monthly and the wife's dues are $1.00 a month. In case of death of the woman the family gets $700. The wife's reasons for belonging to above lodges is that their family may have benefits paid by the lodges in case of a death, either father or mother.

Health:
> This man is in good health. The woman is not in good health, having gone to work too soon after her confinement;

was attended by a midwife. She did not have proper care during her confinement. The children are sickly. One of them had typhoid fever.

Education:

There are four children, the oldest seven years and now attending public school. The only reading matter they have is his Lodge paper, which he gets once a week.

Accidents:

The man had one accident, but no help from the Carnegie fund.

Drink:

The man drinks at home and sometimes at saloons. Pays for himself. He does not get intoxicated. The woman drinks a little when she has it at home.

Amusements:

The man goes only when his lodge gives a dance, it being expected of every member to buy tickets. Neither he nor his wife ever attend theatres, on account of being kept at home with their family. The woman cannot remember having been to any of the parks or amusements of any kind.

It is by such thrift that some of the Slavs attain their ambition to own a home. An official in the foreign department of one bank said he knew of 25 Slavs who had purchased homes in 1907. Sometimes these families continue to live in the Second Ward. One family, for example, had bought an eight-room house on one of these busy streets. The four rear rooms they rented, but with evident regard for appearances lived themselves in the four that faced the front. With the aid of the rent from the rear tenement they had succeeded in freeing the house from the mortgage. The families more often, however, move further from the mill. One I knew bought a house on the hill with two porches and a big yard where they kept chickens. While they had only succeeded in paying $500 on the $1700 the place cost, now that a son was at work they hoped to be able to clear the debt. In the meantime they truly rejoiced in being on the hill above the smoke and away from the bustling courts.

The English-speaking families on such streets rarely extend a cordial welcome. A woman who lives next door to a Slavic family told me that some of the neighbors objected because they were rather noisy and drank a good deal, though she herself found them pleasant enough.

All the Slavs who prosper, however, do not try to buy property here. Some prefer a bank account. It is authoritatively stated that about 1600 Slavs have savings bank accounts in Homestead ranging from $100 to $1000, and even in a few instances to $1500. Occasionally this zeal for saving gets a setback. A few years ago a Slav ran an "exchange bank" in Homestead and when he had secured a goodly sum departed. One family was so discouraged at losing the $400 it had on deposit with him, of hard earned savings, that the woman ceased to take boarders and the man to work hard.

TABLE 38.—AVERAGE EXPENDITURE OF 10 SLAVIC FAMILIES COMPARED WITH 42 OF ALL RACES, SPENDING MORE THAN $15 PER WEEK

	Total	Food	Rent	Fuel	Clothing	Furniture	Minor Household Expenses	Insurance	Tobacco	Liquor	Medicine	Other
Slav . . .	$18.74	$8.08	$2.46	$.42	$2.20	$.04	$.44	$1.51	$.06	$.99	$.27	$2.27
All . . .	21.19	8.14	3.18	.77	2.67	.56	.62	1.42	.06	.39	.53	2.85

TABLE 39.—AVERAGE EXPENDITURES OF TWO GROUPS OF 10 FAMILIES EACH, THOSE SPENDING $15 OR MORE A WEEK AND THOSE SPENDING LESS THAN $12, WITH THE RATIO OF INCREASE

	Total	Food	Rent	Fuel	Clothing	Furniture	Minor Household Expenses	Insurance	Tobacco	Liquor	Medicine	Other
Under $12	$10.03	$4.64	$1.62	$.27	$1.57	..	$.13	$.77	$.07	$.55	..	$.41
Over $15	18.74	8.08	2.46	.42	2.20	$.04	.44	1.51	.06	.99	$.27	2.27
Ratio	189	174	152	155	140	..	..	196	..	180	..	554

Photo by 1

WASHING UP AFTER A DAY IN THE MILL

Photo by Hine

GATHERED FOR A BIT OF GOSSIP

Yet not all the extra money goes into bank accounts and houses. If we compare the budgets * of the 10 Slavic families spending more than $15 a week with the average of the 42 budget families (of all races) in the same expenditure groups, we shall find that the former increase their expenditures along much the same lines as do the other peoples, though it is to be noted here, as in the general averages, that the Slav spends a slightly larger per cent for food and a slightly smaller per cent for rent.

If, on the other hand, we compare the Slavic families spending over $15 with those spending less than $12 (Table 39), we find that the expenditures which have increased less rapidly than the income are the essentials, food, rent, fuel, and clothing; that insurance increases a little more rapidly, but that the great part of the increased pay goes for more distinctly cultural expenditures.

This comparison, though fragmentary, suggests that on the whole these Slavs made a wise use of their increased earnings— that there is an actual increase of expenditure for every item, but that by far the largest gain is in that sphere which stands for the less material side of life, church, education, recreation and savings.

For most Slavic households, however, the increased income which would make such increased expenditure possible must be looked for not from the man's wages, but, at least in the first years, from other sources. We have seen how the first recourse of the young couple is to keep lodgers and the cost to health and childhood that that involves. Time goes on, brings children, and household expenses rise, and even with increased earnings, tends to keep the couple at this double work.

* For average expenditure of all Slavic families by expenditure groups, see Table 37, p. 152.

CHAPTER XII

THE SLAV ORGANIZED

OTHER needs of the Slavs arising out of the industrial situation and out of their isolation, they have attempted to meet co-operatively by various forms of voluntary organization.

The most powerful social institution influencing their lives is the church. Some of the Slavs belong to the Greek Catholic, some to the Roman Catholic communion, and both have an intimate hold upon their adherents. Of their full part in the spiritual life of the people a stranger who cannot even speak the language is unable to judge fairly. When at the crowded church, on Easter morning, I watched the men who could not find room to enter, standing on the steps with bent heads and open prayer books reverently following the service within, I had a vivid sense of the power of the church over these stalwart, slow-moving men. Another day I visited one of the boarding houses. Beneath pictures of Christ on the Cross and "The Last Supper," a group about the table were engaged in a drunken quarrel. With these two scenes in mind,—and scenes of similar character constantly alternated in my experience in Homestead,—it was hard to judge how strong the spiritual influence of the church was, save to realize that it is an intimate part of everyday life.

Undoubtedly priests who are sufficiently intelligent to understand the situation the Slav faces, can exercise a strong influence for good. The one Homestead priest who spoke English fluently was a man of this type, a man who seemed to comprehend the problems of his people and to help in their solution. He not only talked to the women personally but also preached from the pulpit against the ruin of home life that results from taking lodgers; he was organizing a club where the newcomers could meet Slavs who had been longer in this country and could catch from them some American ideas. Priests of this type may be a strong factor in the Americanization of the race. Unfortunately, as many priests speak no English and are little more in touch with American ideas than their people, the church life tends to preserve rather than to remove national distinctions. For their church is not merely a place for religious services; it is an institution with both social and educational functions.

I lived for two months near the Lithuanian church and always enjoyed watching the group of men that gathered outside the gate after service of a Sunday morning. Some came from neighboring towns and looked forward to this weekly chance for a friendly smoke and chat.

Through parochial schools, also, the church exerts a strong influence. Here its activity seems less desirable since all the Slavic parochial schools are distinctly below the standards of the Homestead public schools both in construction and in teaching.* There are far too many pupils in each room, not enough regular school desks, and ventilation, lighting, toilets and water supply are all insufficient. The lower classes are greatly overcrowded and the teaching force is inadequate. One teacher said that they were so busy that instead of giving careful instruction to children ready for higher work they made them repeat the work of the lower grades.

The parochial schools not only fail to provide adequate instruction, but also hinder the work of amalgamation in which public schools are so potent a factor. If the foreign children played and studied with American children, barriers to mutual understanding would be overcome. Moreover, they do not come into contact with intelligent American women. Of the six teachers in the Slavic Roman Catholic school, three spoke English fluently, though not correctly, three spoke almost none. By changing teachers, however, the principal claimed that, save for instruction in religion and the hour a day devoted to the Slavic language, all studies were taught in English. It was obvious,

---

* The St. Magdalene Parochial School, attached to the English-speaking Roman Catholic Church, was held to compare favorably with the public schools in equipment and instruction.

however, that not only was the teaching of English inadequate, but that those simple forms of history and literature which find place in our grammar schools and which are doubly important with foreign children, were missing.

This indifferent work is of course permitted in part by failure of the parents to appreciate the importance of education. Though I heard of one or two Slavic children in the higher grades of the public school, I was told by the principal of the Second Ward school that few went further than the fifth grade. In 1907-8 one Slavic boy was in the eighth grade and the year before there were two. These children are bright, but if they dislike school the parents do not insist upon their remaining, but put them early to work.

In the 29 Slavic budget families were four children from fourteen to sixteen. Two were in school; the other two, both fourteen years old, were at work, one in a glass factory, the other in a bowling alley where he worked from 10 a.m. to 12 p.m. for $4.50 per week. These were both sons of day laborers. My impression was that the Slavs did not yet consider education a good investment. Instead they were usually anxious to secure the addition of the children's wages to an income that was truly slender enough. They felt that what the children learned in school had little relation to practical success in life, and lack of intercourse with Americans made them slow to appreciate its value.

The influence of the church in Slavic life is intensified by its close connection with fraternal orders. The Slavs have developed a system of benefit organizations which fill a large rôle in the life of this isolated portion of the community. While it was difficult to secure comprehensive data, I learned of at least 26 lodges in Homestead. Twenty-two of these had a total membership of 2108, 1765 of whom were men. The Slovaks, Croatians, Poles, Hungarians, and Lithuanians have their independent societies, and intermingling among these groups is rare. How closely most of the organizations are connected with the church is suggested by their names, such as St. Joseph's Croatian Society and St. Mary Magdalena's First Ladies Slovak Catholic Union. That this connection is not merely nominal is shown by the customary

Photo by Hine

Greek Catholic Church

requirement that members shall belong to the church, with the frequent specification that they shall attend mass at least on Easter Sunday. The symbol of the Greek Catholic Union is an eagle bearing the United States flag in one talon and the cross of the church in the other.

Table 40, on the next page, gives the membership, nationality and benefits of these various organizations.

Finding themselves aliens in the community, their habits and customs not understood by their neighbors, and their needs to a large extent a matter of indifference, the Slavs have thus bound themselves together for mutual helpfulness. While such societies are found in most communities where there are a number of people of this race, the tendency to develop them is intensified in Homestead by the constant dangers of work in the mill. There are many accidents among the Slavs. The hazards are accentuated by their ignorance of these dangers and by their difficulty in understanding the orders of English-speaking "bosses." Given this constant peril of accident or death,* and a community which takes little interest in the immigrant's welfare, the extent to which the lodge has been developed is not surprising.

Without exception these lodges are "beneficial" in character; all give a death benefit, and many also a sick benefit. The death benefits are usually larger than those given in the American lodges, amounting in at least one-third of these societies to $1000. In three societies giving this benefit, the average assessment for three months during the winter studied was $1.75. This figure included regular lodge dues and in addition to the sum at death provided a sick benefit of $5.00 a week for thirteen weeks, and $2.50 a week for the succeeding thirteen weeks, thus comparing favorably with the rates of other fraternal insurance orders. The Polish society does not give a regular death benefit, but

---

* If they live abroad, the family of an alien killed at his work in Pennsylvania is barred by state law from recovering damages even when the accident may be due to the gross negligence of his employer. This pernicious law has been properly disregarded by the Carnegie Relief Fund in awarding benefits. The new relief plan of the United States Steel Corporation covers in its stated provisions only "married men living with their families." Awards to the families of aliens living abroad are thus left to the discretion of company managers—a sweeping exception in view of the great numbers of immigrants employed in the mines and mills of the corporation. See Appendix XII, p. 249.

TABLE 40.—MEMBERSHIP, DUES AND BENEFITS OF 9 SLAVIC SOCIETIES IN 1908

Name	Greek Catholic Union	National Croatian Society	National Slavonic Society	Greek Catholic Youths' Union	Slovak Gymnastic Union	First Catholic Slovak Union	First Catholic Union Women Members	Junior Band	Hungarian Reformed Federation
Members; Men	421	130	363		65	460			
Nationality	Russian	Croatian	Slovak	Russian	Slovak	Slovak		Slovak	Hungarian
Church connection	G. or R. C.	None	None	G. or R. C.	None	G. or R. C.	None	G. or R. C.	Hungarian Reform
Age of members	16–45 years	18–45 years	16–45 years	7–16 years	16–35 years	16–45 years	16–50 years	10–16 years	16–55 eyrs
Dues: Initiation	$1.00–$5.00*	$2.00–$4.00*	$1.00–$10.00*	$0.30	$1.00–$3.00*	$1.00–$6.00*	$1.00–$4.50	$0.15	$2.00–$5.00*
Dues for 3 months	$1.80	$1.70	$1.80	$0.15	$0.75	$1.95		$1.00	
Benefits; death	$1000	$800	$1000	$100	$500	$1000	$500		$300 to $750†
Death of wife or husband	$400	$8000	$300		$150	$400	$250		½ death
Total disability	$1000	$400	$1000		$500	$1000	$300		½ death
Loss of limb	$300	$400	$300		$150	$300			$100
Loss of eye	$150		$100		$50	$100			$100
Sick benefit amount per week	$5.00	$5.00	$5.00 for first 13 weeks; $2.50 for second 13 weeks		$5.00 for first 13 weeks; $2.50 for second 13 weeks	$5.00 for first 13 weeks; $2.50 for second 13 weeks	$5.00 for first 13 weeks; $2.50 for second 13 weeks		$5.00 for first 13 weeks; $2.50 for second 13 weeks
Number of weeks sick benefits run	26	39							

* Varies with age of member.
† Varies with number of members in organization. At death of a member each member usually pays one dollar and this constitutes the total death benefit.

162

assesses each member of the lodge $1.00 at the death of any member. Large benefits are scarcely possible save when local lodges are affiliated with national organizations; as the death benefits are then paid from the central treasury, the burden is shared by the entire membership. The contrast between local and national organizations was shown in the mine disaster in 1908 at Monongah, West Virginia. Here, though 27 members of one Slavic lodge were killed, the national organization was able to meet the emergency without serious difficulty. A Polish society, on the other hand, which lost half its members and depended entirely on contributions from the local lodge, could give only a small benefit.

Usually if the wife of a member dies, or if the man receives a serious injury such as the loss of a limb or an eye, a portion of the death benefit may be paid to the beneficiary. If totally disabled, the member receives the entire amount of the death benefit and then ceases to be a member of the organization. With wages so low as to make it practically impossible for a man to save enough to provide for catastrophes, these collective funds are often all that stand between a family and destitution. To help families in temporary difficulties, societies usually give a sick benefit of $5.00 a week for varying periods of time. This practice is less frequent in the women's societies because of the difficulty in determining when a woman is entitled to a sick benefit. In these homes where everything depends upon the mother, she can rarely give up even when she is really ill. That all but two of the Slavic families from whom budgets were secured, belonged to at least one lodge and many to more than one, shows a genuine appreciation of this form of insurance. The administration of the funds of these organizations is thought to be safeguarded by bonds of the officials, especially of the treasurer; and through initiation fees and a special assessment, reserve funds are created to be used in emergencies. Yet a common public prudence should demand state inspection of the insurance operations of these orders.

These lodges also play an important part in social life. They offer some amusement in a community where there is little else available for the Slavs. The meetings themselves, while nominally for business, afford a chance for coming together, while dances and other festivities are held at intervals. Through them the stranger comes quickly into touch with his own people. Especially is this true of the men who move from one part of the country to another in search of work. Traveling cards issued by the home lodge of a society, and recognized by members of the local lodge in any community, assure a man welcome and assistance wherever he goes. This service, a strong feature with any fraternal order, is particularly valuable to the Slav, with his ignorance of the ways of the new country and even of its language. The fellow members of a lodge become nurses who care for the sick or injured during nights of suffering, and friends who give comfort in times of bereavement.

The Slavic lodges are usually limited to the members of one nationality, Slovak, Hungarian, Polish, and in so far as they tend to perpetuate racial and religious feuds, miss their opportunity to amalgamate the immigrant colony. In this they differ from the lodges of the English-speaking community; these usually include representatives of all the English-speaking nationalities, and thus create a common social intercourse. They stop short there, however, and in turn fail to become the unifying force which they might if they were to welcome foreigners to their membership. The Slavs, it is true, prefer to belong to a lodge in which they can speak their own language; but this tendency to form separate societies is intensified by the suspicions aroused by the fact that they have been victims of a number of fraudulent American organizations. The chief reason, however, is the dislike on the part of the English-speaking people to include "Hunkies" in any organization which would bring them into social and personal contact. Even Slavs who have attained a good standing financially have not been welcomed into the American societies.

Nor does the work of the mill, the one common element in the life of the town, afford the relationships which might naturally spring up. There are no labor unions in Homestead as there are in the mines, to give a common interest to Pole, Slav and native born, and pave the way for mutual understanding and citizenship. The policy of the mill thus again becomes a factor in the life of the town, this time to accentuate the failure of its residents to bridge over lines of cleavage, and create a normal community life.

The separation between Slavs and English-speaking people is evident not only in church and school and lodge but also in

Drawn by Joseph Stella

OLD WORLDS IN NEW

politics. Here again, even when Slavs are imbued with our civic ideals, language stands as a barrier to mutual understanding. Ignorant of our forms of political machinery, they can take a real part in the town's political life only after a slow process of education. Few of the Slavs are citizens. Only six per cent of those employed in the mill in 1907 had taken out papers, whereas 63.6 per cent of the other Europeans were naturalized. Many Slavs, of course, are ineligible because of their short residence and others because of their inability to read and write English.

Those who become citizens find it difficult to comprehend our complicated political system or to follow newspaper discussions of party platforms or of aspirants for local offices. As a result, through the simple device of an organization manipulated by the older residents, they fall into line and are instructed which way to vote. Rumors of fraudulent registration and voting are more or less current. Both the Slavic leaders and other local politicians agree that a deal is usually made in Homestead and the Slavic vote goes to the party which promises a place on the police or some other minor office to a Slav. Direct bribery is apparently rare.

That under it all the Slav has a genuine political idealism is whimsically illustrated by quoting from a paper written by a Slav. This idealism is not strange in a people whose political rights have always been restricted whether in Austria, or Poland, or Russia, and it seems deplorable that their genuine enthusiasm for democracy should not be enabled to find early and fair expression:

> The Slav race, and without exception all the Slav nationalities, are the most and sincere patriotic people of our great Republic the United States, because they have found here all that of which they have been robbed in their old countries. They have found in the United States personal and common liberty, free and independent civilization, welfare and all that which the aborigines of the English and other races have there found themselves. Therefore the Slavic races are the most zealous supporters of all the state and social institutions. Because this way, the Slavs are interested in the moral and material development and evolution of this country; they are supporting every time that political party which does seem to them the most honest, moral and virtuous

party. Because now the Republican party and the whole
United States under the most honest, circumspect, and glorious leadership of our most beloved president Mr. Theodore
Roosevelt, are enjoying, just in the latest years, a degree of
evolution in every respect, naturally the Slav are mostly
Republicans and are following the steps which President
Roosevelt does designate. Very small amount of the Slav
is democratic. Socialistic are some, maybe 1000–2000, *but
not a single Anarchist.**

Some general observations may be ventured growing out of
my impressions of the isolated life of these Homestead immigrants.

It is clearly a vital need that the Slavs learn our language.
Sixty per cent of the Slavic workers in the mill in 1907 were reported as illiterate. A night school carried on in 1906–7 in the
labor camp a few miles distant, at Aspinwall, under the auspices of
the Society for Italian Immigrants, demonstrated that the immigrant welcomes instruction in civics and English, and led to the
passage of a state law permitting the opening of such classes in the
public schools upon the petition of twenty residents. Up to 1908,
the schools in Homestead had done nothing in this direction. The
buildings were empty at night, and might easily have been utilized
for teaching English and a simple form of civics. During periods
of slack work, such as that of 1908, men would welcome such
classes as a diversion during the long hours of enforced idleness.

Two attempts to give instruction in English had been made
by other agencies than the schools. A Baptist missionary who
spoke most of the Slavic languages started a class and reported
that the men showed a marked eagerness to learn. The Carnegie
Library made the first considerable effort to reach them by opening
its clubs to the Slavs. Aside from a class in English, however, these
had not been adapted to non-English-speaking people. Even the
Slavic books, which the library bought for their benefit, were
seldom used. I found that a number of the influential Slavs in
Homestead did not know that these books were in the library,
indicating that this failure was due to a lack of successful adver-
tising. The fact that the building is on the hill away from their
homes, and has an imposing entrance which makes the laborer
hesitate to enter, and that there are forms that must be gone

* The complete paper will be found in Appendix XIV, p. 271.

through before the books can be secured, also have doubtless acted as deterrent influences. That a considerable proportion of the members of the Library Club are immigrants, shows that these obstacles have not stood in their way in the use of such practical things as the baths. But if the library is really to reach the foreign population culturally it must not wait for them to come to it; it should go to them. A simple reading room opening into the courts where the people live, where they could drop in after the day's work, find newspapers and books in their own tongue, and where the Americanized Slav could reach his newly arrived brethren, would become an important center of influence.

In such a mill town, great distances do not exist to act as barriers. But education and contact is needed to overcome the deep-rooted prejudices of the resident race. If anything, they are more ignorant of the inherent character of the Slav and his culture, than he is of theirs. Mutual understanding would be achieved the sooner were the American fraternal organizations to adopt the policy of welcoming these aliens; or were the Catholic church to exert a more definite influence to bring men of all races together as well as to hold each race firmly intact, to interpret America to them no less than to preserve the religious heritages they bring from the churches of mid-Europe. In politics, social bonds are less personal, and an aggressive, thoroughly democratic civic movement in Homestead, no less than the ward politics of the proverbial Pennsylvania type, might serve to bring men of all races to touching elbows.

With this lack of intercourse it is now difficult if not impossible for the immigrant to come into a knowledge of our institutions, yet through local legislation certain American standards could be made general. Laws and ordinances are in themselves valuable media of social education. Through them we can make our standards clear to the minds of the newcomers and impose the minimum standards of a community upon all its dwellers. English-speaking residents in Homestead live under fairer conditions than the Slavs, partly because they demand room enough and healthful surroundings. The Slav, coming from a crowded household on a farm, may not understand why overcrowding and unflushed vaults are intolerable in this closely built section where he now lives. The importance of cleanliness and proper sanitary conveniences can be visibly demonstrated by means of well enforced ordinances. Were the health officer to insist that the Slav take fewer lodgers so that there might be air enough for all, and that the landlord put decent plumbing and running water in the house, the Slav would gradually conform to these new requirements. Indeed, both the good and the bad may be new to him, and he may regard the overcrowding as American.

In education, also, effective borough action might help to raise standards. While Homestead has a compulsory school law, it suffers in enforcement because there is a gap between the administration of the public and parochial schools. As a result some children are not in school at all and many are not regular attendants. If the school law were strictly enforced, the Slav would the sooner realize that in the American democracy education is regarded as an absolute essential.

Differences in languages, in customs, in organizations, as we have seen, have made a sharp demarcation between the two halves of this still growing town. The lack of mutual understanding is of course no more marked in Homestead than in many American industrial or commercial centers. But while they are yet towns it seems possible to work out some solution, before such round-about methods as those of social settlements are necessary to bridge the gulf. Through the existing factors of law, of the public schools, of political parties, such contact might be brought about as would hasten the slow process of amalgamation. As it is, the Slavs in Homestead, in their neighborhoods, their schools, their churches, their lodges, their political groups, are a people apart. In isolated groups they are trying to solve the problem set by the economic and social conditions which confront them in this town. Some surer footing and readier fraternity is needed if the Slavic day laborer is to be other than a menace to his own well-being and to that of the community; if in the American sense, he and his family are to "get on" in life.

In conclusion, we may well ask what awaits him if he does; how is life bounded for the households in Homestead, whether of the Slav or native born?

PART IV
THE MILL AND THE HOUSEHOLD

CHAPTER XIII

THE MILL AND THE HOUSEHOLD

THROUGHOUT this study I have referred frequently to the ways in which the one industry in the town through wages, hours and conditions of work limits the fulfillment of the family ideals. This is not because the industry sprang up like a wicked ogre to carry on depredations among the townspeople, but because the employment it offers is the economic basis both of the household life and the town life; it makes both possible; and the terms and conditions on which it offers this employment must directly affect the everyday living of both.

It may be well, therefore, to sum up this discussion in a more definite fashion; first, by defining the limitations due to hours and conditions of work in the Homestead mills (interpreting somewhat the attitude of the men toward this problem); and second, by drawing from our budget study of what can be secured for a given weekly expenditure, some more general conclusions about wages. It is the workman himself who feels the first of these limitations; through him the routine and hazards of the day's work affect the family. The second acts more directly upon the family; to the household no less than to the man, the mill determines the livelihood; it is the housekeeper's purse strings that are tugged with every wage cut and loosened with every advance a man makes in the mill from the pay of common labor to the higher tonnage rates.

The first of these reactions of the mill on the town is subtle and hard to demonstrate. Yet no one who has lived in Homestead can fail to realize how definitely the conditions under which they work influence the mental as well as the physical development of the men.

In an earlier chapter I spoke of the twelve-hour day spent in tumult and in heat, the heavy work, the periodic intensity of labor at the rolls and the furnaces for the skilled steel workers. The onlooker, fascinated by the picturesqueness of it all, sees in the great dim sheds a wonderful revelation of the creative powers of man. To the worker this fascination is gone; heat and grime, noise and effort are his part in the play. The spectacular features may serve only to heighten the over-strain which accompanies continuous processes whenever, as here, the full twenty-four hours is split between two shifts. In the open-hearth department in Homestead in October, 1907, 1517 men worked a twelve-hour day, as against 93 who worked ten. In the Bessemer department, there were nine men who worked an eight-hour day, 19 who worked eleven; the remaining 153 worked the full twelve. In the rolling mills some common laborers were employed eleven hours, but the men in the processes were dividing the twenty-four hours of the day and night between two shifts. (The normal day of the yard laborer was ten hours.) These long hours restrict the development of the individual. They give the men in the two shifts little time for outside interests. The week that a man works on the night turn, from 5.30 p. m. to 7.30 a. m., he has plainly small time to do anything but eat and get such sleep as he can. The other week he has, of course, such leisure as falls to any ten-hour worker. This alternation of shifts lets the men out of consecutive night work, but it interferes with that regularity of meals and of sleep which physicians tell us is essential to health. When a man sleeps in the daytime alternate weeks, it means continual change and adjustment. One week he has supper at 4.30 p. m., works all night, has breakfast at 8 a. m., and has a more or less broken sleep during the day. The alternate week he has supper at 6 p. m., breakfast at 6.30, and a good night's sleep between. Sometimes when sons who are in the mill are on the opposite shift from the father, the family cannot even meet for meals. The irregularity in hours not only adds in the long run to the fatigue of the work and breaks into the family life, but also makes weekly engagements, such as lodge meetings, impossible, and prevents the men from taking much part in other activities.

Some local ministers said they believed that this stiff routine tends to develop steadiness on the part of the mill workers;

Photo by Lewis W. Hine

GOING HOME FROM WORK

This picture sums up Homestead:—the mill at the left; the Carnegie Library on the hill in the center, and the mean houses of the Second Ward to the right.

one clergyman, for instance, told me that most of the hard drinking he knew was among men who had irregular work either as teamsters or in the building trades. Yet the existence of the fifty or more saloons in Homestead indicates that drinking is a prevalent form of excitement in the town. And exhaustion, coupled with the thirst occasioned by the heat in the mills, is at least partly responsible for the number of men who seek stimulus from drink.

A further depressing result of the overwork in the mills is the mental fatigue which accompanies it. The men are too tired to take an active part in family life; they are usually ready after smoking a pipe to go to bed. They have small interest in outside matters and consequently make little effort to increase the provision of amusements in the town, a condition from which their wives and children suffer. Again, with the broken Sunday, which is due either to work on that day or to work Saturday night or Sunday night, it is easy to drift away from church, and many ministers find it almost impossible to secure the attendance of the men. One man who usually had to work at least part time on Saturday night said to me that he was far too tired to get up to go to church on Sunday morning. In the year of our study one man in five worked on seven days in the seven in the steel mills of Allegheny County.*

All this is bound up with perhaps the most serious outcome of conditions in the mill, the tendency to develop in the men a spirit of taking things as they come. As we noted in the chapter dealing with the growth of Homestead, while the industry has attained a marvelous degree of efficiency the town as a political unit has failed. Men weary with long hours of work, men who have been refused any share in determining the conditions under which they work, are not prompted to seize opportunities for

---

* "It is my own deliberate judgment, after a period of almost thirty years' continuous connection with the industry, the early part of which was passed in manual labor in the mills, that the present conditions, which necessitate the employment of the same individual workman twelve hours a day for seven days a week, are a reproach to our great industry and should not in this enlightened age be longer tolerated."—From an address May 27, 1910, by Wm. B. Dickson, First Vice President of the United States Steel Corporation before the American Iron and Steel Institute. As a young man, Mr. Dickson worked at the rolls in the Homestead Mills.

improving the conditions under which they live. Their habitual suppression industrially has meant a loss of initiative. Somehow it is easier to pay a neighbor fifty cents a month for the privilege of bringing drinking water three times a day from his well, than to insist that the borough provide a wholesome supply.

There is, therefore, in the routine of life outside the mill, little to stimulate these men to mental alertness, nor did my talks with them give me the impression that their work within it tended to supply this want. At different points in the process are men upon whose experience and judgment rest heavy responsibilities. But where individual skill was formerly a constant element, little by little that skill, as well as much of the crudest manual labor, is being transferred to the machines. As you watch a crane pick up "buggies" of scrap iron, empty them into a furnace, and then move on to repeat the operation, you feel that the machine itself must be alive until you see the man who pulls lever after lever with strong, steady hand. The demands upon this man's faculties during working hours are not those which had to be met by the old time craftsmen in metals. Improvements in process are, some of them, the result of the men's practical suggestions, which are welcomed eagerly by the superintendents, tested, and when practicable adopted. I was told that the recompense in most instances is small—sometimes a gift of money. Evidence, however, of quickness and ingenuity undoubtedly increases the possibility of promotion. The exceptional man may become an influential official, and the officials of the Steel Corporation state that there is as keen a demand for prize men as ever. Not a few instances, such as Mr. Schwab's rapid rise, are well known. But with 7000 men employed in this one mill,—with half of the payroll made up of unskilled men,—with the tendency at every point to reduce the number of skilled men,—with a majority of the mills in all sections of the country of the same sort practically under the one management, the prospect of rapid advancement for the rank and file becomes more and more uncertain. The sentiment frequently expressed among Homestead people that promotion is due to a pull, may be only a feeling, but it strengthens their belief that for this generation the future will hold little more than the present. The younger men are sometimes ambitious to study and work up, but the older ones feel that there is nothing ahead for them.

On the other hand, the memory of the lost fight of 1892 is still vivid, and the decisions of the corporate employer are not accepted without mental protest.

Probably no outsider can ever know just what the men do think about it all. Certain impressions, however, gathered in talks with many of them may be worth stating, as showing the lines along which Homestead men think. That the older men lack confidence in trade unions is not strange. The strike destroyed the enthusiasm that comes with success, and the hesitation about attempting to reorganize has been intensified by the growth of the Corporation and its policy of repressing any collective action. Its industrial achievements and great strength make it a foe not to be antagonized, and the men have realized its power to the full. Those who were refused re-employment because of their part in the strike, found, as I have said, that they could get no work in any mill of the Carnegie Steel Company and were in some instances unable to get it in any other steel mill. Furthermore, common report has it that anyone who proposes trade unionism in the mill is promptly discharged, and experience has gone to prove this. One phrase current in the town is: "If you want to talk in Homestead, you must talk to yourself." "What is the use?" is apparently the men's feeling. The people who determine their hours, their wages and the conditions under which they work, are to them a small group of men in New York, who know little and perhaps care less what the decision of a 10 per cent cut in his rates means to a man who has been averaging $3.00 a day; still less what it means to his wife and children. While the majority of the workers understand only vaguely the organization of a great industry, or the factors entering into its policies, they feel that their conditions of life are determined by forces too large for them to battle with.

That the men look on the Corporation as a hard taskmaster was shown in many ways. Some even believed that the reason it offered to sell stock to the employes was in order to find out how much money they had saved, an opinion strengthened among them by a cut in wages which followed soon after the men had taken advantage of the first offer. Again, many of them expressed the belief that my own investigation was being made by the Corporation to find out whether wages would stand another reduction. While these people were not among the more intelligent of those I visited, they illustrate an undercurrent of conviction that the Corporation is concerned only with making money and has no interest in the men.

Two states of mind result from this belief. Many simply accept conditions as they are. As one woman said, "I tell my husband that as long as he stays here he has no business to groan at what the company does. If he doesn't like it, he'd better get out." Others, especially men with families, whose own wages may be fair and work steady, feel that it would be foolish to attempt any movement which might result in loss of work in Homestead. This may be common sense, but one regrets the passive attitude which results from the lack of concerted action.

Not all the men, however, thus accept the situation. When, as in 1908, the mills stand idle and the household income ceases, while the Corporation deals out its quarterly dividend, many are not sure that things are as they ought to be. A man whose earnings for two months during the depression had not paid his rent said, "I know the superintendent can't help it. He has done the best he can and tried to see that all of us got a little work. But I think that the men in the New York office are to blame."* A consciousness of the complexity of the situation made this man feel that the concerted action of trade unionism would be helpless to affect the conditions of work. A small but apparently growing group, recognizing that the industry is too large for them to cope with, look toward socialism for a solution. State interference seems to them the only means of changing the situation. Those who think thus are not extremists; they are

---

* An incident occurred recently in which the editor of a local newspaper attempted to shift responsibility as between Homestead and New York, and which may or may not throw some light upon the prevalence of this attitude among the people. In March, 1910, the executive officials of the United States Steel Corporation notified the constituent companies that the rule prohibiting unnecessary Sunday work, which had been a dead letter, must be observed thereafter. Pittsburgh and Homestead newspapers gave local officials credit for this advanced step, and a Homestead paper declined to publish the text of the orders which showed their real origin.

Photo by Hine

TYPE OF STEEL WORKER: THIRTY-FIVE YEARS FROM GERMANY

workingmen who simply can see no other way out. These men held few meetings and attempted no propagandist work; they accepted the socialist program as an individual hope.

The attitude of discontent, however, is not universal. Some who have done well in the mill are loyal to it, and are proud of its reputation; others are won over by the plan by which the Corporation sells stock to its employes. Those who hold shares acknowledge that they have a different attitude toward the business and more zeal for making it pay. One woman, however, whose husband has a few shares, told me with some scorn of herself, that they recognized that their attitude had changed. They realized after all, she said, that the small dividend from the stock did little to make up for the fact that her husband's wages had been cut 20 per cent in the fifteen years of their married life.* Whether or not this sense of rebellion is inevitable or justifiable, it is bound up with complications due to the remoteness and the size of the employing corporation and to the fact that there is no appeal from its decisions.

In Superintendent A. R. Hunt, the local representative of the Corporation in Homestead, the men have a real confidence.† In his younger days he was one of their number and his many personal kindnesses make them trust him. He is, however, responsible to the Pittsburgh office for cheapening the cost of production which is in turn responsible to headquarters in New York for economies, output and profits. Moreover, decisions on many vital points come from a distance, and since they are for the whole industry seem hopelessly unrelated to the local

---

*Among tonnage men changes in process, and improvements in machinery, as well as increased speeding of the work, have notably increased output on many lines, so that adjustments of rates have had to be made from time to time, to fit the new conditions in the different departments. Sometimes these adjustments have not meant a reduction of earnings, in other cases they have; a policy to reduce the pay of the highest paid men has been consistently carried out. These changes are distinct from horizontal decreases and increases in tonnage or day rates affecting the whole force. In all cases, the men have no say as to the new rates. See Fitch, John A.: The Steel Workers, a companion volume in the Pittsburgh Survey series.

† Mr. Hunt, A. C. Dinkey, president of the Carnegie Steel Company, Charles M. Schwab former president, Wm. E. Corey, president, and Wm. B. Dickson first vice-president, of the United States Steel Corporation are all men who have worked up from the ranks in the Homestead plant.

situation. I was told that when Mr. Schwab was made president of the newly organized Steel Corporation, the men, with whom he had been very popular, believed that with "Charlie" in New York, their interests would be safeguarded; but when a new cut in wages was made their hopes fell.

The workers not only have no representatives who can confer with the local management on disputed points, but they have a sense of being utterly outside the great moving center of the industry. The thing that is clear to them is that, for many, rates have been cut and earnings lowered, while the men whose names are linked with steel finance are making fortunes. Nor is this feeling lessened by the part which these same men have actually played in Homestead. Mr. Carnegie has given a library, Mr. Schwab a manual training school, and Mr. Frick a charming little park in the centre of the hill section. These generous gifts beautify Homestead and provide something toward its recreation and intellectual stimulus. Yet, though the people are very proud of them, many a man said to me, "We'd rather they hadn't cut our wages and'd let us spend the money for ourselves. What use has a man who works twelve hours a day for a library, anyway?" They appreciate what the library and manual training offer to them and their children, but they resent a philanthropy which provides opportunities for intellectual and social advancement while it withholds conditions which make it possible to take advantage of them.

Moreover, these men have given money rather than leadership. There is a noticeable contrast between this and some mill communities where the owners live in the town and take a genuine interest in its development. Homestead has no leaders. When in conversation I suggested that some changes in the sanitary ordinances should be made, I was told that only a man of influence could accomplish it. But no one could suggest the man.

On the other hand, as was pointed out in Chapter II, a heavy burden is imposed upon Homestead through the fact that most of the mill property is set off in a separate borough. Munhall, where most of the Carnegie Company's holdings are located, is more attractive, has better water and sewerage, and has no overcrowded section. It is the residence place of the mill officials

Photo by Hine

TYPE OF STEEL WORKER: SLAV

and has the income from the taxation of the mill property. The borough may almost be said to be part of the plant. Here the wealth and influence of the industry make themselves felt in those external conditions which react on the whole life of the residents.

In Munhall the tax rate in 1907 was only 8½ mills, which nevertheless brought $40,000 a year into the town's treasury from the Carnegie Steel Company. In Homestead, across the imaginary borough lines where the greater part of the workers live, the mill owns little property subject to taxation; here the tax rate was 15 mills and the company paid a tax of $7000 only. Through these borough divisions the Corporation has thus been largely relieved of contributing to the maintenance of the community which is necessary to its operation. That burden is borne by the homes of the wage-earners gathered to do its work.

It is through the households themselves that the industrial situation impresses itself indelibly upon the life of the people. The environment of the home afforded by this checkerboard town tilted on the slope back of the mill site, the smoke which pours its depressing fumes to add their extra burden to the housewife's task, the constant interference with orderly routine due to the irregular succession of long hours—these are outward and visible signs of the subordination of household life to industrial life. The mill affects the family even more intimately through the wage scale to which the standards of home making, housekeeping, and child rearing must conform. Here the impressions gained by a season's residence in Homestead are supported by the limited but definite facts as to expenditures afforded by the budget study of ninety families. These were recapitulated in an earlier chapter (page 102), and it is only necessary here to relate them to the standards of the two main groups in the wage-earning population which have been considered in this book. For whatever may be the triumph or failure of the steel plant as a manufactory, it must also be judged by the part it has borne in helping or hindering this town, which has grown up on the farm land at the river bend, in becoming a sound member of the American commonwealth.

By far the largest and most serious group to consider is that of the unskilled workers—earning day laborers' wages.

With unrestricted immigration, and the development of half-automatic processes, the trend as we have seen is toward an increase of this unskilled labor both proportionately and in gross numbers.

The analysis of expenditures indicates that the man who earns $9.90 a week, as do a majority of such laborers, and who has a family of normal size to support, can provide for them only a two-room tenement in a crowded court, with no sanitary conveniences; a supply of food below the minimum sufficient for mere physical well-being; insurance that makes provision which is utterly inadequate for the family left without a breadwinner; a meagre expenditure for clothes and furniture, and an almost negligible margin for recreation, education and savings. Many can, to be sure, add to their earnings by working seven days a week instead of six; by working twelve hours a day instead of ten; but after all, we are talking of standards of life and labor for an American industry, and common sense will scarcely sanction such a week of work. Many, too, as we have seen, take in lodgers, but do it at the cost of decency and health.

It may be claimed that the Slavs are single men and get ahead quickly. But two-thirds of the immigrant Slavs in the Homestead mills are married men. And the exceptional one who gets ahead in the mill only serves to set off the fact that the main body of the employes are unskilled workers and will continue such so long as steel processes remain as they are.

Granted that to the majority of the Slavs, if ambitious, the industry does not afford opportunities to prosper and to become assimilated, still it may be argued that mill work, like gang labor on railway construction, must be regarded as transitional, a stage in the progress of the immigrant until he has learned our language and ways. Nobody knows whether this is true in a large way of the Slavs of the steel district. What we do know is that however the individuals in their ranks change, the unskilled laborers as an economic group persist. They have been a permanent factor in the social life of Homestead. The community as a whole must suffer if this persisting group lives amid an unwholesome environment and undergoes a deterioration in physical efficiency. The wage which the mill pays, while it may bring a little fortune to the single men who herd in a lodging house, offers

Photo by Hine

TYPE OF STEEL WORKER: PENNSYLVANIAN

to the men who bring their families and plan to become American citizens terms which, coupled with their ignorance and ambitions, tend to distort and depress in these formative years the things we hold most precious in every home.

As I waited one day in one of the little railroad stations of Homestead, a Slav came in and sat down beside a woman with a two-year-old child. He made shy advances to the baby, coaxing her in a voice of heart-breaking loneliness. She would not come and finally her mother took her away. The Slav turned to the rest of the company, and taking us all into his confidence said very simply, "Me wife, me babe, Hungar." But were his family in Homestead it would mean death for one baby in three; it would mean hard work in a little, dirty, unsanitary house for the mother; it would mean sickness and evil. With them in Hungary it meant for him isolation and loneliness and the abnormal life of the crowded lodging house.

The terms offered unskilled immigrant labor in the Homestead mills are not, it should be borne in mind, exceptional. The rate paid day labor by the Carnegie Company in 1907 was higher than that paid in some of the independent plants in Pittsburgh; it was 10 per cent higher than the rate paid in 1901; yet it is fair to compare it also with the rate paid unskilled labor in those bituminous mines of western Pennsylvania where the men through the unions have appreciably affected the course of wages and hours. According to Professor Commons, common laborers in the mines were paid $2.36 for an eight-hour day in 1907.* Their weekly earnings exceeded those of a Slavic laborer in a steel mill by two full days' pay a week. They somewhat exceeded the average expenditure ($13.32) of the $12 to $15 budget group among the mill workers which, as we have seen, approximated the amount it is possible for a six-day man to provide for his family on $2.25 a day. In the expenditures of this second budget group of mill workers, we found (Chap. VI) the food cost was about 25 cents

* As against $1.65 for a ten-hour day and $1.98 for a twelve-hour day in the steel mills. See article by Professor John R. Commons, *The Survey*, March 6, 1909, p. 1063. As already noted, the common labor rate in Homestead was raised May 1, 1910, to 17½ cents an hour, or $10.50 per week. This comparison with mine labor, however, still stands.

a day a man—a small leeway for large families or indifferent housekeeping; rent that would give three rooms, though not with sanitary conveniences; clothing sufficient to meet Mr. Chapin's minimum for essentials, and a remaining sum of $1.37 a week for recreation, education, church, savings, and sundries. In other words, such a level, reached by one of the great industries of the region, would seem to afford a foothold of physical sufficiency upon which a newcomer can begin the American struggle without great hazard to his family or to the community in which he casts his fortunes.

As a permanent basis for American life, we must look to a larger budget. We must take account of the fact that the steel industry is on a different footing from the small, quickly developing plants in the early days. There is practically no chance that the steel worker may himself become an employer, and only a lesser chance that he may secure a highly paid administrative position. More than that, while the day labor rate has been raised, steel officials admit that there has been a continued policy of reducing the earnings of the highest paid men, such as heaters and rollers, some of whom in the years when output was increasing by leaps and bounds made very large sums. It is, therefore, only a livelihood after all to which the average man has to look forward if he puts his working years into the steel industry. The steady work offered by the Homestead mill makes it possible for the English-speaking steel worker to develop a household standard with some assurance of what is to be anticipated in the months ahead. But accidental death, injury, sickness or a season of slack work enter in to jeopardize this seeming security. A livelihood cannot be said to be independent which does not provide through insurance and savings for such emergencies; and it falls short of competence if it fails to afford some current share of pleasure as well as toil, of comfort of mind as well as food and shelter. It is within the bounds of practical American idealism to hold that such a livelihood should, within a reasonably short period of years, be reached and maintained by an industrious man.

We found, so far as this group of 90 budget familes could show us (and at the range of prices current in Homestead in

1907) that only when earnings were more than $15 a week ($2.50 per day) could we confidently look for any working margin above those expenditures which should go for actual necessities. It was only in the group earning more than $20 that we found assurance that the average family had reached a point of surplus where, without being unduly spendthrift of the future, they could live well.

Detailed figures for October, 1907, for three representative mills in a large steel plant in the district enable us to relate these standards to the earnings of the men engaged directly in the operations of steel making.* Of the 513 men in these departments, 193, or something over one-third, were paid the same hourly rate as laborers in the yards. Of the 320 men earning more than day laborers' pay, 76, or very nearly a fourth, were earning less than the $2.50 per day without which we found that the average family could not count on a practical margin above actual necessities. About another fourth (82) were earning $20 ($3.33 a day) or over, the positions ranging from that of a roll engineer, whose pay averaged $3.37 per day for the month, to shearmen at $5.58, general foremen at $6.05, heaters at $7.21, and rollers at $8.44. The pay of these men, some of whom were in supervisory positions, averaged that of the most fortunate group of budget families studied.

Thus a full half of the men in these departments earning more than common laborer's pay fell in our intermediate group, earning weekly from $15 to $20. They included, therefore, the largest proportion of the English-speaking workers who, in these departments,† had reached positions of some skill. Here the question whether normal life could be maintained depends, as we saw in our budget studies, on many circumstances—on the size of the

* Twenty-three-inch structural mill, 38-inch blooming mill, 128-inch plate mill. See Appendix IV, p, 215.

† Earnings in the Bessemer department were not so good. Of the 154 men above the day labor rank in October, 1907, only five per cent earned $20 or more, and 50 per cent earned less than $15 per week. In the open-hearth department 262 out of 1610 earned $20 or above—practically the same percentage (16 per cent) as in the three rolling mills cited. Detailed figures were not available as to the earnings of the remainder of the open-hearth departments, but the average rate for the twelve-hour men in the department ($2.76), coupled with the specified earnings of the more important positions, seemed to indicate that the percentage of them earning over $15 was less than in the rolling mills.

family, on the temperance and steadiness of the man, on the skill of the housewife, on freedom from sickness or misfortune. But the margin is so narrow that the appearance of a disturbing factor may seriously depress the family life. Those homely marginal expenditures are at stake which may mean a front room with money to heat and furnish it; washing and sewing machines, and outside help to give the housewife some leisure; the doctor instead of the midwife; the savings account and the insurance policy so that sickness or death, if they come, will not turn sorrow into importunate drudgery for the mother of little children.

Small families may not be unhappily situated in this intermediate wage belt; and with lodgers, or with sons working, or with the practice of an unusual gift of housekeeping, larger families may have some comforts. The more closely, however, that we scrutinize the amount available for marginal expenditures, the clearer does it appear that the average family whose income falls in good times or bad into this intermediate expenditure group, must choose between meeting the family's needs for recreation, its need for providence and its need for that freedom in spending for the home and its furnishings which help develop personal life.

The United States Steel Corporation operates in Homestead one of the largest mills in the country, provided with wonderful machines for producing steel; it has placed in charge a superintendent whose primary object is to produce steel perfectly and cheaply; it offers work on certain terms as to wages and hours which he who wills may accept. Its ignorant Slavic laborers, however, may be exploited by grasping landlords; the wives of many of its workers may find life merely a round of wearisome tasks in the attempt to make both ends meet; its men may be too worn by the stress of the twelve-hour shifts to care for their own individual development or too shorn of self-dependence to exert themselves to maintain a borough government that shall give them better living conditions. "Life, work and happiness,—these three are bound together." The mill offers the one, subject to no effective demand by society nor commercial necessity that the work be done under conditions which make the other two possible.

APPENDICES

APPENDIX I

METHODS OF BUDGET STUDY

FACTS as to wages and labor conditions in the steel district were secured in companion investigations of the Pittsburgh Survey. To get at their full meaning it was necessary to relate them to the household life of the workers; by learning what it costs workingmen's families to live and what the general levels of the wage scale mean to their wives and children. Such was the first purpose of this inquiry. Since in Pittsburgh proper there were complicating factors due to the size of the city and its various commercial activities, it seemed simpler to undertake it in one of the industrial suburbs. The inquiry naturally developed into an analysis of mill town life from the household standpoint, an intimate study of the everyday problems of the workingmen's families. It was not, as early stated in the text, primarily statistical. Yet to determine and illustrate the economic factors entering into family life the budget method of securing data was adopted, as employed in standard of living inquiries since Le Play's first studies.

The investigation extended from October, 1907, to April, 1908. Reference has been made in Chapter III to obstacles which the staff had to overcome in the field work and to the methods adopted for getting into close touch with the homes studied. Through various means friendly relations were established with households of different types, the families were visited weekly and the co-operation of the women was obtained in keeping accounts. The data gathered were transferred to three cards showing: (a) the general history and facts as to the family; (b) expenditures for food; (c) other expenditures (see pages 188–191). In addition notes were kept on any interesting points which cropped out in conversation during the visits, and every opportunity was utilized to become

187

188

No. in household   No. eatin

Hours of work: Day turn

Amount saved by family   Where depo

Relief   Gifts

Articles purchased on instalments

Own home free   Mortgaged   O1

Man had accident?   Use library

House   Rent per mo.   No. rooms   o. dark rooms   Toile

Bath   Size and use of yard

Sleeping rooms

Size	Other use	No. beds	No. occup.	No. wind.
1.				
2.				
3.				
4.				
5.				

CARD A (BACK): FAMILY RECORD

189

NAME   Street

Bakers Fo

Beef

Milk

Butter

Lard

acquainted with the town officials, physicians, business men and others who could correct personal impressions.

It was decided to adopt the account book rather than the budget estimate method of securing data. To secure a budget estimate, a standard of living investigator goes over with a housekeeper her customary items of expenditure, and on the basis of these statements, estimates the outlay for the year. The advantage of this method is that with the housekeeper's help an approximate figure can be secured for disbursements, which are made only at intervals and which vary with the seasons, for clothing, fuel, house furnishings and other things. When the account book method is used, the housekeeper keeps daily records of her expenditures for the period studied. These are totalled and reduced to weekly averages. The advantage of this system is that so far as the figures go, they are actual, and the element of estimate is reduced to a minimum. All accounts included in the budget analysis in this study covered a period of from four to eight weeks; those which showed a five per cent discrepancy between income and expenditure were discarded. They thus register accurately all outlays, such as food, rent, and insurance, which are made frequently, but give only fragmentary indications of the cost of occasional purchases, such as furniture, clothing, medicine, etc. We had neither the time nor the staff to carry them over a period long enough to make these items substantially representative. Nor did we undertake to extend the number of families studied to a total which would satisfy the requirements of a purely statistical inquiry.

Bearing in mind these general limitations of our account book data, and with a further word or two of explanation as to the specific methods employed in gathering and applying them, the reader will be able to form an independent judgment as to (1) how far the group of families studied was representative of the wage-earning population, and (2) to what extent their recorded expenditures were typical.

As Homestead is a homogeneous town of wage-earners, our first task, namely, that of securing families which in economic status, racial make-up and intelligence would be fairly representative of the community, was considerably simplified. At the top of the economic scale is no large high-income group to consider, and at the bottom 60 per cent of the entire working force in the mill are unskilled laborers, getting a common rate per hour. Since, moreover, a majority of the town's people work for the one employer, a recent census of the mill gave us remarkably complete statistical information as to the skill and racial make-up of this working population. This was supplemented by data as to wages in the steel mills of the district secured in the course of a companion investigation for the Pittsburgh Survey. Perhaps no other inquiry of a similar nature has had such inclusive economic and social facts as a local background. Moreover, as the women of Homestead do not go out to labor and as (with the exception of the hard times of 1907 and 1908) work in the mills has been steady, we scarcely encountered two complicating factors which often disturb such budget studies, namely, supplemental incomes and seasonal non-employment. With the exception of the income from lodgers in the low wage groups, the man's weekly earnings form the basis of household life, and by what those earnings afford can the industrial life of the community be judged.

To indicate the gradations from the great underlying mass of day labor to the comparatively small group of highly skilled men, the following classification was adopted:

1. Those receiving less than $12 a week; that is, the unskilled common laborers at 16½ cents an hour, as exemplified in the $1.65 per day for ten hours in the yards or $1.98 per day for twelve hours in the operating departments.

2. Those receiving from $12 to $14.99 per week.

3. Those receiving from $15 to $19.99 per week.

These intermediate groups include, roughly, men paid $2.25 to $3.00 per day on time wages and the less skilled men who are paid by the ton.

4. Those receiving $20 per week and over. The distinctly skilled men, practically all tonnage workers, together with the men above the lowest rounds on the clerical force.

In addition, a few families in each wage group whose breadwinners were not employed in the mill were added to the number studied in order to reflect more accurately the make-up of the community.

It should be borne in mind that the facts presented in Chapter III, Table 5, etc., as to the skill, nationalities, and range of pay of the mill force refer to normal times. So also does Table 6, in which the 90 budget families are classified by their regular income. As tonnage earnings vary from week to week, these latter averages are based on statements made by the families themselves as to the men's usual pay and their income from other sources. They are believed to be fairly accurate except possibly in the case of three colored women who went out to work by the day and apparently gave their maximum rather than their average earnings. According to this table the 90 budget families when classified by normal earnings were about equally divided among the four groups representing the general wage levels in the mill. While the "under $12" group of budget families was numerically no larger than the other three, it of course represented over half the working population. Among the budget families, as in the mill, the Slavs predominated in this lowest group.

To represent, racially, the town's population, it was necessary to include families from three groups: the native born, the old time English-speaking immigrant of a generation ago, and the newcomers of the past decade—the Slavs. A group of colored people was included also, not because numerically important, but for purposes of comparison. It will be noted that for each racial group the percentage of unskilled workers among the budget families is decidedly smaller than in the mill census.* The generalizations with respect to each nationality, therefore, were drawn from families above the average in skill and wages, so that the picture is less dark if anything than the reality. In such a study as the present one, in which the conclusions have been critical of the returns paid to labor, this was a bias on the safe side.

A third requisite was to secure families which in intelligence were representative of the community studied. Here we met a difficulty common to all standard of living inquiries; that as the more intelligent women who can keep accounts or make accurate estimates are usually the more skilful housekeepers, their figures are not thoroughly representative. To overcome this, we kept accounts for families who could not do it for themselves,

Table 1, page 200; also Appendix III.

visiting them daily or every other day for that purpose. Among these were some where the women could neither read nor write. As already noted, the Slavic families included some newly arrived immigrants and were visited by a woman speaking their languages.

On these points then, of economic status, racial make-up, and intelligence, a comparison of the 90 budget families with the census of the mill force shows that, taken as a whole, there were among the former proportionately fewer earning low wages, fewer Slavs and fewer unskilled. We did not attempt, however, to present in the 90 families a miniature of the town's population. Our endeavor was to make sure that the number studied included small sample groups, each of which would represent an important element in that population. In this we were reasonably successful.

The numbers in the different groups were not sufficiently large to make satisfactory cross classifications including size of family as well as race and economic status. For this reason, the conclusions, with few exceptions, have been drawn from the primary classifications. The occurrence of the hard times, to be discussed later, dislodged a number of budget families from their normal economic groups; but the shifting was not so great as altogether to negative the care taken to see that initially they were representative of the different elements in the social make-up. The tables at the close of this appendix and in Appendix II give further indications as to size, occupation, etc., of the families studied.

Turning to our second query—how far the actual expenditures of the families studied were in themselves representative— we must consider several difficulties that were encountered in the course of the work. These, together with the methods employed in overcoming them so far as practicable, should be made clear. The various items of the budget,—rent, food, occasional expenditures,—may be taken up in order.

Under the first heading, that of rent, it is to be noted that 13 of the 90 families whose expenditures were analyzed owned their homes free of mortgage—a proportion which fairly represented the possibilities in this direction which the town's life holds but a number too small to warrant special averages. This complication is inevitable in any study of mill-town expenditures, though usually absent in tenement studies in a city. While such families do not pay rent they have to reckon on the cost of taxes and repairs. No attempt has been made to estimate just what these amounts would be annually for the families studied. The impression gained was that as a whole such families spent for these items less than the equivalent of rent and therefore had more margin for other items than would house-renting families in the same expenditure groups.

To overcome this element of variation the principal tables in the chapter on rent were based on the actual rentals of the house-renting families; and in the chapter on food the test of sufficiency (22 cents per man per day) arrived at by Professor Underhill was accepted as a minimum. Therefore, for these two most important items, we were able to secure units unaffected by this element of house ownership, to use in the final recapitulations as to what a family could get for a given weekly expenditure. With respect to the balance available for the remaining items in the budgets, the effect of the inclusion of the 13 house-owners in our general schedules is not altogether clear. Yet a comparison of the average expenditures of the 90 budget families as a whole (Table 9, page 45), with 77 house renters, classified separately (Table 10), seems to show that their inclusion did not materially alter this remainder. This is illustrated by the following figures for the families spending less than $15 per week for all needs:

	Rent	Food	Total for rent and food
All families (48)	$2.01	$4.73	$6.74
House renters (43)	2.25	4.45	6.70

It was only among those who spent $15 per week or over that the averages for all families (as against the house renters separately) showed an increased outlay for such items as church, education and recreation. The differences even here were very slight.

With respect to the next major item in the budget, food we did not attempt to include in the inquiry any dietetic research as to the food values of provisions used by the families. Such elementary calculations as to food values as could be made from the accounts, indicated that it was reasonable to apply the per diem standard determined by Professor Underhill in his New York estimates the same year, which were based on a careful weighing and chemical analysis of materials and waste. The point is more fully explained in the text, page 70. ·

With the exception of insurance, no satisfactory data were obtained from the account books as to occasional expenditures, as furniture, clothing, expenses of sickness, etc. Such items are at best an unsatisfactory basis of computation unless accounts are kept for the full year. Rather than attempt estimates on the basis of such data as was secured, we made use of conclusions reached in Professor Chapin's exhaustive analysis of the budget estimates of 500 New York families in 1907.

The whole range of expenditures of many families was affected by the industrial depression of 1907 and 1908. As stated in the text, within six weeks after the budget work was started the trouble began and, by the middle of December, the mills were running only about half time, a situation which lasted during the remainder of the investigation. To make up for reduced incomes, rents were allowed to run in arrears, stores gave credit freely to their old customers and money was drawn from the bank. The budget Slavs, for instance, averaged $3.28 per week for credit, one-quarter of their total expenditure of $13.07.

As the depression was regarded as temporary, families did not reduce purchases during this period of waiting as much as would have been anticipated. The items probably farthest from normal were those for clothing and furniture, since these expenditures could easily be postponed. Nevertheless, as few families were receiving full wages, the household accounts fell below what was customary. The elements of uncertainty were sufficient to render out of the question any close statistical deductions as to actual expenditures in prosperous times by families classified by their normal wage groups; as to what proportion of their normal incomes these families would spend for the different budget items; or as to the uses of any surplus which the more prosperous families might be accustomed to. Much larger groups of families, studied for longer and more representative periods, would have been essential.

It looked for a while as if the accounts being kept by our housewives must lose their value also for the simpler comparative uses we had planned to put them to. As time went on this did not prove to be the case. We were seeking light on what elementary household standards are possible on an income, say, of $12 a week in Homestead. If the period covered by the investigation had been a normal one, we could have put opposite each other a family's average earnings and what the money went for as shown by its account book, computed averages, and drawn simple and direct deductions as to the relation between wages and costs of living for each group. Instead, in analyzing the data from the account books, we divided the families, not according to normal wages, but according to the amounts they actually spent per week during the period studied, including what was purchased on credit from landlord, grocer and butcher, and what was drawn from the bank. Rents and the prices of food stuffs did not change appreciably during this period. With these constant, $12 per week would in general buy the same, whether the payments were met out of the lowered earnings of a family during a period of slack times, or out of the total wages of a low-paid man when the mills were running full. For instance, take the household of a semi-skilled man receiving say $2.50 a day, but working only part time and averaging $11.50 instead of $15 per week for the period studied. If this family lived on his $11.50 and paid their bills, the family was entered in the "under $12" per week expenditure group. If they drew money from the bank or secured credit at the store for $2.00 besides, they were entered in the "$12 to $14.99" class.

So far as total weekly expenditures go, it is to be noted that only in the "under $12" and "over $20" groups would the resulting averages probably be appreciably affected by hard times. The latter group is outside the debatable ground: the average expenditure by the former was, it turned out, not far from the customary wages of common labor, with which it was compared. The discussion hinged on the important intermediate groups. The personnel of such an intermediate group, of course, changes, but as a statistical category it remains constant. Half-time employment would throw certain families into the "$12 to $14.99" group from above, and others would drop out below; but the average total expenditure would remain fairly stable.

An element of discrepancy, however, enters into the discussion of items making up this average total. For instance, in the case of the $15 man cited above his fixed expenditures, such as rent, would go on. They would probably be higher than those of a man with an income ordinarily under $12, and the balance free for other expenditures would be less. As affecting this discrepancy, it should be pointed out that these semi-skilled householders often brought a higher grade of managing ability to the purchase and handling of food and other household necessities than would ordinarily be true of the average laborer's family, and also that they would buy, in such a period of depression, only the essentials. With prices normal, the food or other necessities purchased under such circumstances for a dollar were probably as much as could ever be bought in Homestead for such a sum.

Thus by classifying the actual household expenditures into groups corresponding to the range of wages paid in the mills, light was thrown on what an average family at each wage level might reasonably secure from its weekly earnings in ordinary times. The 90 budgets, therefore, afforded a body of specific indications correcting and strengthening the general impressions received, as to how far earnings current in Homestead would go (a) for an unskilled immigrant who seeks a foothold in this country through a job as common laborer, or (b) for the American who looks to his work as a permanent basis for livelihood.

The following tables relating to the budget study supplement those given in the text.

TABLE I.—ANALYSIS OF 90 BUDGET FAMILIES.—BY RACIAL GROUP, OCCUPATION AND NORMAL WEEKLY WAGE OF MAN

Racial and Income Group	Occupation in Mill. No. in Each				Occupation Outside Mill. No. in Each						Total
	Clerical	Tonnage men*	Day men	Laborers	Laborer	Teamster	Building trades	Clerical	Profess.	Other Occupation	
Slav											
Under $12.00			2	19							21
$12.00–$14.99			2								2
$15.00–$19.99		2	2								4
$20.00 and over		1								1	2
Total		3	6	19						1	29
Eng. Sp. Eur.											
Under $12.00				1							1
$12.00–$14.99		1	2	1		1				1	6
$15.00–$19.99	1	1	2								4
$20.00 and over		1	1								2
Total	1	3	5	2		1				1	13
Nat. White											
Under $12.00				1							1
$12.00–$14.99			2				1				3
$15.00–$19.99	1	1	2					1		1	6
$20.00 and over	1	4	5					1	2	2	15
Total	2	5	9	1			1	2	2	3	25
Colored											
Under $12.00					1					1	2
$12.00–$14.99					2	6				1	9
$15.00–$19.99			3				4			1	8
$20.00 and over		3								1	4
Total		3	3		3	6	4			4	23
Total all races	3	14	23	22	3	7	5	2	2	9	90

* In tonnage work the amount earned varies from week to week but pains were taken to estimate earnings closely.

TABLE 2.—AVERAGE NORMAL WEEKLY INCOME AND INCOME FROM SPECIFIED SOURCES, OF 90 BUDGET FAMILIES.—BY RACIAL GROUP

Racial Group	Number of family	Average weekly income	INCOME FROM				
			Man	Sons	Wife	Lodgers	Bank
Slav	29	$13.88	$12.08	$ .52	$ .34	$ .94	..
Eng. Sp. Eur. . .	13	20.53	16.41	3.85	..	.27	..
Nat. White . .	25	22.93	18.95	2.20	.24	.34	$1.20*
Col.	23	17.92	13.27	1.30	2.15	1.20	..

* This family had recently sold a store and were regularly drawing money from bank.

TABLE 3.—90 BUDGET FAMILIES.—BY NUMBER OF FAMILIES HAVING INCOME FROM GIVEN SOURCES IN NORMAL TIMES AND BY RACIAL GROUP

Racial Group	Number of Families	FAMILIES WITH INCOME FROM			
		Man only	Woman	Sons	Lodgers
Slav	29	14	1	6	9
Eng. Sp. Eur. . .	13	9	..	4	1
Nat. White . . .	25	16	2	5	3
Colored . . .	23	14	6	2	5
Total . . .	90	53	9	17	18

TABLE 4.—AVERAGE SIZE OF FAMILIES, AND OF FAMILIES INCLUDING LODGERS.—BY EXPENDITURE AND NATIONALITY GROUPS

Nationality.	UNDER $12		$12.00 TO $14.99		$15.00 TO $19.99		$20 AND OVER		TOTAL	
	Not Including Lodgers	Including Lodgers	Number in Families	With Lodgers	Number in Families	With Lodgers	Number in Families	With Lodgers	Number in Families	With Lodgers
Slav . . .	3.7	3.9	4.2	7.2	4 4	7.1	4.7	4.7	4.1	5.3
Eng. Sp. Eur..	7.0	7.0	7.3	7.3	5.0	5.0	7.7	.7.7	6.8	6.8
Nat. White .	4 0	4.0	7.0	7.0	4.4	4.5	4.8	5.2	4.6	4.8
Colored . .	2.5	3.2	4.3	4.7	4.0	4.0	4.0	4.0	3.4	3.8
Total average	3.7	3.9	5.2	6.3	4.4	5.3	5.2	5.4	4.4	0.5

TABLE 5.—90 BUDGET FAMILIES.   NUMBER OF PERSONS PER ROOM.
—BY RACIAL GROUP

Racial Group	Total Families	Families Having		
		One Person per Room	Two Persons per Room	Three or More Persons per Room
Slav. . . .	29	6	9	14
Nat. White .	25	20	4	1
Eng. Sp. Eur. .	13	7	4	2
Colored . .	23	17	6	0
Total. .	90	50	23	17

TABLE 6.—NUMBER OF HOUSE-OWNING AND HOUSE-RENTING
FAMILIES HAVING WATER IN HOUSE, AND NUMBER HAVING TWO
OR MORE PERSONS PER ROOM.—BY EXPENDITURE GROUP

Expenditure Group	Total Number of Families	Number of Families Having	
		Water in House	Two or More Persons per Room
Under $12.00 .	32	12	16
$12.00–$14.99 .	16	5	10
$15.00–$19.99 .	23	14	9
$20.00 and over	19	16	5
Total . .	90	47	40

TABLE 7.—90 BUDGET FAMILIES OCCUPYING TENEMENTS OF SPECI-
FIED NUMBER OF ROOMS.—BY RACIAL GROUP

Racial Group	Total Families	One Room Number of Families	Two Rooms Number of Families	Three Rooms Number of Families	Four Rooms Number of Families	Five Rooms Number of Families	Six Rooms Number of Families
Slav. . .	29	5	15	5	4	..	..
Eng. Sp. Eur. .	13	..	..	3	5	2	3
Nat. White . .	25	..	..	3	5	7	10
Colored . . .	23	..	6	6	8	2	1

TABLE 8.—90 BUDGET FAMILIES OCCUPYING SPECIFIED NUMBER OF ROOMS.—BY EXPENDITURE GROUP

Expenditure Group	Total Families	One Room	Two Rooms	Three Rooms	Four Rooms	Five Rooms	Six or more
Under $12.00	32	5	10	3	11	1	2
$12.00–$14.99	16	..	3	4	6	1	2
$15.00–$19.99	23	..	6	7	3	5	2
$20.00 and over	19	..	2	3	2	4	8
Total	90	5	21	17	22	11	14

TABLE 9.—COST OF CERTAIN ARTICLES OF FOOD IN NINE CITIES AND RATIO OF THE COST OF THESE ARTICLES IN OTHER CITIES TO THE COST IN PITTSBURGH.—BY CENTS PER POUND*

Article	Baltimore	Boston	Chicago	New York	Philadelphia	San Francisco	St. Louis	Washington	Pittsburgh	Position of Pittsburgh
Beans	.10	.10	.08	.09	.09	.07½	.11	.10	.10	2
Chuck Roast	.13	.11	.06	.12	.12	.10	.13	.12½	.12½	2
Salt Beef	.10	.08	.06	.08	.11	.07	.07	.08	.10	2
Bread (lb.)	.05	.05	.05	.05	.05	.05	.05	.05	.05	..
Butter	.31	.25	.25	.26	.31	.27	.27	.32	.31	2
Cheese	.18	.16	.15	.19	.16	.15	.16	.20	.17	3
Corn meal	.02½	.03	.02½	.04	.02½	.03½	.02½	.02	.02½	4
Lard	.10	.11	.11	.12	.11	.12½	.12	.13	.13	1
Molasses (gal.)	.55	.55	.60	.55	.50	.60	.40	.60	.60	1
Mutton (leg)	.13½	.12	.11	.11	.13	.11	.08½	.13	.13	2
Fresh Pork (chops)	.13	.14	.11	.17	.13	.12½	.13	.14½	.14½	2
Bacon	.15	.17	.16	.18	.15	.20	.17	.17	.18	2
Prunes	.08	.08	.07	.10	.08	.05	.06	.10	.10	1
Rice	.08	.09	.09	.09	.08	.08	.10	.09	.09½	1
Veal Cutlet	.21	.28	.16	.25	.22	.17	.15	.19	.23½	3
Total	2.33	2.32	2.08½	2.40	2.26½	2.21	2.03	2.45	2.49½	1
Ratio	93	93	83	96	91	89	81	98	100	1

*From U. S. Bureau of Labor Report, July, 1907, pp. 175–328.

TABLE 10.—TOTAL AVERAGE WEEKLY EXPENDITURES OF HOUSE-RENTING FAMILIES EXPENDING LESS THAN $12 A WEEK, AND PROPORTIONS SPENT FOR FOOD AND RENT.—BY RACIAL GROUP

Racial Group	Number of Families	Average Total Expenditure	Food Amount	Food Per cent	Rent Amount	Rent Per cent	Total Amount	Total Per cent
Slav	13	$8.85	$4.31	48.7	$1.64	18.5	$5.95	67.2
Eng. Sp. Eur.. . .	2	10.30	4.46	43.3	3.38	31.9	7.84	75.2
Nat. White. . .	2	9.82	3.15	32.1	3.85	39.2	7.00	71.3
Colored	11	8.98	3.22	36.0	2.22	24.7	5.44	60.7
Total average .	28	$9.08	$3.81	42.0	$2.15	23.7	$5.96	65.7

TABLE 11.—AVERAGE EXPENDITURE FOR FOOD PER MAN PER DAY. —BY SIZE OF FAMILY AND EXPENDITURE GROUP

Number in Family	UNDER $12.00		$12.00 TO $14.99		$15.00 TO $19.99		$20.00 AND OVER	
	Number of Families	Average Expenditure	Number of Families	Average Expenditure	Number of Families	Average Expenditure	Number of Families	Average Expenditure
1	..	..	..	..	..	..	..	..
2	10	$ .27	..	..	3	$ .39	3	$ .52
3	10	.22	5	$ .27	7	.45	2	.70
4	5	.22	3	.33	3	.35	4	.33
5	1	.19	3	.27	3	.21	4	.31
6	3	.19	3	.24	3	.29	1	.27
7	1	.22	1	.19	1	.25	2	.27
8	1	.13	1	.15	3	.22	..	..
9	1	.21	1	.10	..	..	3	.39

Expenditure Group	Racial Group	Years in United States	Occupation	Number of Persons in Family	Number of Lodgers	Number of Rooms	Water in House	Remarks
1	Slovak	28	Laborer	7	2	4	No	Are buying home. Son, 21, also a laborer.
2	"	16	"	2	2	3	"	Neither can read nor write even in Slavic. Niece and one other lodger.
3	"	4	"	3	0	3	"	Young couple, married here. Home well furnished. Have made prosperous start.
4	"	3	"	2	0	1	Yes	Young couple.
5	"	8	"	3	0	1	No	Son, 14, at work. Own property in old country.
6	"	2	"	2	0	2	Yes	Man already arrested for intemperance and abusing wife.
7	UNDER $12	"	8	"	3	0	1	Yes	Woman frail. Several children have died.
8		"	8	"	4	0	2	"	Two little children. Have money in bank. Only working part time.
9		"	6	Day man[3]	4	0	2	No	Young couple, married here; two little children. Are furnishing home on instalment plan.
10		"	8	Laborer	2	0	2	"	Poorly furnished home. A child is in old country with relatives.
11		"	14	Day man	5	0	2	"	Inclined to drink. Poorly furnished, unattractive home.
12		"	16	Laborer	6	2	2	Yes	Intemperate man, at one time insane.
13		"	3	"	3	0	1	No	Young couple. Man earns usually about $2.25 a day. One room with but little furniture.
14		"	7	Day man	2	0	1	"	Came to United States when 14. Now an engineer in mill. Married 6 months ago to girl of 17.
15		"	12	Laborer	6	4	4	"	Nephew lives with them. Woman exhausted by hard work.
16		"	14	"	4	0	2	"	Man says his health has been affected by mill work; he must drink to stand it. Home fairly comfortable but small.
17	$12 TO $14.99	Hung.	10	Tonnage	3	0	2	"	Have money in bank and property in old country. Only one little child.
18		Slovak	10	Laborer	4	8	4	Yes	Woman born here. Man intemperate. Home poorly furnished. Woman fairly capable.
19		"	15	"	4	3	2	No	Man of 50. Have to take boarders to manage on his wages.
20		"	19	"	5	8	3	Yes	Family came recently. Have property in old country and also have money in bank.
21		"	7	Tonnage	4	2	2	No	Earns $2 to $3 a day. Says "has two boarders to help earn a living."
22		"	18	Day man	4	0	3	Yes	Naturalized. Own home. Representative older residents.
23	$15 TO $19.99	"	6	"	2	2	2	No	Young couple. Man only 22 but semi-skilled. Are saving for a home.
24		"	3	Laborer	9	2	2	"	Home poor, health not good. Take lodgers to help inadequate income.
25		"	17	Day man	6	0	4	Yes	Man formerly miner. Now earns $3.50 a day in mill. Has rheumatism. One child feeble-minded.
26		"	6	Laborer	3	5	2	No	Man injured in mill, out of work 10 months. $150 from company and income from lodgers supports family.
27	$20 AND OVER	Hung.	7	Tonnage	4	0	3	Yes	Thrifty Protestant family. Home simple, but attractive.
28		Slovak	2	Laborer	4	0	2	No	Married in Hungary. Man came over first.
29		Hung.	6	"	6	0	2	"	Son also laborer. Has savings; drew on them for extra expenses at death of child recently.

II

WEEKLY EXPENDITURE OF EACH OF THE NINETY FAMILIES

SLAVS

No. of Weeks Account Kept	Ave.¹ Available Income Weeks Studied	Average² Weekly Credit	Average Weekly from Bank	Average Weekly Expenditures	AVERAGE WEEKLY EXPENDITURE FOR										
					Food	Rent	Fuel	Clothing	Furniture	Household Expenses	Insurance	Tobacco	Liquor	Health	Sundries
8	$10.60	..	..	$10.58	$6.60	*	$ .03	..	..	$ .02	$2.00	$ .39	..	..	$1.54
6	11.43	..	..	11.47	5.35	$2.75	.28	$1.46	..	.27	.79	..	$ .25	..	.32
4	11.90	..	..	11.86	4.90	2.25	.02	2.44	..	.10	1.00	..	1.00	..	.15
4	6.02	$5.80	..	6.03	4.80	1.00	..	..	..	.18	..	..	..	..	.05
7	6.86	.50	$2.37	6.87	3.80	1.14	.39	.79	$ .07	.05	.43	..	.14	..	.06
4	8.48	3.55	..	8.49	.3.30	2.00	.06	3.02	..	.09	..	..	..	..	.02
4	5.25	.50	..	5.22	3.40	1.12	.06	.54	..	.10	..	..	..	..	..
4	10.46	3.87	..	10.46	5.89	2.00	.04	1.27	..	.06	.40	..	.80	..	..
4	9.48	2.48	..	9.48	4.81	1.62	.53	..	..	.26	1.18	..	1.00	..	.08
4	9.85	4.41	..	9.93	3.66	1.87	.05	1.96	..	.06	.45	.06	.41	..	1.41
7	7.26	.75	..	7.30	4.25	1.89	.05	.32	..	.14	.25	.02	.32	..	.09
5	8.95	4.75	..	8.92	4.35	2.00	.42	1.31	..	.09	.38	.02	.16	..	.19
7	9.74	..	.75	9.70	3.87	.86	.59	2.74	..	.10	.74	.09	.57	..	.14
7	9.36	..	..	9.35	3.86	.86	.66	1.50	..	.26	.74	.09	1.28	..	.28
6	13.86	.75	..	13.87	6.96	3.50	..	2.31	.23	.33	..	..	.54	..	..
7	13.68	..	..	13.68	5.81	2.29	.57	3.08	..	.90	..	..	..	$ .71	.32
9	13.74	..	..	13.73	3.79	2.50	1.15	.78	..	.12	..	.10	.78	.56	3.95
8	12.58	.75	..	12.60	5.84	2.00	.89	1.95	.19	.12	.25	.15	.82	..	.39
8	12.24	7.57	..	13.24	7.57	1.75	1.17	.25	..	.23	1.75	..	..	..	.52
5	17.68	2.10	5.60	17.67	7.17	3.50	.82	2.12	..	.44	.98	.09	.90	..	1.65
7	19.46	1.00	..	19.61	11.06	2.28	.54	2.36	..	1.22	..	.05	1.42	.04	.64
9	19.93*	..	..	19.95	8.26	*	1.40	1.21	..	.03	.63	.08	1.35	.65	6.34
7	15.71	..	..	15.68	7.92	2.86	.78	1.85	..	.22	.49	.09	1.47	..	..
8	15.85	3.75	..	15.65	7.56	1.75	.30	1.75	.38	.42	.65	.01	.91	.04	1.88
4	17.00	..	..	16.26	6.61	3.75	..	1.97	..	.04	1.15	.05	2.12	.50	.07
4	17.46	..	13.71	17.45	10.77	2.50	.10	1.32	..	.36	1.47	..	.63	..	.30
4	20.34	..	..	20.34	7.19	2.37	.05	5.20	..	1.06	2.19	.10	.19	.43	1.56
..	20.29	4.49	10.00	20.21	6.89	1.50	.13	.70	..	.34	.50	.05	..	..	10.10
..	24.10	6.64	6.66	24.11	7.28	4.00	.04	3.43	..	.27	6.97	..	.92	1.00	.20

¹ Including credit.
² Average amount purchased on credit.
³ Paid per day instead of per ton.
* Families owned home.

ENGLISH SPEAK-

Expenditure Group		Racial Group	Years in United States	Occupation	Number of Persons in Family	Number of Lodgers	Number of Rooms	Water in House	Remarks
30	UNDER $12	Irish	14	Day man	6	0	4	No	Rather shiftless family, always buy on credit. No insurance.
31		Scotch	35	Tonnage	9	0	6	"	Two boys at work. Have good income in ordinary times. Own house, free.
32		German	30		6	0	4	Yes	Relatives giving food during depression.
33	$12 !TO $14.99	English	25	Day man	5	0	4	No	Three young children. Own home.
34		"		"	8	0	4	Yes	Man formerly glass blower. Irregularly employed in mill. Church gave a little assistance.
35		Irish	35	Conductor	5	0	6	"	One girl at home, two children in school.
36		English	12	Laborer	11	0	4	"	Son at work, pays $5.00 a week board when working. Thrifty family.
37	$15 TO $19.99	"	29	Tonnage	3	0	4	No	Once a miner. Earns $2.50 to $3.00 a day. Owns home, free.
38		Scotch	27	Office	4	0	3	Yes	Prosperous home, musical family. Have savings.
39		English	12	Day man	8	0	3	No	Six children under 14.
40	$20 AND OVER	Irish	23	Laborer	11	0	8	Yes	Two grown sons at work. Originally miners.
41		Scotch		Teamster	7	0	5	"	Thrifty family. Home well furnished. 3 sons at work. Own property in another town.
42		"		Tonnage	5	0	5	"	Man earns over $25 a week. Girl over 14 at home and boy in school. Have savings. Attractive home.

208

ING EUROPEANS

No. of Weeks Account Kept	Ave.[1] Available Income Weeks Studied	Average[2] Weekly Credit	Average Weekly from Bank	Average Weekly Expenditures	AVERAGE WEEKLY EXPENDITURE FOR											
					Food	Rent	Fuel	Clothing	Furniture	Household Expenses	Insurance	Tobacco	Liquor	Health	Sundries	
4	$10.22	$3.97	..	$10.12	$5.98	$3.00	..	$ .12	..	$ .21	$ .46	$ .21	..	..	$ .14	30
5	10.69	5.00	..	10.90	3.86	*	$1.05	.34	..	.20	..	.21	$ .20	..	.04	31
4	10.30	1.50	..	10.48	2.94	3.75	..	.27	..	.06	2.52	.15	.20	..	.59	32
7	14.28	2.25	..	14.28	6.49	2.25	.80	.09	..	..	.39	..	..	$ .19	4.07	33
5	13.92	..	..	13.93	5.06	2.50	..	5.04	..	.24	.30	.02	..	..	.77	34
4	14.68	1.23	..	14.69	9.27	*	1.50	3.29	..	.27	..	..	..	..	.36	35
4	13.82	4.73	..	14.11	4.72	2.75	.83	.50	$ .27	.06	2.80	.32	..	..	1.86	36
7	15.96	..	$2.14	15.93	6.80	*	..	8.85	..	.29	..	..	..	..	.02	37
6	18.63	..	..	18.64	5.19	5.00	.83	1.00	.87	2.65	.53	..	..	.52	2.05	38
4	15.04	5.53	..	15.02	5.53	2.50	..	3.12	.56	.07	1.73	..	.50	.22	.79	39
4	29.34	..	..	29.35	20.15	7.50	..	.10	.20	.58	.12	..	..	..	.70	40
4	33.14	..	..	33.16	8.59	6.00	.87	9.06	.29	.28	1.47	.02	..	..	6.58	41
13	20.11	..	..	19.91	8.60	2.54	.02	2.24	.76	.27	3.02	.11	..	.29	2.06	42

[1] Including credit.
[2] Average amount purchased on credit.
* Families owned home.

NATIVE

Expenditure Group	Racial Group	Occupation	Number of Persons in Family	Number of Lodgers	Number of Rooms	Water in House	Remarks
43	American	Tonnage	3	0	4	No	Young man brought up on farm. Fairly comfortable home.
44	"	Boatman	3	0	4	Yes	Man away a good deal. Live comfortably.
45	"	Tonnage	6	0	6	No	In Homestead since a boy. Woman earns a little. Own home.
46	"	"	4	0	5	Yes	Man ill, unable to work, family live on sick benefits, savings and credit. Own home.
47	"	Day man	7	0	4	"	Man began work at 16 as clerk; now pencil job, shiftless. Son messenger in mill.
48	"	Laborer	8	0	5	"	
49	"	Clerical	3	0	3	No	Young German-American couple. Wife formerly dressmaker. Neat attractive home.
50	"	"	4	0	5	Yes	Prosperous young couple, thrifty, attractive home.
51	"	Professional	2	0	5	"	Spend money freely. Entertain. Pay cash for everything.
52	"	Day man	3	1	4	"	Earns about $3 a day. Have roomy house so take a lodger. Home well cared for.
53	"	"	5	0	6	"	Two young sons in mill help support family. Own home free. Well insured.
54	"	"	8	0	6	"	Have bought home in suburb. Woman competent.
55	"	"	2	0	5	"	Man has fair salary. Spend freely for what they want. Good home.
56	"	Day man	9	0	3	"	Old residents of Homestead. Man worked here before strike. Boy works in mill irregularly.
57	"	Clerical	2	2	7	"	Middle aged couple. Man semi-official position. Had some unusual expenses so took lodgers.
58	"	Tonnage	6	0	6	"	Man not much good. Two sons practically support family. Own home.
59	"	Day man	2	0	4	"	Old residents of Homestead. Have comfortable, small home.
60	"	"	2	0	6	"	Went to school till 17. Since in mill. Earns about $3.50 a day. Very nice home.
61	"	Clerical	5	0	6	"	Man has small business of his own. Family prosperous, own home, have bank account. Son 16 in school.
62	"	"	7	0	6	"	Own home in suburb. Son in mill. Daughter at home.
63	"	Day man	5	3	5	"	German descent. Man earns about $2.25 a day.
64	"	"	3	0	3	"	Earns about $3 a day. One child. Small home, have savings.
65	"	Professional	4	0	6	"	Live well.
66	"	Tonnage	3	0	5	"	Ten years in Homestead. Man earns about $3.50 a day. Savings in bank. Well furnished home. Irish-American.
67	"	..	9	0	6	"	Man had small store which he sold. Family living on savings. One son at work, pays $5 a week board.

Expenditure Group brackets: 44–46 Under $12; 47 $12–$14.99; 48–55 $15 to $19.99; 56–67 $20 and over.

WHITE

No. of Weeks Account Kept	Ave.¹ Available Income Weeks Studied	Average² Weekly Credit	Average Weekly from Bank	Average Weekly Expenditures	AVERAGE WEEKLY EXPENDITURE FOR											
					Food	Rent	Fuel	Clothing	Furniture	Household Expenses	Insurance	Tobacco	Liquor	Health	Sundries	
5	$ 9.20	$ .50	..	$ 9.14	$ 4.50	$ 2.50	$ .05	$ .64	$ .30	$ .06	$.38	..	$ .06	..	$ .65	43
5	10.49	..	..	10.49	1.79	5.20	.35	1.04	1.40	.11	..	$ .05	..	$ .02	.53	44
4	9.29	.50	..	8.75	6.50	*	..	.63	..	.06	.67	.14	..	..	.75	45
5	9.35	2.62	..	9.35	4.38	*	.40	1.41	.08	.20	1.20	.13	..	.60	.95	46
10	12.80	1.75	..	12.80	5.92	3.00	.51	.77	.40	.25	1.07	..	..	.03	.85	47
8	19.37	2.50	$ 3.12	19.33	8.33	2.50	..	2.13	.03	.64	1.51	.04	..	.73	3.42	48
4	16.96	..	..	16.94	6.19	3.33	..	5.30	.17	.26	1.00	..	..	..	.69	49
13	18.04	.50	..	18.07	6.31	4.84	1.11	1.18	.48	.68	.36	..	..	1.82	1.29	50
4	17.39	..	..	17.38	5.41	5.00	.82	.31	..	.49	1.75	..	..	.12	3.48	51
12	19.53	..	..	19.51	6.52	3.75	.48	3.08	1.88	.83	1.51	.05	..	.59	.82	52
4	18.16	..	..	18.12	6.22	*	.76	1.20	2.43	.29	1.08	..	..	..	6.14	53
4	15.09	1.06	..	15.07	8.64	*	1.35	1.33	..	.76	2.27	.12	..	.50	.10	54
..	19.05	..	..	19.03	4.21	4.52	.58	2.82	.91	1.01	.98	.21	.20	.37	3.22	55
5	21.09	..	..	21.03	8.02	2.21	.45	5.37	1.44	.60	.34	.29	..	.75	1.56	56
10	22.00	..	..	21.97	3.62	*	1.00	.28	..	.17	.35	..	..	..	16.55	57
5	20.92	..	..	20.92	8.56	*	1.00	1.39	2.75	.22	2.55	..	..	.90	3.55	58
4	22.42	1.00	..	22.46	6.83	5.00	1.00	1.52	2.50	.32	..	.28	..	.04	4.97	59
5	22.57	..	..	22.56	9.22	5.00	3.43	.80	..	..	1.02	..	..	2.50	.59	60
4	24.84	..	..	24.84	7.97	*	..	7.15	..	3.71	3.04	..	..	..	2.97	61
5	23.59	3.12	..	23.57	9.94	*	1.44	9.02	.83	.99	.20	..	..	.04	1.11	62
5	28.95	..	..	28.95	8.50	11.20	1.82	1.34	.84	.38	.15	.08	.28	.40	3.96	63
4	29.24	..	8.00	29.24	8.37	5.00	.69	3.74	..	.77	4.50	..	.21	1.84	4.12	64
5	29.81	..	..	29.81	5.21	7.05	.66	2.46	..	.99	2.23	..	..	.92	10.29	65
4	34.14	4.00	..	34.18	14.04	4.00	2.47	1.62	5.57	.31	.66	.35	..	1.25	3.91	66
5	38.29	1.00	36.49	38.29	20.89	5.00	.53	8.47	..	.31	1.47	.19	.46	..	.97	67

¹ Including credit.
² Average amount purchased on credit.
* Families owned home.

COLORED

Expenditure Group	Racial Group	Occupation	Number of Persons in Family	Number of Lodgers	Number of Rooms	Water in House	Remarks
68	Negro	..	2	2	4	Yes	Widow, earns living by laundry work and taking boarders. One child at home.
69	"	Window cleaner	3	0	2	No	Man began work as chore boy. Work irregular. Rooms poorly furnished and unsanitary.
70	"	Janitor	2	0	2	"	Man out of work. Woman earns a little. Married children help.
71	"	Teamster	3	0	4	"	Young couple with one child. Wife good natured but totally ignorant.
72	Under $12	"	2	0	2	"	Young couple. Home neat and well furnished but dark and unsanitary.
73		Laborer	2	0	4	"	Middle aged couple. Pleasant home.
74	"	Mason	2	1	4	Yes	Man formerly miner. Two dark rooms.
75	"	"	4	0	3	"	Man intemperate. Woman largely supports home. Son unruly.
76	"	Day man	3	0	2	No	Small dark tenement but neatly furnished and well cared for. One small child.
77	"	Housework	2	5	4	"	One son at work, rest of income from five men lodgers.
78	"	Tonnage	2	0	4	Yes	Small pay comparatively. Have comfortable home on hill, good garden.
79		"	Teamster	3	0	3	No	Here only a few years, from Virginia. Little house. Six families share one yard.
80	"	"	3	0	3	"	Small shabby unsanitary home. Man's work irregular in winter.
81	$12 TO $14.99	"	Tonnage	3	2	5	"	Earns $2.50 to $3 a day. Nice home, well furnished.
82	"	Hod carrier	6	0	3	"	Man's work very irregular. Home unsanitary; children sickly.
83	"	Tonnage	6	0	6	"	Began work on a farm, now earning about $2.50 a day. Simple but well furnished and cheerful home, good garden.
84	"	Laborer	5	0	4	"	
85		"	Teamster	3	0	2	Yes	Young married couple with one child. Small neat home.
86	"	Tonnage	6	0	5	"	Exceptionally attractive home with large garden. Woman competent, man devoted to home.
87	$15 TO $19.99	"	Housework	4	2	3	No	Woman supports family, washing and lodgers. One son idle. Family rather degenerate.
88	"	Day man	2	0	3	"	Went to work at 10 picking cotton, at 18 into mines, now semi-skilled in mill; live over store.
89	"	Painter	3	0	2	Yes	Woman helps support family. Here from South 8 years.
90	$20 AND OVER	"	Teamster	4	0	4	No	Elderly couple. Two grown sons also teamsters. Rather poor home.

COLORED

No. of Weeks Account Kept	Ave.¹ Available Income Weeks Studied	Average² Weekly Credit	Average Weekly from Bank	Average Weekly Expenditures	Average Weekly Expenditure for											
					Food	Rent	Fuel	Clothing	Furniture	Household Expenses	Insurance	Tobacco	Liquor	Health	Sundries	
6	$ 7.93	$1.33	..	$ 7.90	$3.02	$2.50	$ .08	$ .51	$ .50	$ .16	$ .18	$ .02	..	$ .06	$ .87	68
4	9.93	1.25	..	9.92	4.32	1.75	.78	.69	..	.03	1.02	.27	..	.97	.09	69
4	3.24	..	..	3.32	1.21	1.50	.04	.25	..	.05	..	.03	..	..	.24	70
5	10.13	.50	..	10.07	3.01	2.50	.69	.92	..	.53	.99	..	..	.67	.76	71
..	9.50	..	..	9.50	3.19	2.00	.71	.92	..	.33	.57	.19	..	.30	1.29	72
4	11.79	..	..	11.79	4.12	2.50	1.39	.64	..	.25	1.80	.14	..	.25	.70	73
5	7.05	..	..	7.06	2.52	2.00	.21	..	..	.13	1.18	..	..	..	1.02	74
7	7.70	..	..	7.69	4.30	2.00	.30	.29	.08	.13	.29	..	..	.05	.25	75
5	11.34	3.07	..	11.38	3.07	2.20	1.00	3.15	.20	.28	.26	.02	$ .07	..	1.13	76
5	11.18	.50	..	11.18	3.76	2.50	1.76	..	.30	.12	1.61	..	..	.30	.83	77
4	8.90	..	..	8.99	2.93	3.00	.02	1.62	..	.06	.98	..	..	..	.98	78
4	12.32	..	..	12.27	4.27	1.81	1.28	.79	.37	.23	.65	..	.06	.41	2.40	79
4	12.36	..	..	12.36	6.32	2.00	1.45	.56	..	.21	.37	..	..	..	1.45	80
8	14.68	..	..	14.78	3.99	4.00	.68	2.38	1.75	.12	.17	.11	.05	.43	1.10	81
5	12.42	8.42	..	12.47	3.51	1.88	.03	2.09	..	.17	.07	..	..	4.12	.60	82
4	12.09	4.56	..	12.12	8.06	2.50	..	1.17	..	.30	..	..	..	..	.09	83
4	12.28	2.73	..	12.29	6.23	2.00	1.45	..	..	.09	.39	.08	..	1.09	.96	84
6	16.86	..	..	16.88	6.88	2.80	.40	1.77	..	.11	1.41	.01	5.00	1.50	2.00	85
4	19.80	..	..	19.80	8.27	4.00	.38	1.13	..	.59	2.50	..	.	.69	2.27	86
..	18.39	1.30	..	18.41	5.16	2.50	.71	1.05	..	.85	1.04	.01	5.00	.74	1.35	87
4	15.77	1.75	..	15.84	5.00	2.50	1.17	1.38	.62	.73	.81	.18	..	1.98	1.47	88
4	18.27	8.00	..	18.27	9.68	3.00	2.65	..	..	.25	.37	.18	..	..	2.14	89
4	20.74	..	..	20.74	8.45	2.50	1.62	..	..	.97	4.60	..	..	.62	1.98	90

¹ Including credit.
² Average amount purchased on credit.
* Families owned home.

APPENDIX III

EMPLOYES IN HOMESTEAD PLANT OF THE UNITED STATES STEEL CORPORATION CLASSIFIED ACCORDING TO SKILL, CITIZENSHIP, CONJUGAL CONDITION, ETC., MARCH 1, 1907

Nationality	Skilled	Semi-skilled	Un-skilled	Total	Naturalized	Not naturalized	Married	Single	English speaking	Non-English speaking	Under 16 years	16–19 years	20–29 years	30–39 years	40 years and over
U. S. White	767	707	451	1925	1925	...	984	941	1925	...	61	311	716	469	368
U. S. Col.	21	32	68	121	121	...	64	57	121	...	...	2	42	58	19
English	182	149	66	397	273	124	294	103	397	...	1	13	105	114	164
Irish	62	91	106	259	182	77	182	77	259	...	...	4	57	72	126
Scotch	66	43	20	129	91	38	98	31	129	...	...	4	24	47	54
German	56	48	72	176	100	76	147	29	154	22	1	9	42	55	69
Italian	1	2	72	75	9	66	49	26	14	61	...	3	34	24	14
Other Eur. except Slavs	31	25	33	89	41	48	56	33	66	24	...	2	35	30	22
Slovak	45	275	1542	1862	128	1734	1381	481	919	943	...	160	797	615	290
Magyar	12	37	483	532	37	495	375	157	189	343	...	24	224	204	80
Polish	10	39	166	215	20	195	134	81	87	128	...	4	102	68	41
Russian	3	71	271	345	2	343	243	102	103	242	...	15	194	119	17
Lithuanian	7	26	97	130	24	106	72	58	66	64	...	3	56	48	23
Roumanian	1	7	361	369	3	366	209	160	31	338	...	59	146	103	61
Other Slavs	2	4	142	148	3	145	96	52	17	131	1	15	57	52	23
Total	1266	1556	3950	6772	2959	3813	4384	2388	4477	2295	64	628	2631	2078	1371

APPENDIX IV

CLASSIFICATION AND EARNINGS OF EMPLOYES IN THREE REPRESENTATIVE STEEL PLANTS OF THE PITTSBURGH DISTRICT, OCTOBER 1, 1907

128-INCH PLATE MILL

Men Earning Over $3.33 Per Day (i. e., over $20 for six-day week)	Number	Earnings Per Day
Supts., General Foremen, 30"—42"—128" . .	2	$6.05
Heaters	4	7.21
Rollers	2	8.44
Rollers' Assistants	10	4.40
Shearmen	6	5.58
Heaters' Helpers	2	4.09
Markers	12	3.50
Roll Engineers	2	3.37
Crane and Machine Operators	6	4.18

Men Earning $2.50 to $3.33 Per Day (i. e., $15 to $19.99 for six-day week)		
Clerks, Timekeepers and Weighers	18	$2.63
Rollers' Assistants	4	2.83
Shearmen	3	3.13
Shearmen Helpers	38	3.30
Inspectors	7	2.70
Millwrights	6	2.68
Shippers and Checkers	7	2.89

Men Earning $2.00 to $2.49 Per Day (i. e., $12 to $14.99 for six-day week)		
Markers	3	$2.17
Shearmen Helpers	4	2.07
Crane and Machine Operators	10	2.33
Common Labor, Unspecified Positions . . .	20	2.40

Men Earning Under $2.00 Per Day (i. e., under $12 for six-day week)		
Common Labor (16½ cents per hour) . . .	49	$1.82

23-INCH STRUCTURAL MILL

MEN EARNING OVER $3.33 PER DAY (i. e., over $20 for six-day week)	Number	Earnings Per Day
Supts., General Foremen	1	$4.61
Heaters	6	4.98
Rollers	2	7.38
Rollers' Assistants	8	3.83

MEN EARNING $2.50 TO $3.33 PER DAY (i. e., $15 to $19.99 for six-day week)	Number	Earnings Per Day
Foremen	5	$2.80
Clerks, Timekeepers and Weighers	4	2.53
Heaters' Helpers	6	2.99
Hot Sawyer and Push Over	2	2.77
Straighteners	10	2.79
Cold Sawyers	8	2.70
Crane and Machine Operators	4	3.23
Engineers, Stationary	4	2.76
Inspectors	2	2.70

MEN EARNING $2.00 TO $2.49 PER DAY (i. e., $12 to $14.99 for six-day week)	Number	Earnings Per Day
Clerks, Timekeepers and Weighers	4	$2.33
" " " " . . .	4	2.47
Crane and Machine Operators	8	2.16
Checkers	2	2.04

MEN EARNING UNDER $2.00 PER DAY (i. e., under $12 for six-day week)	Number	Earnings Per Day
Common Labor (16½ cents an hour) . . .	50	$1.98
" " Unspecified Positions . .	23	1.65

38-INCH BLOOMING MILL

MEN EARNING OVER $3.33 PER DAY (i. e., over $20 for six-day week)	Number	Earnings Per Day
Rollers	2	$6.47
Heaters	2	6.47
Supts., General Foremen	1	3.65
Foremen	4	3.52
Heaters' Helpers	8	3.77
Shearmen	2	3.77

MEN EARNING $2.50 TO $3.33 PER DAY (i. e., $15 to $19.99 for six-day week)	Number	Earnings Per Day
Clerks, Timekeepers and Weighers	4	$2.67
Rollers' Assistants	4	3.06
Shear Helpers	8	2.58
Inspectors	2	2.70
Engineers, Roll Engine	4	3.04
Crane and Machine Operators	4	3.19
Engineers, Narrow Gauge.	2	2.94
Millwrights	6	2.66

MEN EARNING $2.00 TO $2.49 PER DAY (i. e., $12 to $14.99 for six-day week)		
Clerks, Timekeepers and Weighers	7	$2.48
Engineers, Stationary	2	2.37
Common Labor Unspecified Positions per 100 tons	2	2.16
Crane and Machine Operators	10	2.02

MEN EARNING UNDER $2.00 PER DAY (i. e., under $12 for six-day week)		
Common Labor (16½ cents per hour) . . .	58	$1.98
" " Unspecified Positions . . .	13	1.90

APPENDIX V

AN ACT TO ENABLE BOROUGH COUNCILS TO ESTABLISH BOARDS OF HEALTH. STATE OF PENNSYLVANIA, 1893

Town Council or Burgess shall appoint a Board of Health to consist of five persons.

Section 1. Be it enacted, etc., that it shall be the duty of the President of the town council, or burgess where he is the presiding officer, of every borough in this Commonwealth, within six months after the passage of this Act, to nominate and by and with the consent of the council to appoint a board of health of such borough to consist of five persons not members of the council, one of whom shall be a reputable physician of not less than two years' standing in the practice of his profession. At the first appointment the president of the town council, or burgess where he is the presiding officer, shall designate one of the members to serve for one year, one to serve for two years, one to serve for **Length of term of first appointees.** three years, one to serve for four years and one to serve for five years, and thereafter one member of said board shall be appointed annually to serve for five years. The board shall be appointed by districts to be fixed by the town council, representing **Shall be appointed by districts.** as equally as may be all portions of the borough. The members shall serve without compensation.

Duties, etc., of board, how regulated.

Section 2. The duties, responsibilities, powers and prerogatives of said board shall be identical with those assigned to boards of health of cities of the third class by sections three, four, five, six and seven of article eleven of the Act of May twenty-third, one thousand eight hundred and eighty-nine, entitled "An act providing for the incorporation and government of cities of the third class," which reads as follows, due allowance being made for the difference in the municipal government of cities and boroughs.

Members to be sworn and shall organize annually.

Section 3. The members of the board shall severally take and subscribe the oath prescribed for

218

borough officers, and shall annually organize by the choice of one of their number as president. They shall elect a secretary, who shall keep the minutes of their proceedings and perform such other duties as may be directed by the board, and a health officer who shall execute the orders of the board, and for that purpose the said health officer shall have and exercise the powers and authority of a policeman

Salaries.

of the borough. The secretary and the health officer shall receive such salary as may be fixed by the board, and they shall hold their offices during

Bonds.

the pleasure of the board. They shall severally give bond to the borough in such sums as may be fixed by ordinance for the faithful discharge of their duties, and shall also take and subscribe the oath required by members of the board. All fees which shall be collected or received by the board or by

Fee to be paid into the borough treasury.

any officer thereof in his official capacity, shall be paid over into the borough treasury monthly, together with all penalties which shall be recovered for the violation of any regulation of the board. The

President and secretary shall have power to administer oaths.

president and secretary shall have full power to administer oaths of affirmation in any proceedings or investigation touching upon the regulation of the board, but shall not be entitled to receive any fee therefor.

Powers and duties of board as to infectious diseases.

Section 4. The said board of health shall have power, and it shall be their duty, to make and enforce all needful rules and regulations to prevent the introduction and spread of infectious or contagious diseases, by the regulation of intercourse with infected places, by the arrest, separation and treatment of infected persons, and persons who shall have been exposed to any infectious or contagious disease, and by abating and removing all nuisances which they shall deem prejudicial to public health; to enforce vaccination, to mark infected houses or places, to prescribe rules for the construction and maintenance of house drains, water pipes, soil pipes and cess-pools, and to make all such other regulations as they shall deem necessary for the preserva-

May establish hospitals.

tion of the public health. They shall also have power with the consent of the councils in any case of the prevalence of any contagious or infectious diseases within the borough to establish one or more hospitals and to make provisions and regu-

May appoint district physicians and sanitary agents.

lations for the management of same. The board may in such cases appoint as many ward or district physicians and other sanitary agents as they may deem necessary whose salaries shall be fixed by the

Duties of all practicing physicians.

board before their appointment. It shall be the duty of all physicians practicing in the borough to report to the secretary of said board of health the names and residences of all persons coming under their professional care afflicted with such contagious or infectious diseases, in the manner directed by said board.

Abatement of nuisances.

Section 5. The said board of health shall have power, as a body or by committee, as well as the health officer, together with his subordinates, assistants and workmen, under and by orders of the said board, to enter at any time upon any premises in the borough upon which there is suspected to be any infectious or contagious disease or nuisance detrimental to the public health for the purpose of examining and abating the same; and all written orders for the removal of nuisance issued to the said health officer by order of said board, attested by the secretary, shall be executed by him

Costs and expenses.

and his subordinates and workmen, and the costs and expenses thereof shall be recoverable from the owner or owners of the premises from which the nuisance shall be removed or from any person or persons causing or maintaining the same, in the same manner as debts of like account are now by law collected.

May maintain system of registration of marriages and births and deaths.

Section 6. The said board of health shall have power to create and maintain a complete and accurate system of the registration of all marriages, births and deaths which may occur within the borough and to compel obedience of the same upon the part of all physicians and other medical practitioners, clergymen, magistrates, undertakers, sextons and all other persons from whom information for such purposes may properly be required. The board shall make and cause to be published, all

Board shall publish necessary rules and regulations.

necessary rules and regulations for carrying into effect the powers and functions with which they are hereby invested, which rules and regulations, when approved by the borough council and chief burgess, and when advertised in the same manner as other ordinances, shall have the force of ordinances of the borough, and all penalties for the violation thereof, as well as the expenses necessarily incurred, in carrying the same into effect, shall be recoverable for the use of the borough in the same manner as penalties for the·violation of borough ordinances subject to the like limitations as to the amount thereof.

How penalties, etc., shall be recovered.

Section 7. It shall be the duty of the board of health to submit annually to the council before the commencement of the fiscal year, an estimate of the probable receipts and expenditures of the board during the ensuing year, and the council shall then proceed to make such appropriation thereto as they shall deem necessary; and the said board shall in the month of January of each year submit a report in writing to the council of its operations for the preceding year with the necessary statistics, together with such information or suggestions relative to the sanitary conditions and requirements of the borough as it may deem proper, and the council shall publish the same, in its official Journal. It shall also be the duty of the board to communicate to the State (Board) Commissioner of Health, at least annually notice of its organization and membership, and copies of all its reports and publications, together with such sanitary information as may from time to time be required by said State (Board) Department.

Board shall submit estimate of probable receipts and expenditures.

Council to make appropriation.

Shall submit an annual report.

Communication with State (Board) Commissioner of Health.

Repeal.

Section 8. All acts or parts of acts inconsistent with or contrary to the provisions of this act are hereby repealed.

Approved—The 11th day of May, A. D. 1893.

ROBT. E. PATTISON

APPENDIX VI

REPORT OF THE BOARD OF HEALTH OF THE BOROUGH OF HOMESTEAD FOR THE YEAR ENDING DEC. 31, 1908*

To the President and Members of the Council of the Borough of Homestead.

Gentlemen:—

We submit to your honorable body a report of the work accomplished by your Board during the past year. The Sanitary Work as reviewed in our last report has been carried on as vigorously as at any time in the past, and the work done in this respect will speak for itself in figures compiled for that purpose hereinafter incorporated. Besides taking care of the regular work of our department, we have given no little attention to the milk question. With the help of the Council we have been able to have passed and approved a set of Model Rules and Regulations governing every phase of conditions whereby the town can be kept in a clean and sanitary condition if the same are obeyed, and giving us power to punish the offender if the same are not obeyed. As we have said before, the milk question has been given more attention than has been customary in the past, as this question has become a real live one, and there are not many users of milk in a municipality who ever give the question a thought as to what the conditions and surroundings are at the barns from which they derive their milk supply. There is no commodity that is so susceptible to surrounding conditions and which is so easily contaminated as milk. If barns and their surroundings are not kept in an extraordinary sanitary condition the odors arising from the filth contaminate the milk and make it unwholesome. Your Board has gone into this phase of the question thoroughly and had one of the Inspectors from the State Board investigate every

*For an interesting comment on The Pittsburgh Survey see p. 224.

dairy from which Homestead draws its milk supply and make a written report of each one separately to us, and on an average the majority of the dairies were in a fair condition. A few were above the average and are model dairies, while a few were in a filthy condition and were given the option by your Board of either bringing the same up to the standard within a specified period or cease selling milk within the corporate limits of the Borough. We are pleased to say that there is a steady improvement going on in the few real bad dairies, and we shall not cease our crusade against them until they are up to the standard required by law. We have also had some prosecutions against local dealers for selling adulterated milk, and in all prosecutions disposed of to date, conviction has been secured and the guilty parties fined. This is the worst feature of the milk business we have to contend with. During the summer months formaldehyde, a rank poison, is put in the milk by unscrupulous dealers for the purpose of preserving it, and as a general rule the amount of formaldehyde used for preserving purposes when drank with the milk, will not injure an adult person, but is, without a doubt, fatal to children. This has been demonstrated by our most eminent medical men, and we are determined to continue prosecutions against all violators of the law in this respect. As no human being could conceive of a more dastardly or contemptible piece of work under the guise of modern business methods than this, any contamination of food to be consumed by human beings, and especially that used by infants, should be, and we are determined shall be, prosecuted to the limit of the law. We have made a start in this direction and we shall continue until the law is fully respected in this particular. We have also begun an innovation by requesting the milk dealers to co-operate with us in the thorough cleansing of the milk bottles before refilling, and in this respect we have demanded that they be not allowed to deliver milk in bottles to houses where a contagious or infectious disease has developed, believing that by this method we can prevent, to a certain extent, the spread of these diseases, as milk bottles used in houses, where contagious or infectious diseases have developed, if not thoroughly cleansed, are liable to become contaminated and carry these diseases into other homes. So we believe much good will come from this order if properly lived up to, and if any violators of this order are caught we propose to destroy the bottles in question, as we consider this necessary for the preservation of the good health of the community.

SANITARY CONDITIONS

With respect to the general sanitary conditions of the town we are of the opinion that the work we have accomplished since our last report justifies us in saying that the general conditions are considerably better than they were one year ago. During the first part of the year we requested the co-operation of the public in general to assist us in making the sanitary conditions of the Borough the best in its history by procuring garbage cans that would not leak, and keep the same covered at all times, and to keep all garbage and refuse matter in these cans, and have the same emptied at least once each week, as specified in the Borough Ordinance, and urged them not to throw these substances, so deleterious and dangerous to the public health, around openly in the yard, and in this respect we can say we have reason to compliment the largest portion of our population for complying with this order and co-operating with the Board for the benefit of not only themselves, but for the entire community. While, on the other hand, certain classes of people, as you will find in every community pay no attention whatever to sanitary measures and have to be compelled by our Inspectors to even keep clean the inside of the house in which they live. This condition is unwarranted in a civilized community, but nevertheless true. In some instances to get them to obey the law in this respect we are compelled to resort to prosecution, but we are determined to keep the Borough in a clean, sanitary condition at any cost.

A LITTLE ABOUT THE PITTSBURG SURVEY WITH REGARD TO CONDITIONS IN HOMESTEAD

The conditions portrayed by this Survey had a tendency to exaggerate to a certain degree. It is not our intention to criticize the work done by this Survey or to do anything to interfere in any manner with the good the originators of this Survey expect to accomplish. In what manner they expected to accomplish any good is beyond our comprehension. The mere fact of going into a locality and portraying the conditions existing there, and then producing them in miniature and exhibiting them in large centers of population away from where the actual conditions exist, does not in any way improve the conditions of that particular locality. It has been true ever since the world began that to accomplish or to succeed in any way or in any thing one must work intelligently and industriously, and the only way that we can conceive that conditions can be bettered in the Second Ward, Homestead, is by work such as your Board has been doing, and not by exhibition, as done by the Pittsburg Survey. And then again conditions exhibited by them are not the true conditions as existing today. This survey was taken nearly two years ago, and if you will peruse our last annual report you will perceive that we had undertaken during the year 1907 to disseminate the occupants of overcrowded houses, and an inspection of the locality referred to will reveal the fact as to what extent we have succeeded in relieving the congestion of overcrowded houses. We have been carrying this work along without abatement during the past two years, and we realize even at this time that conditions are not ideal by any means. Yet we have accomplished so much along this line that the real bad conditions found two years ago, are not to be found to-day. Occasionally it is brought to our notice that there is an overcrowded house, and our officers are immediately dispatched with orders to compel the vacation of some of the occupants, and in all cases the orders have been obeyed. It is impossible to prevent the over-crowding of houses, as the occupants can move in while the officers are not in that immediate vicinity. But when we discover such conditions exist we promptly have them remedied. It is hard to keep conditions as they should be in this particular locality, but we can truly say we are doing our best along this line, and we are of the opinion that we are accomplishing something. So, with all due respect to the Pittsburg Survey, we are still of the opinion that conditions found by them to exist in the Second Ward and exhibited by them in the Pittsburg Carnegie Library are not the true conditions as exist in the Second Ward to-day.

THE SPITTING ORDINANCE

In our last report we congratulated Council on the enactment of an ordinance prohibiting spitting on the sidewalks and in public places, and endeavored to demonstrate why such an ordinance should be rigidly enforced for the good of the entire community. Some little work has been done along this line, but not enough to justify the assertion. We are still of the opinion that this is a splendid measure, and believe much good will come from its enforcement. Our greatest authorities on scientific matters have demonstrated and tell us, that germs of disease are communicated from one person to another in this manner, thereby causing a larger majority of communicable diseases than we otherwise would have if this measure was enforced. It is an unsightly thing to observe where people have expectorated all along the sidewalk, and should be stopped, if for no other reason than this. But when the influences for contagion are taken into consideration there should be no hesitancy in a strict enforcement of this ordinance. We therefore recommend that the proper officers be authorized to give this matter their careful attention by enforcing this measure, as we believe the results obtained from such a crusade will justify our confidence in this ordinance from a sanitary point of view.

CONTAGIOUS DISEASES

Jan. 1, 1908, to Jan. 1, 1909

Measles	112
Typhoid Fever	28
Pneumonia	24
Chicken Pox	18
Diphtheria	14
Scarlet Fever	15
Pulmonary Tuberculosis	16
Cerebro-spinal Meningitis	6
Erysipelas	5
Whooping Cough	4
Tetanus	1
Mumps	4
Incipient Tuberculosis	1
Total	248

WORK OF OUR OFFICERS

We especially ask that a careful perusal be given to the work accomplished by our officers during the past year. Our officers have done all the fumigating, as in the previous year, and following is a complete review of the work accomplished, and we will leave it to the opinion of the reader as to whether or not the work done and the results obtained justify the amount expended for this purpose.

Fumigated after the abatement of contagious diseases, 135 rooms; dead animals hauled from off the streets, 111; compelled the cleaning of 2,158 yards; compelled the cleaning of 337 cellars; made owners clean in entirety 89 houses; compelled the putting in a sanitary condition 79 stables; supervised the cleaning of 391 closets; compelled the abandonment of 42 closets; had 55 closets in yards discontinued and placed in the houses instead; compelled the opening of 206 clogged sewers; condemned 3 buildings; tacked up 300 garbage notices; succeeded in installing 78 new garbage cans; visited 56 families in quest of contagious diseases; served 70 notices to principals of schools of contagious diseases existing in families whose children were school pupils; served 494 written notices and 2,125 verbal ones to landlords, agents and tenants to remove garbage and rubbish from premises; compelled the removal of 54 boarders and 25 beds from overcrowded houses; had 7 manure boxes removed from alleys; notified and compelled 31 persons to procure proper receptacles for garbage; served 45 copies of the new Milk Ordinance to milk dealers and 30 copies to milk shippers, and collected for analysis 24 samples of milk from dealers.

Outside of the work enumerated above our officers have given quite a little attention to sanitary conditions relative to proper sewering facilities in the Borough proper and more especially in the Third Ward. Conditions in some parts of this ward were exceedingly bad at the beginning of last year, but with a proper portrayal of conditions by our officers to the Street Committee of Council, we succeeded in having Council remedy the conditions by the extension of sewers to these districts, the result being that we were enabled thereby to make some wonderful improvements along a sanitary line in this ward. Our officers are yet of the opinion that conditions could and should be benefited still farther by the construction of sewers on Maple street and Seventeenth avenue, and we respectfully submit this opinion to the Council for their consideration. As a whole we are of the opinion that our officers have done remarkably well during the past year and we believe a study of the work accomplished will verify and justify our belief along this line. We therefore submit this part of the report to your respectful consideration.

WITH RESPECT TO EPIDEMICS

Measles was our leading contagious disease during the past year which was also true of the previous year. Out of the 112 cases for the entire year 55 of them developed in the month of January, and the large majority of these cases being in the hill district or Third Ward. These cases developed in so close proximity to one another and so fast that they gave your board some little concern, but it was finally gotten under control without the inconvenience of resorting to any measures of a harsh nature. Epidemics of this disease are caused through the carelessness of some person and we desire to ask and persuade all parents to be very careful and not allow their children to mingle with any member of the family or to allow any outsider to come into the house while there is a case of measles in the household. We desire to inform everybody that the majority of people look upon measles as a harmless disease, and in fact they have every reason to do so, as the death rate from measles has been very low in the past. But the continual negligence in the care of patients suffering with measles, by allowing them to come in contact with other people, will result in an epidemic of this disease which will result in a harvest of deaths and compel your Board to institute a quarantine as rigid as in cases of smallpox, thereby inconveniencing the whole community. So for the good of the whole people we ask the co-operation of the entire citizenship of the Borough to appoint themselves a committee to enforce the health regulations with respect to contagious diseases by agreeing to keep all patients afflicted with contagious or infectious diseases isolated in such a manner that it will be impossible for these diseases to spread beyond the house in which it developed. This can be done with very little effort on the part of the people, and by so doing a more healthful condition can be established and much concern and anxiety eliminated for not only your Board but for the entire populace. Let us get together and have co-operation in this respect and ascertain what result can be obtained in the coming year.

ANOTHER WORD TO PHYSICIANS

In our last annual report we gave a short talk to the physicians of the Borough with respect to their negligence in reporting contagious diseases, and when we inserted that paragraph in our last report we did not think it would be necessary for us to again resume this advice one year hence. But we still believe, as we did one year ago, that there has developed and existed quite a number of diseases designated as contagious under the law, that have not been reported as required by the Act of Assembly. The diseases that seem to compare the worse are pneumonia, mumps and whooping cough. There is no physician in the Borough who would care to be accused of being a law breaker, still some of them are doing that very thing every month in the year. The diseases enumerated above are exceedingly prevalent in some seasons of the year, and we ask the physicians to peruse the table appearing in this report and see if it is his opinion that this is the correct number of these diseases existing in the Borough during the past year. We think each one will agree with us that a considerable portion of said diseases have never been reported. And on the other hand the physicians not only owe it to themselves as law abiding citizens, but they owe it more so to the community at large. For in the event of a physician not reporting a very dangerous contagious disease, the Health Board not having knowledge of its existence, some unscrupulous person allows the child infected to enter school. Said action may result in an epidemic of this disease, and death may result. This is not a square deal, gentlemen. You are not doing your duty in the manner provided by law, and you are doing an injustice by so neglecting, to every citizen of this Borough. The law requires that these diseases be reported and provides a penalty for a violation. We warned you a year ago about your neglect in this respect and we again inform you that our advice was not heeded and you have again been negligent.   We have concluded that we are, and have been wasting time and energy in being lenient with you, and if this warning does not result in stricter application to the letter of the law in reporting the diseases therein specified, we have concluded that we will detail an officer on this line of the work and arrest all violators irrespective of who they are.   We did not think when we issued a warning a year ago that it would be necessary for us to institute a threat in order to get the physicians of this Borough to obey the law in this respect, and we feel sorry to have to acknowledge that our confidence was misplaced with regard to this issue.   We are of the opinion that we have come to the point when patience has ceased to be a virtue, and harsher measures must be employed.   The measures agreed upon have been recited previously in this letter.   We therefore would advise that the physicians give this their attention and govern themselves accordingly.

BIRTHS

Born of American parents	360
Born of foreign parents	558
Total	918
Of these were white	877
Of these were black	41
Total	918

BIRTHS SEPARATED ACCORDING TO NATIONALITY OF PARENTS

American	360
Austrian	341
Russian	54
English	33
Irish	26
Italian	25
Polish	22
Slavish	21
German	18
Scotch	10
Roumanian	2
Welsh	2
Arabian	1
Syrian	1
Swede	1
Greek	1
Total	918

A comparison of this table with the one of last year will reveal the fact that identically the same number of children were born as during the previous year, and a comparison of the births and deaths for two years certainly shows that there is no race suicide in Homestead, as we have almost three times as many births as we have deaths.

DEATHS

Jan. 1, 1908, to Jan. 1, 1909

Still-born and premature births	77
Pneumonia	72
Castro-enteritis and Marasmus, Enterocolitis	67
Tuberculosis	28
Nephritis	16
Convulsions	15
Meningitis, now specific	14
Heart Disease	13
Bronchitis	13
Cirrhosis of liver	10
Accidental and Suicide	9
Acute Indigestion	4
Apoplexy	3
Cerebral Hemorrhage	3
Membranous Croup	2
Typhoid Fever	2
Alcoholism	2
La Grippe	2
Puerperal Fever	2
Acute Peritonitis	2
Erysipelas	1
Necrosis	1
Scarlet Fever	1
Asthma	1
Pleurisy	1
Jaundice, Acute	1
Whooping Cough	1
Meningitis, Malignant	1
Paralysis	1
Tonsillitis	1
Progressive Anemia	1
Cholera Morbus	1
Total	368

A comparison with the report of last year shows a decrease in the death rate of 48. In 1907 the total deaths were 416 and in 1908 it was 368, which is very gratifying. In 1907 we had 6 deaths from typhoid fever, in 1908 we had only 2. This is a condition that is almost beyond belief. Two deaths from typhoid fever is certainly a low estimate for a population of 17,000, and we believe bears out our statement that the general sanitary conditions of the Borough have improved considerably. During very prevalent epidemics of measles, such as we experienced last January, many children die of pneumonia, and while no deaths are recorded with measles as the primary cause, still in a large number of cases it was the contributory cause. The same is true of some cases of typhoid fever. Only two deaths are recorded from this disease as the primary cause, yet a few deaths are recorded from pneumonia where typhoid fever was the contributory cause. But even at that we consider we have been fortunate with this disease.

COST AND EXPENSE FOR THE YEAR

Officers' and Secretary's Salaries	$1,730.00
Printing	224.20
Formaldehyde	86.40
Inspecting Dairies	49.84
Hauling Dead Animals	31.50
General Expense	26.00
Supplies	15.93
Freight	1.89
Total	$2,165.76

The cost of carrying on the work of the department is nearly five hundred dollars less than it was for the year 1907. Attention to smallpox cases was a large item in our expense during the previous year. There being no cases of this disease during the past year gave us a saving in this respect. The printing bill is a large item in this year's expense account and we desire this shall be understood. The model rules and regulations adopted by your Board during the past year we had printed in book form and distributed throughout the community, a sort of publicity campaign for the enlightenment and education of the people to the methods employed by your Board for the preservation of the good health of the community, and we believe the literature issued has justified the expense incurred.

Respectfully submitted,

ANDREW HILL, Secretary.

APPENDIX VII

RECORD OF CASUALTIES ON UNPROTECTED GRADE CROSSINGS, HOMESTEAD, 1905–1907*

THE Board of Trade has compiled a record of the grade crossing accidents which have taken place in Homestead from Jan. 1, 1905, up to the present time, which will be used in an effort they propose to put forth to secure safety gates. The record shows that 23 people have met death and 25 have been permanently injured on grade crossings.

Just how to proceed to get safety gates seems hard to determine. Some citizens argue that the borough can compel the railroads to construct safety gates by legislation and some that it cannot, and as there is no state law covering the point there seems to be nothing to go by.

McKeesport has at last forced the railroad companies to come to time simply by passing an ordinance declaring that the safety gates must be constructed at all the crossings by a certain time. When the ordinance was first passed the railroad officials only laughed at it and declared the city could not enforce the ordinance, but when the time for action came and they found the city officials determined, they came around and agreed to put up the gates and the material is now on the grounds ready for construction to begin.

Mayor Coleman, when he was in Homestead Thursday night, said the safety gate ordinance was one of the first ordinances he signed, and while the railroads had demurred and delayed matters as much as possible they were slowly but surely coming to time, and that the gates would be up within a comparatively short time. The mayor, in conversation with a *Daily Messenger* reporter, said:

"The material for the gates is now on the ground and I do

* Reprinted from the *Homestead Daily Messenger*.

not think the railroad companies will delay work much longer. When we first passed the ordinance the railroad people declared they would ignore it altogether, but later on they came around and wanted to compromise. They declared it was unfair to make them put gates up at every crossing and wanted to compromise by agreeing to put gates at the principal crossings but we stood pat and it now looks as if we would win out."

When asked if he thought Homestead could compel the railroad companies to put up gates by legislation, he said he did, and added further, that we would never get safety gates unless the borough officials forced the companies to construct them.

The record of the railroads, in killed and injured, as compiled by the Board of Trade, from January 1, 1905, to the present date, is as follows:

1905

Killed	12
Injured	13
Horses killed	6
Wagons demolished	3

1906

Killed	6
Injured	10
Horses killed	3
Wagons demolished	1

1907

Killed	5
Injured	2
Horses killed	4

P. V. & C., 1905—Persons killed, 8; injured, 9; horses and mules killed, 5.
P. & L. E., 1905—Persons killed, 3; injured, 2; horses killed, 1.
P. V. & C., 1906—Persons killed, 3; injured, 2.
P. & L. E., 1906—Persons killed, 4; injured, 2.

Date and name of those killed and injured. Also newspaper reports of narrow escapes:

1905

John Stahl, Jan. 30, 1905, P. V. & C., injured.
Empire Laundry wagon, Feb. 1, 1905, P. V. & C., two mules killed.
Jos. Peters (Slav), Feb. 7, 1905, P. V. & C., Gold alley, killed.
Jos. Dobrosky, Feb. 7, 1905, Gold alley, P. V. & C., injured.
P. J. Crawford, Mar. 7, 1905, P. V. & C.
John J. Hughes, May 2, 1905, Union, killed.
Walter Hight, May 4, 1905, P. V. & C., not seriously.
Cleveland Prov. Co. of Pittsburgh, May 8, 1905, P. V. & C., horse killed, driver escaped
Lawrence Johnston, May 29, 1905, P. V. & C., Munhall, seriously injured.
M. Bellot (Hun.), June 12, 1905, P. V. & C., Amity street, killed.
Willie Schuette, July 3, 1905, P. & L. E., West Homestead, killed.

John Uhrin, sr., July 12, 1905, P. V. & C., City Farm Lane, killed.
Frank Kovaic, Aug. 3, 1905, P. & L. E., killed.
Mrs. B. McDonough, Aug. 10, 1905, P. & L. E., City Farm Lane, killed.
Jacob Bernstein, Aug. 14, 1905, P. V. & C., Heisel street, seriously injured, horse killed, wagon demolished.
Samuel Walker, Aug. 24, 1905, P. V. & C., McClure street, hurt, horse killed.
Jos. Sinclair, Sept. 5, 1905, P. & L. E., West street, injured, wagon struck.
Eugene Freidman, Sept. 10, 1905, P. V. & C., Ann street, killed.
George Verdo, Sept. 14, 1905, P. & L. E., Heisel street, seriously injured.
John Zahornaski, Sept. 16, 1905, P. V. & C., Fifth avenue, killed.
Mike Metro, Sept. 23, 1905, P. V. & C., Heisel street, struck, injured.
H. F. Botsford & Bro., Oct. 28, 1905, P. & L .E., Amity street, horse killed.
Peter Kilosky, Nov. 1, 1905, P. V. & C., Dickson street, injured, wagon demolished.
Henry Elicker, Nov. 21, 1905, P. V. & C., Amity street, arm cut off.
Jacob Rushe, Nov. 27, 1905, P. V. & C., Dickson street, killed.
S. B. White, Dec. 13, 1905, P. V. & C., Munhall; killed.
Michael Medzyi, Dec. 21, 1905, P. V. & C., McClure street, killed.

1906

Mary Sipas, Jan. 9, P. V. & C., Dickson street, leg cut off.
Three young girls, Feb. 13, P. V. & C., Amity street, narrow escape.
Thomas Roach, Mar. 31, P. & L. E., Heisel street, fatally injured.   Three companions had narrow escape.
Trolley car, Apr. 12, P. & L. E., Amity street, fender taken off.
Three valuable dogs, Apr. 25, P. V. & C., Amity street, killed.
Loaded street car, Apr. 27, P. & L. E., Amity street, narrow escape.
John Milache, May 10, P. &. L. E., West Homestead, seriously hurt.
Street car, May 14, P. & L. E., Amity street, struck.
Frank McCarley, June 13, dragged from McClure to Howard works, P. & L. E., seriously hurt.
Street car, July 16, P. & L. E., Amity street, Motorman H. C. Smith and G. H. Hall, conductor, seriously injured; three passengers cut and bruised.
Joseph Sogat, July 21, P. & L. E., Heisel street, killed instantly, horse killed, wagon wrecked.
W. H. Gould's team, July 24, P. & L. E., Amity street, killed.
Street car, July 30, P. V. & C., Amity street, narrow escape.   Two passengers injured in jumping from car.
Thomas Saunders, July 31, P. V. & C., Hays street, killed.
Bernard Smith, July 31, P. V. & C., killed.
Bolo Kovachy, Aug. 6, P. & L. E., Dickson street, killed.
Repair trolley car, Aug. 16, P. & L. E., Amity street, narrow escape.
John Warko, Aug. 15, P. V. & C., Heisel street, pulled from tracks in time.

1907

John Such, killed at the McClure street crossing of the P. V. & C., Tuesday evening, January 11.
Robert E. O'Connor, killed on Sixth avenue, Thursday, Jan. 10, P. V. & C.
Sunday, Feb. 24, Penn & Shady car struck by fast train at Amity street, 25 lives endangered.
Monday, Feb. 25, Patrick O'Mara killed at Ammon street crossing, P. V. & C.
Tuesday, July 9, John Dryer had one horse killed and another injured at Heisel street crossing, P. V. & C.
Stephen Sweeney and Al. Woodside, killed Sept. 21, at West street.   Two horses killed.
Max Rosen, lost leg at Amity street crossing, Sept. 21.
Clyde Graham, aged 4 years, struck by train.   Badly injured.

APPENDIX VIII

SEVEN-DAY LABOR

ORDERS ISSUED BY UNITED STATES STEEL CORPORATION OFFICIALS RELATIVE TO SUNDAY LABOR

Resolution with regard to Sunday labor passed by the Finance Committee of the United States Steel Corporation at a meeting held on April 23, 1907:

On motion, it was voted to recommend to all subsidiary companies that Sunday labor be reduced to the minimum; that all work (excepting such repair work as cannot be done while operating) be suspended on Sunday at all steel works, rolling mills, shops, quarries and docks; that there shall be no construction work, loading or unloading of materials.

It is understood that it is not at present practicable to apply the recommendation to all Departments, notably the Blast Furnaces, but it is desirable that the spirit of the recommendation be observed to the fullest extent within reason.

Copy of telegram sent to presidents of constituent companies of United States Steel Corporation by Chairman Gary, March 21, 1910:

Mr. Corey, Mr. Dickson and I have lately given much serious thought to the subject-matter of resolution passed by Finance Committee April 23rd, 1907. concerning Sunday or Seventh Day Labor. Mr. Corey has written you on the subject within a day or two. The object of this telegram is to say that all of us expect and insist that hereafter the spirit of the resolution will be observed and carried into effect. There should and must be no unnecessary deviation without first taking up the question with our Finance Committee and asking for a change of the views of the Committee which proabbly will not under any circumstances be secured. I emphasize the fact that there should be at least twenty-four continuous hours interval during each week in the production of ingots.

E. H. GARY.

APPENDIX IX

COST OF LIVING IN PITTSBURGH

A Report of the Committee on Trade and Commerce to the Chamber of Commerce of Pittsburgh on the Comparative Cost of Food and House Rent in Pittsburgh and Other Cities

November 18, 1909

AT a meeting of the Chamber of Commerce on May 13th, 1909, your Committee on Trade and Commerce was instructed to consider the matter of cost of living in the city of Pittsburgh in comparison with other cities similarly located.

Your committee took up the subject assigned to it and had an investigation made, but owing to the adjournment for the summer season occurring immediately upon this matter being placed in the hands of the committee, and the fact that several members of the committee were absent from the first fall session, we were unable to have our report prepared until this time.

In accordance with the instructions, your committee had a list prepared of standard essentials in food stuffs and a representative of the Chamber of Commerce was sent about our city to obtain the retail prices for these articles of food in various districts. Taking the Diamond Market as a center, visits were made in districts diverging in all directions from the established center. It was found that there was a great variation in the prices of these commodities without regard to location and in most cases without any apparent well-founded commercial reason. In some cases we found the prices prevailing at the Diamond Market higher than the same articles were sold at some distance away from this center. It was also observed that in similarly located sections a different range of prices was given, ranging both higher and lower. In fact, there does not seem to be anything approaching a consistent uniformity of prices on food stuffs asked by our mer-

237

chants for the same quality. There was also a tendency in many cases on the part of the merchant, or his representative, to dicker with prices in order to make sale.

After having investigated the conditions in Pittsburgh, a representative of the Chamber visited the cities of Buffalo, Cleveland and Cincinnati, and we hereto attach a copy of the items on which prices were asked with the average price in these cities.

A calculation has been made of the cost at which a family of five persons could be subsisted for a week in any one of the cities under consideration, using a liberal quantity of all the articles of food considered, which is as follows:

Cincinnati	$10.33
Buffalo	10.90
Pittsburgh	11.88
Cleveland	11.81

While this gives a reasonable comparison of cost, it is not probable that any family of five would use the quantities and the same varieties as used in this estimate; the probabilities are that in actual use in each case it would show a less aggregate cost.

Consideration was given to the matter of house rents in the cities named. It is apparent from investigation made that the rents in the city of Pittsburgh and the city of Cincinnati are about the same for like accommodations, while in Buffalo and Cleveland the rents would range slightly less. There are some physical conditions that account for this—the topography of Pittsburgh is very irregular and the many heavy grades with rock formation to contend with make the cost of construction of buildings necessarily higher than in cities located as are Cleveland and Buffalo on almost level territory. Furthermore, in Cleveland and Buffalo the majority of the houses are constructed of wood, while in Pittsburgh a great many of our houses are constructed of more substantial material and necessarily more costly, but more durable and should cost less to maintain. The increased earning capacity of the wage-worker of the Pittsburgh district materially overcomes any such difference that may appear.

A very important factor to be considered in this comparison is the earning power of our people. The national government report of wages earned in Pittsburgh is $574 per annum, in Buffalo $508, Cleveland $522, and Cincinnati $466. Therefore, the average wages earned in Pittsburgh are $52 higher than the highest and $108 higher than the lowest of the cities referred to, which makes a liberal offset on any increase that may appear in the cost of rents.

The cost of provisions in Pittsburgh, as compared with other cities, is so trifling that it is hardly worth considering. In fact, it is apparent to your committee, from the information obtained, that a prudent and careful buyer of the necessities will be able to purchase what is desired on an average, at Pittsburgh, as low as at any of the cities taken in comparison, and the greater earning capacity of our wage-earners makes living in Pittsburgh fully as advantageous as in any of the cities considered, if not superior. This investigation has brought to the knowledge of your committee that the average buyer of food stuffs in Pittsburgh, especially meats, demands a higher standard of quality than in many other locations, which of course has a tendency to increase the cost of living. It might be noted that many of the plainer but substantial articles of food are offered in Pittsburgh at prices equally as low as in any of the places referred to, articles such as Ham, Dried Salt Pork, Pickled Pork, Boiling Beef, Cabbage, Onions, Potatoes, Molasses, Sugar, Dairy Butter, Coffee, and some other items.

Your committee is of the opinion that the matter of our public markets, in which the sale of perishable food stuffs is conducted, should have early attention, and better facilities should be provided to offer such goods to buyers than now exist, both as to improvement of the market buildings we now have, and the establishing of others in suitable locations, so that buyers would have an opportunity of comparison as to quality and prices offered. There is a tendency on the part of the many dealers in these commodities to vary the price on a certain commodity in order to encourage a hesitating buyer, which leads your committee to believe that the less aggressive buyer pays the excessive prices. City ordinances should provide that where food stuffs are offered for sale, especially in market buildings provided by the city, plain figure prices should be displayed thereon, and if a lower price is accepted on any article, that would become the selling price and be so displayed.

Your committee is of the opinion that the frequently made allegations that articles of food stuffs are much higher in Pittsburgh than many other cities are not well-founded. When taken as a whole, it is doubtless true that certain articles at particular times may be purchased in other cities at lower figures than we are accustomed to buying them in Pittsburgh, but as has been indicated in this report, if buyers will be more careful to investigate the quality and to demand fair prices, we feel that our merchants handling these goods are in position to furnish like goods at as low prices as in similarly located communities in this country.

Referring to the matter of fruits and vegetables, we labor under some slight disadvantages in the Pittsburgh District. Adjacent to the cities we are using for comparison and many other of the great cities of our country, are territories that produce fruit and vegetables in large quantities on account of being specially adapted to the growing of such articles. From the fact that the hills and valleys surrounding Pittsburgh have been so bountifully supplied with valuable minerals, oil and gas, the production of these commodities is more profitable to the owners and has driven out agricultural pursuits. This, to some extent, puts us far away from the growing territory, but with all this, the up-to-date facilities for transporting these commodities materially offset the advantages of the close-to-city grown products. There is a lack of interest on the part of many of our wage-earners, as compared with those of other localities and countries, in utilizing small garden plots for the raising of vegetables on their own account. This may appear to be a small matter and not worthy of consideration, but investigation will show, not only in this country, but in many foreign countries, that great results have been obtained for the workers of a small garden plot, the labor being furnished at practically no cost, being done in leisure hours and producing profitable returns for the labor. The work should be encouraged by our employers and land owners and such gardens should receive ample police protection. Encouragement should be given to the workingman to have his own garden plot on which he would doubtless be able to raise all the vegetables required for his family during the growing seasons of this section. This would not only be a saving,

SCHEDULE SHOWING QUANTITY OF FOOD ESTIMATED FOR SUBSISTENCE OF FAMILY OF FIVE PERSONS FOR ONE WEEK

Average price per unit obtained from six different inquiries during July, 1909, in each of the cities compared.

	Pittsburgh			Buffalo		Cleveland		Cincinnati	
Article	*Quantity*	*Av. price per unit*	*Total cost*	*Av. price per unit*	*Total cost*	*Av. price per unit*	*Total cost*	*Av. price per unit*	*Total cost*
Cod Fish	1 lb.	$13\frac{3}{4}$	$13\frac{3}{4}$	14	14	$16\frac{1}{2}$	$16\frac{1}{2}$	12	12
Mackerel	1 lb.	14	14	12	12	10	10	$12\frac{1}{2}$	$12\frac{1}{2}$
Poultry	3 lb.	22	66	20	60	$20\frac{1}{3}$	61	20	60
Bacon	3 lb.	19	57	18	54	$18\frac{1}{2}$	$55\frac{1}{2}$	$18\frac{2}{5}$	$55\frac{1}{5}$
Tenderloin	6 lb.	25	1.50	$19\frac{3}{4}$	$118\frac{1}{2}$	$23\frac{4}{5}$	143	$17\frac{3}{5}$	$105\frac{3}{5}$
Boiling Beef	4 lb.	10	40	$9\frac{4}{5}$	$39\frac{1}{5}$	$10\frac{1}{5}$	$40\frac{4}{5}$	$9\frac{2}{5}$	$37\frac{3}{5}$
Mutton	4 lb.	$17\frac{3}{8}$	$69\frac{1}{2}$	14	56	17	68	$13\frac{3}{5}$	$54\frac{2}{5}$
Pork, pickled	4 lb.	$15\frac{3}{8}$	$61\frac{1}{2}$	$14\frac{2}{3}$	$58\frac{2}{3}$	16	64	$15\frac{3}{5}$	$62\frac{2}{5}$
Ham	7 lb.	16	112	16	112	16	112	$16\frac{2}{5}$	115
Bread	12 lb.	5	60	5	60	5	60	$3\frac{4}{5}$	$45\frac{3}{5}$
Flour	6 lb.	4	24	$3\frac{7}{25}$	20	$3\frac{22}{25}$	23	$3\frac{23}{25}$	24
Lard	1 lb.	$15\frac{9}{10}$	$15\frac{9}{10}$	15	15	$16\frac{1}{4}$	$16\frac{1}{4}$	13	13
Molasses, 1 Qt.	$1\frac{1}{2}$ lb.	10	10	10	10	10	10	10	10
Oat Meal	1 lb.	5	5	5	5	5	5	$4\frac{1}{5}$	$4\frac{1}{5}$
Butter, Creamery	2 lb.	$32\frac{1}{2}$	65	$30\frac{4}{5}$	$61\frac{1}{5}$	$32\frac{2}{5}$	$64\frac{4}{5}$	$31\frac{4}{5}$	$63\frac{3}{5}$
Butter, Oleo.	2 lb.	19	38	21	42	19	38	$18\frac{1}{2}$	37
Eggs	1 lb.	27	27	28	28	30	30	26	26
Cheese, Cream	$\frac{1}{2}$ lb.	$19\frac{2}{5}$	$9\frac{9}{10}$	$19\frac{3}{5}$	$9\frac{4}{5}$	$20\frac{3}{4}$	$10\frac{3}{8}$	$18\frac{4}{5}$	$9\frac{2}{5}$
Beans, Qt.	2 lb.	10	10	10	10	$11\frac{1}{5}$	$11\frac{1}{5}$	$9\frac{2}{5}$	$9\frac{2}{5}$
Prunes	1 lb.	12	12	09	09	10	10	09	09
Rice	1 lb.	09	09	08	08	$08\frac{1}{5}$	$8\frac{1}{5}$	7	7
Potatoes	30 lb.	$1\frac{2}{3}$	50	$1\frac{14}{15}$	58	$2\frac{2}{15}$	64	$1\frac{2}{5}$	42
Cabbage	3 lb.	5	15	$5\frac{4}{5}$	$17\frac{2}{5}$	05	15	05	15
Onions, $\frac{1}{4}$ Pk.	4 lb.	12	12	$10\frac{4}{5}$	$10\frac{4}{5}$	10	10	$11\frac{2}{5}$	$11\frac{2}{5}$
Lettuce, 6 hds.	$1\frac{1}{2}$ lb.	03	18	$02\frac{3}{5}$	$15\frac{3}{5}$	05	30	03	18
Carrots, 2 bun.	$1\frac{1}{2}$ lb.	03	06	$02\frac{3}{5}$	$5\frac{1}{5}$	02	04	$1\frac{2}{3}$	$3\frac{1}{3}$
Tomatoes, 2 Qt.	6 lb.	15	30	10	20	10	20	10	20
Radishes, 2 bun.	1 lb.	03	06	02	04	$02\frac{2}{5}$	$4\frac{4}{5}$	02	04
Beets, 2 bun.	2 lb.	03	06	$02\frac{3}{5}$	$5\frac{1}{5}$	02	04	01	02
Cucumbers, two	1 lb.	05	10	04	08	03	06	02	04
Coffee	3 lb.	$18\frac{5}{8}$	$55\frac{7}{8}$	$17\frac{1}{4}$	$51\frac{3}{4}$	20	60	$16\frac{2}{5}$	$49\frac{1}{5}$
Sugar	5 lb.	$5\frac{7}{8}$	$29\frac{3}{8}$	$5\frac{1}{2}$	$27\frac{1}{2}$	$05\frac{3}{5}$	28	$05\frac{1}{2}$	$27\frac{1}{2}$
Milk, 7 Qts.	$17\frac{1}{2}$ lb.	07	49	07	49	$06\frac{2}{3}$	$46\frac{2}{3}$	08	56
Tea	$\frac{1}{2}$ lb.	$56\frac{5}{9}$	$28\frac{3}{9}$	45	$22\frac{1}{2}$	58	29	51	$25\frac{1}{2}$
Vinegar, $\frac{1}{8}$ Gal.	1 lb.	25	$3\frac{1}{8}$	21	$2\frac{5}{8}$	25	$3\frac{1}{8}$	$21\frac{4}{5}$	$2\frac{3}{4}$
			11.88		10.90		11.81		10.33

but would furnish fresher and better qualities than are ordinarily obtained under the present system by which he is supplied.

Committee on Trade and Commerce

(Signed) ALBERT J. LOGAN, Chairman,
E. A. KITZMILLER, Vice-Chairman,
ROBT. GARLAND,
WM. CAMPBELL,
MARCUS RAUH,
W. A. ROBERTS,
W. L. HIRSCH.

APPENDIX X

RATINGS ON MEN EMPLOYED IN IRON AND STEEL INDUSTRY, BY PRUDENTIAL INSURANCE COMPANY OF AMERICA

[Excerpts from Current Rate Book]

28. *Ratings on Account of Occupation* have been divided into three general classes, and a separate set of premium rates is provided for each class.

The special rating provides for that class whose occupation makes it necessary to charge a slightly higher rate than the regular ordinary rate.

The intermediate rating is the regular Intermediate rate on pages 95 to 97, and covers that class where the occupation is attended by some hazard.

The hazardous rating is higher than the Intermediate rate, and covers all the extra hazardous risks. Age 55 nearest birthday is the highest age for which these rates are quoted.

The special and hazardous tables are found on pages 148 and 149.

Applications for $500 where the occupation is rated will be issued only at Intermediate rates. Applicants belonging in the hazardous class must apply for $1,000 or more.

Where the rating is "Intermediate only," $500 policies, or multiples thereof up to $1,500, will only be issued.

The regular rate charged to all applicants at any given age is the basis, to which an addition is made of an average of $3.20 per $1,000 of insurance for Special rating, $6.39 for Intermediate, and $13.23 for Hazardous rating, in the case of whole life policies. By reference to the following illustration you will be able to determine what the charge would be for any group at the ages stated:

Whole Life Policy—$1,000 Insurance

Age	Regular Rate	Special Rate	Intermediate Rate	Hazardous Rate
20	$14.96	$16.24	$17.52	$25.36
30	19.08	21.34	23.60	31.63
40	26.09	29.90	33.70	40.10
50	38.83	44.79	50.74	54.50

Iron and Steel Industry.

Superintendents and Foremen in all departments not exposed to extreme heat—*No rating.*

Blast Furnace Employes—*Hazardous.*

Puddlers and Cupola Tenders—*Hazardous.*

Heaters and Melters—*Intermediate.*

Rollers and Roll Tenders not exposed to considerable heat—*Special.*

Bessemer Converting Department, except Blowers—*Hazardous.*

Blowers, Bessemer Department—*Special.*

Open Hearth Furnaces—*Hazardous.*

Charging Machine Operators—*Intermediate.*

Crucible Steel Manufacture—*Hazardous.*

243

Tube Mill Employes—*Intermediate.*
Crane and Hoist Men, outdoor—*Special.*
Crane and Hoist Men, indoor—*Intermediate.*
Gas Producers—*Intermediate.*
Ladle Men—*Intermediate.*
Lever Men, not exposed to heat—*Special.*
Lever Men, exposed to considerable heat—*Intermediate.*
Shear Men, not exposed to heat—*Special.*
Shear Men, exposed to considerable heat—*Intermediate.*
Molders, pit and floor—*Intermediate.*
Molders, bench—*No rating.*
All other employees exposed to considerable heat—*Hazardous.*
All other employees exposed to moderate heat—*Intermediate.*
All other employees not exposed to heat—*Special.*

APPENDIX XI

CARNEGIE RELIEF FUND

Extract from Letter of Mr. Andrew Carnegie Relative to Relief Fund.

NEW YORK, N. Y., March 12, 1901.

To the President and Board of Directors,
The Carnegie Company,
Pittsburgh, Pa.

GENTLEMEN:—Mr. Robert A. Franks, my cashier, will hand over to you, upon your acceptance of the trust, Four Million Dollars ($4,000,000) of The Carnegie Company bonds, in trust for the following purposes:

The income of the Four Million Dollars ($4,000,000) is to be applied:

1st. To provide for employees of The Carnegie Company, in all its works, mines, railways, shops, etc., injured in its service, and for those dependent upon such employees as are killed.

2nd. To provide small pensions or aids to such employees as after long and creditable service, through exceptional circumstances, need such help in their old age, and who make a good use of it.

3rd. This fund is not intended to be used as a substitute for what the Company has been in the habit of doing in such cases—far from it—it is intended to go still further and give to the injured or their families, or to employees who are needy in old age, through no fault of their own, some provision against want as long as needed, or until young children can become self-supporting.

4th. A report is to be made at the end of each year, giving an account of the fund and its distribution, and published in two papers in Pittsburgh, and copies posted freely at the several works, that every employee may know what is being done. Publicity in this matter will, I am sure, have a beneficial effect.

5th. I make this first use of surplus wealth upon retiring from business as an acknowledgement of the deep debt which I owe to the workmen who have contributed so greatly to my success.

(Signed)   ANDREW CARNEGIE.

NOTE.—On April 1st, 1903, The Carnegie Company was succeeded by Carnegie Steel Company.

ACCEPTANCE OF TRUST

Extract from minutes of meeting of the Board of Directors of The Carnegie Company held at the offices of this Company, Pittsburgh, Pa., on March 20th, 1901.

"WHEREAS, Mr. Andrew Carnegie has generously offered to this Company Four Million Dollars ($4,000,000) in bonds of The Carnegie Company, to be held in trust and the income therefrom applied to the purposes set forth in his letter of March 12th, 1901, provided this Company accept the trust; therefore.

"*Resolved,* That the Board of Directors of The Carnegie Company hereby accepts the trust, so tendered by Mr. Carnegie, and agrees to hold said bonds in trust, and to apply the income therefrom to the purposes and in accordance with the terms and conditions set forth in his letter of March 12th, 1901:

"*Resolved,* Further, That the Secretary is directed to communicate this action of the Board to Mr. Carnegie, accompanied with a copy of these resolutions, expressing our deep appreciation for his munificent gift for the welfare of the employees of this Company, and reciprocating the kindly expressions of his personal interest in those with whom he has been so long associated, though no words can adequately express our feelings of love, loyalty, admiration, and inspiration, which have been so much a part of our service for him."

GENERAL NOTICE

Mr. Andrew Carnegie having munificently tendered to the Board of Directors of The Carnegie Company, Four Million Dollars ($4,000,000), the income therefrom to be applied, as set forth in his letter of March 12th, 1901, in the establishment of a Relief Fund, and the trust having been accepted by the said Board of Directors, as recited in the foregoing paragraphs, the "Andrew Carnegie Relief Fund" was created for the purpose of carrying out the intent of Mr. Carnegie's benefaction, and became effective January 1st, 1902.

On January 1st, 1905, the name of the Fund was changed to Carnegie Relief Fund.

Employees of Carnegie Steel Company and its constituent Companies, as given below, will participate in this Fund in accordance with the prescribed Regulations:

Carnegie Steel Company.
Carnegie Natural Gas Company.
Pittsburgh Limestone Company, Limited.
H. C. Frick Coke Company.
Oliver Iron Mining Company.
Bessemer & Lake Erie Railroad Company.
Union Railroad Company.
Pittsburgh Steamship Company.
Pittsburgh & Conneaut Dock Company.
Union Supply Company.
Mingo Coal Company.
National Mining Company.

NOTICE

On May 14th, 1906, (after the printing of this edition of the Regulations), a body known as the "Board of Trustees of Carnegie Relief and Library Fund," appointed by the Court of Common Pleas, No. 2, of Allegheny County, Pennsylvania, succeeded the Board of Directors of Carnegie Steel Company as trustees of the Carnegie Relief Fund. The Board of Trustees of Carnegie Relief and Library Fund adopted, by resolution, the Regulations governing the Carnegie Relief Fund as they had been adopted by the Board of Directors of Carnegie Steel Company and as they appear in the following pages, and appointed the same persons to be members of the Advisory Board as named on the opposite page.

Wherever in these Regulations, therefore, the terms "President of Carnegie Steel Company" and "Board of Directors of Carnegie Steel Company" appear, they will be understood to mean "President of Board of Trustees of Carnegie Relief and Library Fund" and "Board of Trustees of Carnegie Relief and Library Fund," respectively.

246

DATA AS TO BENEFICIARIES OF CARNEGIE RELIEF FUND AMONG EMPLOYEES OF HOMESTEAD WORKS

(a) Total payments on account of the deaths of employees of Homestead Works from January 1, 1902, to December 31, 1909, inclusive $74,230.00

Total death benefit payments to beneficiaries residing in Europe, and in the United States in places other than Homestead 24,700.00

Total death benefit payments to beneficiaries residing in Homestead $49,530.00

(b) Total death benefit payments in 1907 paid to account of Homestead Works $11,398.00

Total death benefit payments in 1907 to beneficiaries residing outside of Homestead 5,000.00

Total death benefit payments to beneficiaries residing in Homestead $6,398.00

(c) New cases of accidental injuries at Homestead Works reported in 1907 3

(d) Accident benefits paid to account of 3 cases reported in 1907 . . . . $623.00

(e) Number of families in Homestead to whom Accident Benefits were paid in 1907 . . . . 6 amount $2,218.95

Number of families outside Homestead to whom Accident Benefits were paid in 1907 . . . . 1 " 365.00

$2,583.95

Number of families in Homestead to whom Death Benefits were paid in 1907 . . . . . 30 " $6,398.00

Number of families outside Homestead to whom Death Benefits were paid in 1907 . . . 8 ¨ 5,000.00

$11,398.00

Number of families in Homestead to whom Pension Allowances were paid in 1907 . . . . 21 $2,286.10

Number of families outside Homestead to whom Pension Allowances were paid in 1907 . . . 15 ¨ 2,470.10

$4,756.20

Total Accident Benefits paid to account of Homestead Works $79,759.91

Total Death Benefits paid to account of Homestead Works 74,230.00

Total Pension Allowances paid to account of Homestead Works . . . 30,540.75

$184,530.66

PENSIONERS, CARNEGIE RELIEF FUND, HOMESTEAD, 1907

Case Number	Works	Last Occupation	Age at Retirement	Length of Service	Average Earnings	Monthly Allowance
1	Homestead Works	Janitor	75 years	23 years	$40.50	$9.30
2	" "	Laborer	64 "	15 "	37.75	5.65
3	" "	"	72 "	19 "	37.30	7.10
4	" "	"	60 "	20 "	54.60	10.90
5	" "	Sta. Engr.	60 "	23 "	66.43	15.25
6	" "	Laborer	64 "	18 "	46.28	8.35
7	" "	"	61 "	18 "	40.80	7.35
8	" "	"	69 "	21 "	38.35	8.05
9	" "	"	69 "	20 "	38.07	7.60
10	" "	"	63 "	24 "	62.69	15.05
11	" "	Clerk	70 "	18 "	73.60	13.25
12	" "	1st Pitman	51 "	21 "	70.22	14.75
13	" "	Heater	61 "	17 "	71.86	12.20
14	" "	Blacksmith	52 "	21 "	81.72	17.15
15	" "	Toolman	63 "	17 "	71.00	12.00
16	" "	Laborer	57 "	21 "	34.58	7.25
17	" "	"	66 "	26 "	60.50	15.75
18	" "	"	66 "	22 "	40.00	8.80
19	" "	"	70 "	21 "	41.08	8.65
20	" "	"	63 "	27 "	36.42	9.85
21	Duquesne Works	Blacksmith	61 "	25 "	72.07	18.00

APPENDIX XII

ACCIDENT RELIEF PLAN OF THE UNITED STATES STEEL CORPORATION*
MAY 1, 1910

THE United States Steel Corporation has announced a plan for relief of men injured and the families of men killed in work accidents. The plan is a distinct advance over any existing system of relief carried out under any of the constituent companies; it puts all the employes of the biggest payroll in America—225,000 men—on the same footing, and it establishes a system which can be adjusted to the new legislation that will probably be enacted in the next ten years in the different states in which the corporation operates.

In more ways than one, then, the new plan, which will go into effect May 1 for an experimental year, is a step in advance. The exact provisions are published below. While some of them do not measure up to the proposals made by the various state commissions which have been considering the subject, many of them are a radical departure from contemporary practice, and as a voluntary act show both foresight and liberality. The plan disregards the idea of negligence entirely and may be said to recognize that a share of the income loss due to work-accidents should be a charge on the industry; it covers hazardous and non-dangerous employments alike; it puts the entire cost of the plan on the business without any contribution whatsoever from the men. No relief will be paid if suit is brought. It naturally requires a release from legal liability upon payment of the relief, but it avoids the involved and questionable relationships created by such relief associations as, for instance, the Pennsylvania Railroad Relief Department, to which, like a mutual insurance association, the

* Reprinted from *The Survey*, April 23, 1910.

employes pay dues, and from which they can receive no benefits from their dues until they sign a paper releasing the company from any legal liability.

The Steel Corporation makes a point in its announcement that the payments it proposes are "for relief and not as compensation." "There can be no real compensation for permanent injuries, and the notion of compensation is necessarily based on legal liability, which is entirely disregarded in this plan as all men are to receive the relief, even though there be no legal liability to pay them anything. . . ." In line with this position, there are no death benefits for single men and extremely low disability benefits for them. Large numbers of immigrant laborers fall in this class. Moreover, in death cases the wording of paragraph 24 specifies that relief will be granted "married men living with their families." This would exclude the non-resident families of aliens unless the manager of the relief sees fit to exercise his discretionary power in their favor. But it is understood that wide latitude has been left the company managers in cases where single men have old people or others demonstrably dependent upon them. The death benefit for a married man is eighteen months' wages, and this is increased ten per cent for every child under sixteen; an adjustment of relief to need which is noteworthy. The plan includes medical and hospital treatment. It is a statement of a consistent policy which will give the man who goes to his work in the morning a fair knowledge as to what will happen in case he is killed. Much of the ill name of claim departments in all industries in years past has been due to the incentive to claim agents to "make a good showing" by keeping down awards. Here definite standards are set.

The most serious question raised by a first reading of the prospectus of the plan is as to the sufficiency of the benefits provided. In comparison with the three years' wages, which is the death benefit under the English system, and the four years' wages proposed by the New York State Commission, the Steel Corporation announces eighteen months' wages for a married man in case of death. By a sliding scale this is increased with an increased number of children and with length of service in the company. Yet the family of an employe of ten years' standing with five children would still get but two and one-half years' wages. If such a man were temporarily disabled, however, he would get eighty-five per cent of his weekly wages as against the flat rate of fifty per cent for all disabled men under the New York bill. The highest injury benefit specified in the Steel Corporation's announcement is for the loss of an arm—eighteen months' wages. The highest benefit for permanent disability under the proposed New York state law is half wages for eight years; that under the English law is half wages for life. But here again the discretion of the company managers enters in, and in the case of loss of both limbs or other more complete permanent disability, larger amounts would doubtless be paid. At several important points, therefore, the plan is flexible and results will be dependent upon the spirit in which the company managers carry out its provisions. It would be impossible to forecast these practical workings of the plan until after it has had at least the year's trial and until detailed statements are available as to the nature of injuries and actual benefits paid. The minimum provisions for death in the case of married men are in themselves higher than were the average benefits paid by any large employer in the steel district the year of the Pittsburgh Survey.

Nor is it likely that the Steel Corporation will know either the cost of the new policy or its acceptability to its employes earlier than after such a probationary year. The Corporation has been able in the past to settle most cases out of court, yet the new plan may effect economies in gathering legal evidence, etc. Such a large plan of relief would scarcely have been attempted were it not for the energetic measures to lessen accidents which have been carried out in the plants of the constituent companies during the last two years. From the managers' standpoint, the plan has merit in its probable attraction to the men—a considerable point in keeping intact a non-union working force. From the public standpoint it is widely significant that the operating corporation, which has probably the largest accident experience in America upon which to base its plan, and which has spent a million dollars a year on accident payments in the past, should adopt a plan which it describes as "similar in principle to the German and other foreign laws and to recommendations which have been made by employers' liability commissions in New York and other states since our work upon this plan was begun (December, 1908)."

The plan was put into operation tentatively by the National Tube Company last December. A further plan for the payment of pensions to disabled and superannuated employes is under consideration.

Following is the plan in full:

ACCIDENT RELIEF

1. This plan of relief is a purely voluntary provision made by the company for the benefit of employes injured and the families of employes killed in the service of the company and constitutes no contract and confers no right of action. The entire amount of money required to carry out the plan will be provided by the company with no contribution whatsoever from the employes.

2. Where the word "manager" appears in this plan of relief it means that official of the company who has charge of this relief for his company.

3. The decision of the manager of this relief shall be final with respect to all questions arising under this plan of relief, and he shall have full discretionary power in paying relief to meet any conditions which may arise and may not be covered by this statement.

4. The privilege of this relief will take effect as soon as an employe enters the service of the company, will continue so long as the plan remains in operation during such service, and will terminate when he leaves the service.

5. Payment of this relief will be made only for disablement which has been caused solely by accidents to employes during and in direct and proper connection with the performance of duties to which the employes are assigned in the service of the company, or which they are directed to perform by proper authority, or from accidents which occur in voluntarily protecting the company's property or interests. Relief will not be paid unless investigation of the causes and circumstances of the injury show that it was accidentally inflicted and that it renders the employe unable to perform his duties in the service of the company or in any other occupation.

6. No relief will be paid for the first ten days of disablement nor for a period longer than fifty-two weeks.

7. No employe will be entitled to receive relief except for the time during which the surgeon certifies that he is unable to follow his usual or any other occupation.

8. Employes will not be entitled to receive disablement relief for any time for which wages are paid them.

9. The company will provide treatment by surgeons and hospitals of its selection.

10. The company will furnish artificial limbs and trusses in cases where these are needed.

11. All men injured in the service of the company must obey the surgeon's instructions in reporting for examination, using the remedies and following the

treatment prescribed, and going to the hospital if directed. No relief will be paid unless these instructions are obeyed. All employes who are disabled but not confined to the house must report in person at the surgeon's office, from time to time, as reasonably requested, and must keep any other appointments made by the surgeon.

12. All employes who wish, while disabled, to go away from their usual place of residence, must first arrange with their employing officer and with the surgeon in charge as to the absence and the evidence of continued disablement to be furnished. Such employes must report as often and in such manner as may be required of them.

13. No relief will be paid to any employe or his family if suit is brought against the company. In no case whatsoever will the company deal with an attorney or with anyone except the injured man or some member of his family in the matter of relief to be paid under this plan, because it is part of the plan that the whole amount paid shall be received by the employe and his family.

14. No relief will be paid for injuries caused or contributed to by the intoxication of the employe injured or his use of stimulants or narcotics or his taking part in any illegal or immoral acts.

15. All employes of the company who accept and receive any of this relief will be required to sign a release to the company.

TEMPORARY DISABLEMENT

16. Under the terms and conditions stated here, employes shall be entitled to the following temporary disablement relief (but no relief will be paid for the first ten days nor for longer than fifty-two weeks, as stated in paragraph six):

Single Men: Single men who have been five years or less in the service of the company shall receive thirty-five per cent of the daily wages they were receiving at the time of the accident. Single men of more than five years' service shall receive an additional two per cent for each year of service over five years. But in no case shall single men receive more than $1.50 per day.

Married Men: Married men living with their families who have been in the service of the company five years or less shall receive fifty per cent of the daily wages they were receiving at the time of the accident. For each additional year of service above five years two per cent shall be added to the relief. For each child under sixteen years five per cent shall be added to the relief. But in no case shall this relief exceed two dollars per day for married men.

PERMANENT DISABLEMENT

17. The amount of relief which will be paid to employes who have sustained some permanent disablement, such as the loss of an arm or leg, will depend upon the extent to which such disablement renders it difficult for them to obtain employment. The kinds of disablement that may occur and the extent to which each interferes with employment differ so greatly that it is impossible to provide any adequate schedule of relief which will be paid in all cases of permanent disablement. The amounts which will be paid in cases not specifically mentioned here must of

necessity be left to the discretion of the manager; but it is the intention of the company that this discretion shall be so exercised in all cases as to afford substantial relief corresponding as far as possible with the amounts stated below, considering the special circumstances of each case and the character and extent of the injury.

(a) For the loss of a hand, twelve months' wages.

(b) For the loss of arm, eighteen months' wages.

(c) For the loss of a foot, nine months' wages.

(d) For the loss of a leg, twelve months' wages.

(e) For the loss of one eye, six months' wages.

DEATH

18. Relief for the families of employes killed in accidents which happen in the work of the company will be paid only where the death of the employe is shown to have resulted from an accident (or sunstroke or heat exhaustion) in the work of the company during and in direct and proper connection with the performance of duties to which the employe had been assigned in the service of the company or which he had been directed to perform by proper authority, or from accidents which occur in voluntarily protecting the company's property or interests.

19. Death relief will be paid as soon as possible after the required proof of cause of death is obtained and a satisfactory release given.

20. The company will pay reasonable funeral expenses, not to exceed $100.

21. No relief will be paid for death caused or contributed to by the intoxication of the employe killed or his use of stimulants or narcotics or his taking part in any illegal or immoral acts.

22. No relief will be paid to the family of any employe if suit is brought against the company.

23. In no case will this relief be paid until the receipt by the company of a satisfactory release properly executed.

24. Under the terms and conditions stated here, the widows and children of the employes killed in accidents which happen in the work of the company shall be entitled to the following death relief:

In the case of married men living with their families, who have been in the service of the company five (5) years or less and leave widows or children under sixteen (16) years of age, the company will pay relief to an amount equal to eighteen months' wages of the deceased employe. For each additional year of service above five years, three per cent shall be added to this relief. For each child under sixteen (16) years, ten per cent shall be added to this relief.

But in no case shall this death relief exceed three thousand dollars ($3,000.00).

26. This plan of relief will be in operation for only one year from May 1, 1910. If the plan meets with success, it is hoped that some similar plan may be put in operation for succeeding years.

APPENDIX XIII

THE CARNEGIE LIBRARY, HOMESTEAD

By W. F. STEVENS, Librarian

THE Carnegie Library of Homestead was founded and endowed by Andrew Carnegie in 1898. The steel mills that contributed most toward Mr. Carnegie's experience and success as an iron-master were located at Homestead, Braddock and Duquesne, Pennsylvania. To show his good will toward the people who had worked with him during the more aggressive period of his career as a manufacturer, he conceived the idea of giving them an institution that would contribute toward the essential needs of all the people all the time. The composite nature of the mill town libraries is well outlined in Mr. Carnegie's dedicatory address as quoted in the following form in the Homestead Library reports:

THE PURPOSE

The three natures in the make-up of every human being that must be developed in order that the Divine purpose may be realized, are the mental, moral and physical. In founding this institution Mr. Carnegie discerned these necessities and provided a building and funds to accomplish this end.

THE LIBRARY

"The library filled with the most precious legacy the past can bequeath to the present—a collection of good books."

To educate the people of this community by—
Supplying readable literature to the masses of the people.
Making provision for the student.
Encouraging societies formed for self culture.
Supplementing the work of the public schools.

THE CLUB

"How a man spends his time at work may be taken for granted, but how he spends his hours of recreation is really the key of his progress in all the virtues."

To provide a place where one may occupy his time—
In systematic physical development.
In amateur athletics.
In healthful games and profitable intercourse.

EDUCATIONAL

"Here you will have your educational classes. In music you have a great field."

To conduct classes
Where students may be directed in their studies by competent instructors.

MUSIC HALL

"Here you will have your entertainments and meetings for educational and philanthropic purposes."

To contribute toward the ethical and moral spirit of the community by providing a meeting place for—
Free musicales and entertainments.
A suitable hall for public gatherings.

"The best return to the giver is to make a proper and steady use of all which is sought here to place within their reach."

Mr. Carnegie's first library gift was to Braddock, Pennsylvania, in 1889. The library at Duquesne was opened in 1904. These three libraries were endowed by the founder with one million dollars, which produces an income of fifty thousand dollars annually. The preference in the distribution of this income is based upon the age of the respective institutions. The care of this fund is in the hands of a board of trustees composed of officials of the Carnegie Steel Company. The disposition of the income is by the separate boards of directors of the three different libraries. These boards are selected mostly from the officials and employes in the mills. The board of directors of the Homestead library is composed of Azor R. Hunt, general superintendent of the Homestead Steel Works, Allan A. Corey, assistant general superintendent,

Ralph W. Watson, second assistant general superintendent, Isaac L. Irwin, chief clerk of the Homestead Steel Works, John Bell, metallurgist, Thomas R. Davies, superintendent of re-heating furnaces, Rev. John J. Bullion, pastor St. Mary's Roman Catholic Church, and Rev. Nathan D. Hynson, pastor First Presbyterian Church.

The old catechetical idea that the chief end of man was to "glorify God and to enjoy Him forever" is not at variance with the idea that the purpose of life is to enjoy all that is good and beautiful. To accomplish this great end we are given intellects to guide us, bodies to execute the will of the mind, and a moral nature to guard both. To develop these three functions is the purpose of educational institutions, religious organizations, the exercise of daily life, and the directed physical culture of athletic associations and physical development. The founder of this institution did not aim to duplicate the work of the organizations that have this same motive, but to supplement them.

How well our own library has contributed toward the general good of the community may be seen from these figures relating to its usefulness for 1909:

In the library the circulation of books was 245,800. This is equivalent to circulating the total of 37,000 volumes in the library 8.5 times, or 10 books for every man, woman and child in this community, or 21 volumes for every reader. Of this circulation 77,500 was at the adult desk; 51,600 at the juvenile desk; 116,600 in the schools, 90,000 of which is supplementary reading; the remaining 26,600 at stations located in the schools throughout the township. The total attendance was 133,700.

The athletic department reports an average membership of 1,170 per month or 3,705 different members for the year. This, in all probability, places the Homestead Carnegie Library Club in the lead among organizations of its kind in western Pennsylvania. The total attendance was 97,750. The gymnasium shows an attendance of 21,000 by 1,043 members in classes. Basket ball holds its own with 30 teams with a membership of 270. There are at least ten teams not belonging to the club, making a total of 40 teams credited to this community. While basket ball seems very prominent, it is conducted as a secondary exercise. The classes

17   257

that occupy first place are those for men, women, misses, girls, boys, with special classes for working boys. There are also special classes in wrestling, fencing and boxing, and many hours each week are given to individual work. Seventy-three physical examinations were given. The man, girl and boy that shows the best physical progress is given a valuable prize. Prizes were given in different branches of athletics amounting in value to over $250. There were 1,838 games bowled in the alleys. Eight teams contested in the league games.

The natatorium includes a swimming pool with a capacity of 100,000 gallons, 20 bath tubs and 8 showers. Swimming classes are conducted for boys, girls and women. Out of a membership of 864 boys, fully 700 have been taught to swim. If the old adage that "cleanlinesss is next to godliness" be true, then it must be admitted that the natatorium does a righteous business. The total number of baths was 69,570. This is 19 baths for each member for the year or one bath every three weeks; so there is still room for improvement. In the billiard and pool room 60,000 games were played at no extra expense to the members.

The music hall was used more than ever before in a single year, the total attendance being 31,600. The several musical organizations give free concerts from time to time. We are taught to believe that Heaven is full of music; then, who can estimate the good coming from these numerous concerts that have lifted many for the time being above the cares and sorrows of this mundane sphere.

Besides the concerts by the several musical organizations, the library organist gives free recitals that are well attended. The music hall is used also for the high school commencements and plays, memorials, minstrel shows by local organizations, dramas, and lecture course. A course of lectures was given after the manner of the university extension lectures by professors from the Carnegie Technical Schools. There were thirteen lectures with an attendance of 900. The use of the hall is granted free to all religious, patriotic, literary and musical events at which no admission is charged. Other affairs pay a nominal rate of $15 to $25, including the use of the organ, piano and the services of the ushers.

Balcony and Entrance, Carnegie Library, Homestead

The value of the library in meeting the needs of the people is no better shown than in the educational department.

Knowledge is of two kinds, the kind you know and the kind you know where to find. The teacher's duty is to lead the scholar in search of the former, and the librarian's office to conduct the reader in search of the latter. The ultimate aim is the same; hence the work of the teacher and librarian go hand in hand. If it is proper for the library to furnish books for the people, it is right that they should be good books. If the library has the right to control the character of the reading, it has a right to direct the reader to the desired information which supplements the work of the teacher. The educational department is but the outgrowth of this idea. As the work in this instance must necessarily be limited, it is confined largely to studies of practical use to the students in their daily work.

In what are designated as scientific and literary classes, during this season there were 187 students. The attendance was 2,887. There were in all 55 students enrolled in the mechanical drawing class. The attendance was 1,136. Eighteen of these pupils attended 75 per cent of the possible sessions. In the common branch class, where grammar, arithmetic, spelling and history were taught, the enrollment was 54 and the attendance 790. In the higher branch class, where trigonometry, geometry, algebra, physics, higher arithmetic, and beginning Latin were taught, the enrollment was 23 and attendance 293. The metallurgy class consisted of ten lectures by steel works officials. The class for foreigners had an enrollment of 24, and an attendance of 386. Twenty-one students were enrolled in the penmanship class, which had an attendance of 230.

The interest in the musical department is equally gratifying. The band has a membership of 35 with an attendance for the year of 1,500. Free concerts were given in the Music Hall with an attendance of 2,100. Many more concerts were given in the band stand in the park in front of the library to audiences of equal size. The Junior Orchestra has had during the winter an enrollment of 31 and an attendance of 673. This orchestra has given free concerts with an attendance of 1,750. The Symphony Orchestra composed of 25 members did excellent advance work and contributed its share toward entertaining the public. The Children's Chorus with a membership of 125 and an attendance of 1,300 closes its season with a grand concert. The Mandolin and Guitar Club with 25 members is credited with its share of success. The Male Chorus, which is composed of 30 members, is an attraction at home and has won honors abroad at the national eisteddfods.

The total enrollment in all classes was 388, with an attendance of 6,437.

The total attendance in the four departments of the library was 274,300, an average gain of 17.5 per cent.

USE OF THE LIBRARY BY FOREIGNERS

Homestead has a population of 25,000, forty per cent of which may be classified as foreign. The foreigners are attracted to this community by the Homestead steel works, which employ 10,000 men, one-half of whom are foreign born. The Carnegie Library aims to benefit this population, intellectually, physically, and morally. For this purpose the privileges of library, night school, athletic club, and music hall are granted to all classes of people alike; hence, it may be said that no special work is conducted in the interest of the foreigners. This class of citizens is, however, reached in more ways than one.

In the library a collection of Lithuanian books is provided for the Lithuanians, the male portion of whom compose a large part of the laboring class in the mills. This collection was loaned to a society of the Lithuanian church and was conducted as a station for some time and with some degree of success.

A collection of books by Catholic authors is very well used. It is, however, difficult to determine what percentage of the readers might be classed as foreigners. A catalogue of this collection was distributed in the parochial schools. Other collections in French, German, and Italian are used freely. The assistant librarian speaks these languages and is instrumental in creating and maintaining interest in the books. A station is conducted by a mission in the "foreign" ward. This collection is composed largely of well-worn books that are not expected to be returned.

It can hardly be expected that the library will have a marked influence on the "grown ups" among the foreigners, but the influence over the children is most gratifying. In certain cases where the families were visited it was ascertained that the fathers and mothers listened eagerly to their children as they read aloud from the library books. This fact is interesting and becomes a hopeful sign when it is known that these children read mostly fairy tales, religious books, such as the life of Christ in one syllable, and United States history. It is safe to say that the reading of fiction by foreign children is less than the average.

In the night school classes are conducted for the foreigners where they may learn English and the common branches. The talent in this class is so varied that most of the instruction has to be individual. One of the students is forty years of age and when he began did not know his a b c's. In three months he could read as well as a second grade pupil in the public schools. By the side of the forty-year-old pupil sat an orphan boy ten years old who was adopted by a poor widow. The boy delivered milk during the day and attended night school two nights each week. Some of the students come year after year; others drop out in a few weeks. This is the experience with one-half of the night school students. Two years ago the class for foreigners was composed almost entirely of Transylvanians. In their own language they were well educated, and they came to the library for the English only. However contradictory it may seem, our best teachers for foreigners speak only the English language.

In the public and parochial schools, the library is able to benefit the foreigners by furnishing supplementary reading. In the second ward, the primary room may begin the term with fifty pupils, not half a dozen of whom can speak English. By the time these pupils are in the second grade they are reading library books at least two days each week. They are taught that it is a privilege to use the library books. The theory is that the text-book is of use in teaching the mechanics of reading; that is, in teaching how to read. The supplementary reading is encouraged because it is interesting first, and instructive second. It is usually much easier reading than the text-book; hence, is read without the usual effort in pronunciation. It frequently happens that a pupil will tell his brothers or sisters about the library book he is reading in school, and the brother or sister forthwith goes to the library for the book. When a set of books is ordered for the schools, extra copies of the same books are ordered for the children's room. Small libraries of about 25 volumes each are loaned to the principals in the several wards and 300 to the high school. Small libraries of 200 volumes each, as well as supplementary reading sets, are furnished the village and country schools throughout the township. The books sent to the country schools in the mining districts are those discarded by the library, and this is their final mission.

Out of a total circulation of 246,000 last year, 75,000 are credited to foreign readers, which indicates that about one-third of the foreigners use the library books. The male foreigners receive further benefits from the athletic department, where they pay one dollar for three months for the use of the billiard room, game room, gymnasium, swimming pool, and bowling alleys. Out of a membership of 3,700 last year, 1,200 were foreigners, mostly Slavs. What seems to be a most hopeful indication is that these men and boys make the most use of the baths. Out of 70,000 baths taken last year, fully 23,000 were taken by foreigners at a cost of three and one-half cents per bath. The city furnishes the water—cheerfully.

Out of a total attendance of 32,000 in the Music Hall, at least 5,000 may be credited to the foreigners who come to enjoy the free organ recitals, band and orchestra concerts, and choruses. Two of the plays given by local talent were by foreigners. The children's librarian told stories to the school children to an attendance aggregating 6,000. The library conducted at the children's playground has its share of influence upon the foreign children. Out of a total attendance of 275,000 in all departments connected with the library, it is probable that 90,000 were foreigners.

TECHNOLOGICAL USE OF THE HOMESTEAD LIBRARY

The technology department is composed of approximately 3,000 volumes. The use during the past year amounted to 7,500. The use of periodicals would make this, in all, 10,000. This usefulness has been encouraged by the semi-annual bulletin in which is printed a list of books on special subjects. The mill books come in for their share of publicity. Quantities of these bulletins are sent to the numerous offices through the mills as well as to the general offices.

Several years past an annotated list of "mill books for mill men" was issued with marked success as to its results. The local paper prints freely any lists that are furnished by the library. The most satisfactory selection is made by the readers who come to the library and select books for themselves. The open shelves make it convenient for the reader to find a book that is "just as good" when he fails to find the one he wants.

A well-known author said he did not care what the critics said about his books, but he did care what the people said to each other. The same principle is true in the use of technical books. When Campbell's Iron and Steel was reissued a few years ago it became necessary for us to add fifteen copies, and that did not fully satisfy the demand. This occurred not because of any special effort on the part of the library but because of personal testimony of the readers themselves.

In the case of employes of the Mesta Machine Company, the books are taken to the men by conducting a small library of 200 volumes in their reading room. Many of these books are on the subjects of iron, steel, founding and machinery. This like all other stations is renewed upon request. The collection at the C. M. Schwab Industrial School is composed of 200 volumes on mechanical drawing, carpentry, blacksmithing and domestic economy, and shows an annual use of nearly 1,000.

Out of 27 study and literary clubs, only one gave all its time to the study of mill subjects. It was composed of 15 young men and known as the Iron and Steel Club. The Superintendents' Club is not classed as a literary club, but it is a fact that most of the discussions are on iron and steel subjects, which because of their current nature require a marked amount of periodical reading of a technical character.

The educational department enrolled last year 388 students, 187 of whom were in scientific classes. During the past five years there have been not less than 325 men in this department who were studying technical subjects and reading technical books on such subjects as physics, chemistry, metallurgy and mechanical drawing. During the same period a single correspondence school claims 900 students in this community. If this be true, there are in Homestead probably not less than 1,500 users of technical books. This is equal to one-half of the technical employes in the mills.

The athletic department has no doubt the effect of attracting men to the books in the library. The Music Hall with an attendance of 31,000 likewise brings people to the library. The extent to which these two departments influence the use of technical literature is not known.

The close proximity of the libraries in the Monongahela Valley to the Carnegie Library of Pittsburgh makes it futile to build up large collections in technical literature. When the case is important, the readers in Homestead are almost invariably referred to this library for literature that is final on the subject.

STUDY AND LITERARY CLUBS

The first club in Homestead was the Woman's Club, which was organized in 1897. This club includes thirty-five members. The subjects from year to year have been broad and comprehensive. For the past few years, Shakespeare, Norway and Sweden, Egypt, Famous Women, together with various modern topics, have been the objects of discussion. For two years the children's playground work was conducted and sustained by this club.

The Outlook Club is composed of business and professional men. The subjects discussed are miscellaneous in their character. Some of the subjects for the past year were: "Gain as an incentive to progress," "Everyday psychology," "Justice in taxation," "The function of government," "Poe's place in literature," "If I had a million dollars," "The Panama Canal," "The Jewish Nation," "Child Labor," "Robert Burns," and "The spirit of speculation." The Outlook Club, like most of these clubs, is entertained by its members. The lunch is usually composed of three items, but the topics for this social period are without number. The membership is limited to 15.

The Thursday Night Study Club was organized in 1902 and is composed of 25 teachers. In the beginning the membership was limited to 15, but the demand for admittance was so great that the membership was increased to 25. For six successive years this club has studied Shakespeare. The Prytaneum Club is composed of the wives of business and professional men. The programs have included "Italy," "American topics," "Ancient History" and miscellaneous topics. This club has 15 members.

The Principals' Association is composed of the principals of the several ward schools and the teachers in art, music, domestic economy, commercial and manual training. The topics used in this association are, for the most part, literary and pedagogical. The Teachers' Association is similar in its character. Its membership consists of the grade teachers and their papers are on subjects relating to their profession. Speakers of national reputation are invited to address these two associations when they hold joint sessions.

The Platonian Literary Society with 70 members is virtually the Munhall high school. The value of the literary society cannot be overestimated. The majority of the members in study clubs were at some time identified with a school literary society. The Munhall Teachers' Study Club consists of the teachers in the school of the borough of Munhall. The topics discussed are literary and pedagogical. The Monongahela Valley Library Association is composed of the librarians in Braddock, Homestead, Duquesne, and McKeesport. The programs are mostly professional and literary. Five out of a membership of 25 live in Homestead.

The Thebian is a literary society conducted at Lincoln Place, about three miles from Homestead. The Excelsior Class is a Sunday-school class that devotes certain evenings to literary work. This plan not only benefits the members intellectually but helps to solve the problem of retaining the Sunday-school membership of young people from thirteen to eighteen years of age. Although the Thebians are in Lincoln Place and the Excelsiors in Munhall, the distance does not prevent them from locking horns in debate. The West Homestead Teachers' Club studies the reading designated by the county superintendent. The programs are interspersed with current event topics. In four of the Homestead ward schools literary societies are conducted in the seventh and eighth grades.

Two organizations that are closely allied to the study clubs are the Men's Association of the First Presbyterian Church with 100 members and the Wesleyan Brotherhood of the First M. E. Church with 50 members. The literary work of these organizations is conducted on the lecture plan, and consists of addresses on historical, literary and religious subjects.

The Homeville Literary Society has a membership of 50. The Philakalon is the name of the society of young ladies in the Homestead high school. The membership numbers 15. The subjects are current topics and self culture. The Lincoln Place Teachers' Club, with a membership of seven, discusses literary and pedagogical subjects. The Brilliant Circle of Whitaker is composed of ladies who discuss current topics.

In all there are 22 literary and study clubs with a membership of 787. Not all the clubs that have been organized have lived. Some ceased because their purpose had been accomplished; others disbanded "because"—and that is all the reason a woman needs to give. The Woman's Improvement Club, the Steel Club, the Gwal, the Chautauqua Circle, the Criterion Club, the Ancient History Club, the Atheneum Club and the Audubon Society are in this class.

These literary clubs are unified in the United Literary Clubs of Homestead and vicinity. This organization was formed in 1902 for the purposes of (1) interchange of experience, (2) obtaining the stimulus derived from the assemblage of a large number of people having the same purpose, (3) stimulating the ethical and literary spirit of the community, (4) forming new clubs. The annual function of this organization has attracted a thousand of the club members and their friends. The best talent that can be secured is obtained for these occasions. The first annual meeting was held in the smallest church in town and now the meetings must be held in the Carnegie Music Hall.

The Carnegie Library aims to take a helpful interest in the club spirit of this community. The books that may be of service to any club with a program made out for the year are placed on a shelf in "club corner" where they may be consulted or selected for home use. In the case of the Audubon Society a list of books and magazine articles was printed for free distribution. The

A YEAR'S USE, COMPARATIVE STATISTICS FOR 1908 AND 1909

Departments	1908	1909	Gain	Loss
LIBRARY				
Inventory	33,961	36,942	2,981	..
Accessions	3,753	4,220	467	..
Withdrawn	944	1,239	295	..
CIRCULATION	235,247	245,831	10,584	..
Adult Desk	77,774	77,512	..	262
Juvenile Desk . . .	49,575	51,665	1,090	..
Schools	78,058	90,195	12,137	..
Stations	29,840	26,459	..	3,381
PERCENTAGE OF FICTION. .	53	51	..	2
ATTENDANCE	131,869	133,700	1,821	..
Adult	79,111	80,500	1,389	..
Juvenile	52,768	53,200	432	..
READERS.	11,000	11,500	500	..
READING ROOM USE . . .	93,000	97,500	4,500	..
EDUCATION—Attendance .	5,900	7,126	1,226	8
Scientific	2,895	2,887	..	..
Musical	2,561	3,550	989	..
Number Students . . .	364	388	24	..
STUDY CLUBS	25	27	2	..
Membership	750	800	50	..
THE CLUB				
MEMBERSHIP. Av. Monthly .	994	1,179	185	..
Employees	374	424	50	..
Non-Employees . . .	262	291	29	..
Boys.	224	285	61	..
Girls	55	99	44	..
Ladies	79	80	1	..
Different Members . .	2,732	3,705	973	..
ATTENDANCE	89,042	97,754	8,712	..
Gymnasium . . .	19,721	21,013	1,292	..
Gymnasium Members . .	950	1,043	93	..
Natatorium	55,356	69,569	14,213	..
BOWLING GAMES . . .	2,216	1,832	..	384
MUSIC HALL				
Events	22	34	12	..
Attendance	13,370	31,625	18,255	..
Attendance—Grand Totals .	240,390	274,350	33,960	..
Percentage of Gain . . .	12.4	17.5	5.1	..

percentage of fiction circulated is 51. Before these clubs were organized the percentage of fiction was 63.

While figures are considered conclusive, they do not always tell all the story. The value of the clubs to the individuals, to society, to the public schools, and to the library would make a book if it could be written. To accomplish this general good through organized reading is what the United Literary Clubs aim to do.

A CATECHETICAL CONCLUSION

What points are most essential in comparing the usefulness of libraries?

1. Volumes per capita. Because it indicates that the library has or has not enough books.

2. The percentage of readers per population. Because it indicates that the library is or is not covering its field.

3. The per capita circulation. Because it indicates that the readers are or are not making sufficient use of the books.

4. Percentage of fiction read. Because it indicates, in a measure, the quality of reading done.

5. The cost of circulating each volume. Because it indicates that the funds are or are not being used economically.

How many volumes should our library have?

According to the average of ten well-known libraries one volume per capita is sufficient. We have 37,000 volumes and about 30,000 population in that part of Mifflin Township which we supply with books to a greater or less degree. This is 1.2 volumes per capita.

How many readers ought our library have?

If the average is a criterion we should have 7,510 readers or 25 per cent of our population. The fact is we have 11,500 readers or 38 per cent of our population.

How well are these readers using the library?

Each reader draws on an average of 22 volumes. This is 7 more than the average. Out of 22 volumes drawn by each reader only 51 per cent is fiction. Since the fiction is of the best, it does not count much against the quality of reading. The average percentage of fiction read in libraries is 63.

Is it costing us more to get our books read than it does other cities?

It costs us 5 cents to get a book read. This is 7 cents less than the average.

How does our club compare with other similar organizations?

By comparing our club with the average of 450 similar organizations, our operating expenses are $2,400 less; our membership is 459 more; our attendance is the same; we have 215 more in the gymnasium; and we have 26 more organized teams.

How does our educational work compare with other similar work?

By comparing the same as in the athletic club, we have three more teachers, 205 more scholars, and a per capita expense of $3.00 less.

The Pittsburgh *Gazette-Times* considers the annual report of Homestead Carnegie Library of sufficient importance for a very complimentary editorial notice.

"Special significance attaches to the eleventh annual report of the Homestead Carnegie library. It is generally believed that an industrial community must be intellectually stagnant, and also that a large admixture of foreign element in the population acts as a drawback upon the so-called 'higher life.' So far as this higher life is made up of bridge whist and new thought, there may be truth in the general belief; but, judging by such indices of social and mental activity as the Homestead library affords, neither the presence of aliens nor preoccupation with material interests interferes with the most gratifying progress. In fact, comparison with other communities and similar institutions gives rise to the suspicion that these factors promote instead of hamper the 'higher life.'

"The Homestead library contains 37,000 volumes and serves a community of about 30,000. Over 77,000 volumes were circulated at the adult desk last year among 11,500 readers. The total circulation in all departments was 246,000, an increase of 11,000 over the previous year. Most significant of all is the percentage of fiction read, which is only 51, being 14 per cent lower than the average library. The report tells of 27 literary and study clubs in the community with a membership of about 800, while the Carnegie Library club listed 3,705 members in the course of the year.

It should be understood that the Homestead library is largely institutional, with swimming pools and billiard tables, brass bands, and evening classes to supplement the books upon the shelves.

"Librarian Stevens is to be congratulated upon the excellent showing of his 'plant.' But Homestead is even more to be congratulated upon the excellent use made of its opportunities to upset the theory that an industrial community is necessarily unintellectual and materialistic."

The library management and the good people of Homestead appreciate the recognition of the advancement the citizens here are making intellectually and trust the wider circulation of the fact will have a good influence on "benighted" industrial communities.

APPENDIX XIV

SLAVIC ORGANIZATIONS IN HOMESTEAD

Patriotic Statement by a Slav

A CLERKLY Slav, who had lived in Homestead for some years, put down the following in answer to some questions about the fraternal organizations of his own people.* It was his expressed wish to write his answers rather than to "speak them," saying of them:

Please excuse me, if I have done in this my letter some grammatical or linguistical errors. I can work in six languages, but in the English I am working seldom. I have learnt the English language mostly from books, and have had very small opportunity to go deeper into this most beautyfull American language. If I can not write and speak it as Milton or Shakespeare, You must excuse me. It is sometime no good, to take from good to much. And this is true with the knowledge of to much languages. One You are neglecting for the other. But as You see please, I am not neglecting very much the beautyfull language of my adopted American country.

His letter, despite its quaint formalism, breathes a spirit toward America which it would be sheer wantonness to mar by attempting to edit out his phrases. It is worth printing here for itself:

There are in Homestead following:—not foreign but decidedly American, non-english, indigenous, public organizations of the Slavic race, respectively of the Slovak nation.

1. National Slovak Society In the United States and Canada, 37,000 members. Slovak organization.
2. Roman Catholic Slovak Union in the United States and Canada, 36,000 members. Slovak organization.
3. Greek Catholic Union called Sojedinenje, all over the United States and Canada, 22,000 members. Slovak organization.
4. Greek Catholic Union called Sojur, in the United States and Canada, 8,000 members. Russian organization.

* For a thoroughly interesting and exhaustive interpretation of organized social life among the Slavs, and their assimilation in this country, the reader is referred to Our Slavic Fellow Citizens by Emily Greene Balch, recently issued by Charities Publication Committee, New York.

5. Greek Catholic Union, called Obscestvo, in the United States and Canada, 5,000 members. Russian organization.

6. Roman and Greek Catholic Union of Pennsylvania, in the United States and Canada, 8,000 members. Slovak organization.

7. Slovak Evangelical Lutheran Union, in the United States and Canada, 6,000 members. Slovak organization.

How many members have these organizations in the town of Homestead, Pa., separately, I cannot state, and this statement if I would or could do it could not be correct, because all these organizations have in Homestead, 1, 2, 3, 4, branches called assemblys and from these some have 200–400 members, but there are such, which have 50–60 members only.

The accounting of the membership of the Assemblys cannot be made correctly, because the members are migrating every month from one place to another, from one town to another, searching for work and occupation. There-fore in the account of the membership of Assemblys is sometime big difference every year, every month and every week.

These organizations are paying death benefits from $600.00 to $1,000,000. Accident benefits from $100.00 to $400.00 and benefits in sickness from $5.00 to $7.00 weekly. Every member of these organizations does pay monthly dues from 80 cents to $1.30. These dues are changing in their amount nearly monthly according to how many expenses are there in the organization, and how many deaths, accidents and sickness occur. These organizations are mostly organizations of men, but in some, as in all the Greek Catholic Unions, are included women too, which are organized in separate assemblys belonging to their respective organizations.

The Slavic race has separate women organizations too; and these, mostly are by the Slovaks, these:

1. Slovak National Women's Union called "Jivena" in the United States and Canada, with active membership of nearly 8,000.

2. Slovak Roman Catholic Women's Union in the United States and Canada with active membership of nearly 10,000 women and girls.

3. The Roman and Greek Catholic Women Union of Pennsylvania in the United States and Canada a membership of 3,000 women and girls.

"There are Young Men Associations in the United States and Canada.

1. Roman Catholic Young Mens Association with nearly 4,000 members. This organization is a branch of the big "Roman Catholic Slovak Union."

2. Greek Catholic Young Men Association with nearly 1,500 members. This organization is a branch of the Greek Catholic Union called Sojedinenije.

There is the "Gymnastical Slovak Union" called Sokol in the United States and Canada, with a membership of 5,000 young men. Independent of any organization.

Besides these American, Slovak Organizations, there are in Homestead and all over the United States more organizations of Polish, Russian, Croation, Chech, Servian, Bulgariass, nationality but regarding these I can state only, that these nationalities of the Slav race have very strong and rich organizations.

The organization of the Lituanian nationality are in number 4 or 5 and these must be reckoned to the Slav race, too, because the Lituanians are only a branch of the very big Slav race, and they are one of the Slav nations.

I have there stated the membership of the organizations a little higher, because I know that until your book will be ready, the organizations will have nearly the same number of members, which I state here. This does occur irrevocably, because the immigration of all these nations to this most glorious our American Republic, to the United States, is just now enormous and it will be in a short time more stronger.

The Slav race, and without exception all the Slav nationalities are the most and sincere patriotic people of our great Republic, the United States, because they have found there all that of which they have been robbed in their old countries. They have found in United States personal and common liberty, free and independent civilization, wellfare and all that which the aborigines of the English and other races have there found themselves. Therefore the Slavic races is the most zealous supporter of all the state and social institutions. Because this way, the Slavs are interested in the material and moral development and evolution of this country, they are supporting every time that political party, which does seem to them the most honest, moral, and virtuous party. Because now the Republican party and the whole United States under the most honest, circumspect and glorious leadership of our most beloved president Mr. Theodore Roosevelt are enjoying, just in the latest years, a degree of evolution in every respect, naturally the Slav are mostly Republicans and are following the steps which president Roosevelt does designate. Very small amount of the Slavs is democratic. Socialist are some may be 1000–2000, may be a little more, *but not a single Anarchist.* The Anarchists are mostly Russian Jews.

"There are in Homestead and vicinity plenty of English speaking Slavs, and if you want, you can go to whichever finer

Slav or Slovak home and personally ask regarding the cost of living. But you must have somebody with you from the Slavs or Slovaks themselves, who is among them good, versatilic and known as their priminent or honest man or woman. If you have not done this, you cannot get some information and not the smallest, because the people are every time secluded and reserved in their giving of information to one, whom they do not know, who he or she is.

I can state only that, that this step from you would be of no use, because our people is living in every respect as the American English people is living, except that the Slavs are liking to eat dumples with fine cheese of their country and disregard the eating of half cooked or baked english beafsteak. The yearly costs of living are by the Slavs the same as by the English people which is varying according the degrees of wellfare of the family. From my experience I state that a family of working people now in the United States does need yearly $600–$800 for support and from this can save very very small amount or nothing.

Our people the Slavs are not holding or registering accounts regarding their income or expenses. This does not do nobody from the poorer classes in the whole world, except in some very rich and very popular families. Some European rich Barons, Counts, and Princes are doing this, but not a single from the poorer class. If there is one or two cases that is exception only.

The Greek Catholic Union is doing the same, what are doing the all other Slav or Slovak organizations. This is enlightening the people and members in every respect on the true principals of the christian civilization. To develop from the members the most true, honest, moral, citizens of the United States, and therefore, the members are compelled to become citizens of the United States to help each other in the case of death, accidents or sickness. To support the United States and their christian civilization in every possible regard. To develop their own civilization by the means of cultivation of their own the English American, but not English European language? To reach this purpose not only the Greek Catholic Union, but all the Slav organizations and all the Slav race have spent millions of dollars to build christian schools and churches which are standing now in every part of the United States where there are living the Slavs. There will be built more.

In Homestead the Greek Catholic Union called Sojedinenije has two Assemblys, of men with 260 and 130 members, respective subscribers, and one Assembly of women with 60 members or subscribers. The official organ is the weekly Amerikansky Russky Viertnik but I must there make the observation that because this weekly is the property of the whole organization, the members are supporting this weekly themselves and for this purpose are paying monthly 8 cents for the paper into the treasury of the organization and for this reason the members of the organizations cannot be considered as subscribers, but as proprietors of the paper. In the right sense of word they are not subscribers, but proprietors of the paper. Subscribers we have not very much but supporters or proprietors of the paper there are as many as how many members there are in the organization; that is just now 20,500 in round numbers, but in some three or four months there will be over 22,000.

Some Observation: The organizations of the Slavic race are not foreign organizations but indigenous, because the organizations are chartered by the American, United States authorities, courts and governmental delegations, and to these organizations are belonging adopted citizens of United States, mostly, or such individuals who in short time would be citizens.

Adopted, naturalized citizens of United States is not a foreigner, whatever language he does speak. A English speaking Canadian, or a subject of the European United English Kingdom, if not naturalized, is more foreigner in the United States, as a naturalized and only slightly English speaking, Slav or German.

To know to read and write is not a sign of civilization, but the manner and habits, the moral degree of a individual. One who is good educated, but is a scoundrel, rascal or wrong doer, is not a civilized or at least wrongly civilized and educated individual. One who is good educated and is a human beast, is more dangerous to the humanity as a Bengal tiger, and for this reason cannot be called civilized individual.

The national civilization of the Slavs is the same christian civilization as that of the English race, because the source of both is the same, Jesus Christ, the distinction exist only in some national traits and habits.

No one nation does exist which has not some black sheep. In every nation are fine and good men and women, but in every nation there are some bad men.

The science of sociology has the commencement in the marriage then in the family, then in the tribe then does spread in the nation, then in the race and finally in the whole humanity.

Sociology is a very young science and is very different from "Cultural History" which is a young science too.

The first cultivator of the true and right science of sociology was Jesus Christ, the true fundamental ideas of sociology are in the Holy Bible.

Every science must be based on christian philosophy, because the most true philosophy are the revelations of God, and the source of every science is God, because every true wisdom does come directly from God.

If a science is not in harmony with the laws of morality and the laws of God and of nature, such science is not science but fraud and prostitution of reason and human soul.

It is impossible for me to supply you with the data of all the organizations of the Slavic race, because to get this data, I would be compelled to work diligently for months and give myself in connection with every Slav organization and with every Assembly, with every president or officer of the organizations and Assemblys.

If you are sometime writing regarding the Slavs, never do you forget that the Slavs have been every time and are until today the most brave and gallant, heroic defenders of the western European civilization and of all the Western European nations. If there is not Slav blood, and if there have not been the Slav heroes in Eastern Europe, the civilization of the Western European Nations, the French, German, English national civilizations would have been crashed under the hard blows of Tartarism, Mohammedanism and Mongolism. The newest example of this truth is the most eloquent Russo-Japanese war.

APPENDIX XV

POPULATION OF HOMESTEAD AND MUNHALL, 1910

The United States census of 1910 gives Homestead borough a population of 18,713, as against 12,554 in 1900, and 7911 in 1890. The population of Munhall is given as 5185.

INDEX

INDEX

279

57; wages of skilled and unskilled, (Table) 40; weekly wage of, (Table) 38. See also general tables and Appendix II

Negroes—
Expenditures of, for food, 70, (Tables) 44, 68, 69, 72; expenditures of, for fuel, insurance, and other items, (Table) 44; expenditures of, for rent, (Tables) 44, 50, 52; expenditures per week by, (Table) 44; infant mortality among, (Table) 146; owning homes, (Table) 57; social position of, 14; wages of skilled and unskilled, (Table) 40; weekly wage of, (Table) 38. See also general tables and Appendix II

New York Central System, 29

Newspapers—
Attitude of, toward mill, 88, 176; expenditures for, during depression of 1907–08, (Table) 98

Nickelodeons. See *Amusements*

Nurses—
No school, 120; no visiting, 87

Nutrition Investigation, Report on—
By Frank P. Underhill, Ph. D., 70, 71, 141

Odd Fellows, 115

Officers—
Mill, formerly workmen, 177

Offices—
Women in, 125

Order of Elks, 113

Ordinance—
Borough, regulating sanitary conditions, 25; affecting railroads ineffective, 29. See also *Housing ordinances; Sanitary ordinances*

Other expenditures: The budget as a whole, 81–106. See also *Sundries*

Overcrowding—
Absence of specific regulation concerning, 25; decreases with higher wages, 52, 53; effect of, on Slavic children, 145, 146, 147; in Slavic

families, 136, 137, 138, 139, 140, 143, 144; number of persons per room in 21 courts—Families which took lodgers compared with families which did not, (Table) 144. See also *Congestion*

Parents—
Interest of, in school, 118, 119, 120; ambition for daughters, 127, 128; ambition for sons, 126, 127, 128

Parlor. See *"Front Room"*

Pay Friday, 37

Pennsylvania Act—
To enable borough councils to establish, Appendix V, 218

Pennsylvania lines, 29

Pensions—
Fund set aside by United States Steel Corporation to provide, 95, Appendix XII, 249

Philanthropic movements—
Attitude of workmen toward, 178

Pinkertons—
In strike of 1892, 9

Pittsburgh—
Cost of living in, Appendix IX, 237; water supply, 24

Pittsburgh and Lake Erie tracks, 29

Pittsburgh, Virginia and Charleston tracks, 29

Playgrounds—
School, 120, 121

Poles. See *Slavs*

Political divisions. See *Borough divisions*

Political situation, 22, 23

Politics—
Among Slavs, 165, 166

Population—
Congestion of, 46, 47; congestion of, among Slavs, 135, 136, 137; effect of transient, on civic efficiency, 15;

THE SURVEY

SOCIAL   CHARITABLE   CIVIC

A JOURNAL OF CONSTRUCTIVE PHILANTHROPY

THE SURVEY is a weekly magazine for all those who believe that progress in this country hinges on social service: that legislation, city government, the care of the unfortunate, the cure of the sick, the education of children, the work of men and the homes of women, must pass muster in their relation to the common welfare.

As Critic, THE SURVEY examines conditions of life and labor, and points where they fail: how long hours, low pay, insanitary housing, disease, intemperance, indiscriminate charity, and lack of recreation, break down character and efficiency.

As Student, THE SURVEY examines immigration, industry, congestion, unemployment, to furnish a solid basis of fact for intelligent and permanent betterment.

As Program, THE SURVEY stands for Prevention: *Prevention of Poverty* through wider opportunity and adequate charity; *Prevention of Disease* through long-range systems of sanitation, of hospitals and sanatoriums, of good homes, pure food and water, a chance for play out-of-doors; *Prevention of Crime*, through fair laws, juvenile courts, real reformatories, indeterminate sentence, segregation, discipline and probation; *Prevention of Inefficiency*, both industrial and civic, through practice in democracy, restriction of child labor, fair hours, fair wages, enough leisure for reading and recreation, compulsory school laws and schools that fit for life and labor, for the earning of income and for rational spending.

EDWARD T. DEVINE - - - EDITOR

GRAHAM TAYLOR - - ASSOCIATE EDITOR

105 EAST 22D
STREET
NEW YORK

$2.^{00} YEARLY

RUSSELL SAGE FOUNDATION PUBLICATIONS

THE PITTSBURGH SURVEY

The most significant piece of investigation the country has seen.
—"American Magazine."

The findings of the Pittsburgh Survey are to be published in six volumes during 1910, under the editorial direction of Paul U. Kellogg, Director of the Pittsburgh Survey. Four of these books are now ready:

WOMEN AND THE TRADES
By ELIZABETH BEARDSLEY BUTLER
Former Secretary of the Consumers' League of New Jersey

The first general survey of the occupations open to wage-earning women in an American city.

8vo, 440 pages; 40 full-page illustrations of women at their work, by Lewis W. Hine. **Price, Postpaid, $1.72**

WORK-ACCIDENTS AND THE LAW
By CRYSTAL EASTMAN
Attorney-at-Law; Secretary New York State Industrial Accident Commission

During the year studied, five hundred industrial wage-earners were killed at their work in Allegheny County, Pa. The story of their hazards is dramatic and compelling.

8vo, 350 pages; 38 full-page illustrations by Lewis W. Hine, Joseph Stella, and others. **Price, Postpaid, $1.71**

HOMESTEAD: THE HOUSEHOLDS OF A MILL TOWN
By MARGARET F. BYINGTON
Assistant Secretary, Charity Organization Department, Russell Sage Foundation

A clearly drawn picture of the home and community life of the steel workers.

8vo, 310 pages; 41 full-page illustrations by Lewis W. Hine, Joseph Stella and others. **Price, Postpaid, $1.70**

THE STEEL WORKERS
By JOHN A. FITCH
Formerly Expert, New York Department of Labor

A study of the men who make steel by one who lived among them.

8vo, 350 pages; 39 full-page illustrations by Lewis W. Hine, Joseph Stella and others. **Price, Postpaid, $1.71**

The entire set of the Pittsburgh Survey volumes, to be issued at $1.50 net each, will be as follows:

THE PITTSBURGH DISTRICT—Symposium by John R. Commons, Florence Kelley, Robert A. Woods, Peter Roberts, Charles Mulford Robinson and others.
THE STEEL WORKERS—John A. Fitch.
HOMESTEAD: THE HOUSEHOLDS OF A MILL TOWN—Margaret F. Byington.
WOMEN AND THE TRADES—Elizabeth Beardsley Butler.
WORK-ACCIDENTS AND THE LAW—Crystal Eastman.
PITTSBURGH: THE GIST OF THE SURVEY—Paul U. Kellogg.

CHARITIES PUBLICATION COMMITTEE
105 East 22d Street, New York

RUSSELL SAGE FOUNDATION PUBLICATIONS

MEDICAL INSPECTION OF SCHOOLS

By LUTHER HALSEY GULICK, M.D., AND LEONARD P. AYRES, Ph.D.

THE first American work on a subject of the utmost importance to educators, physicians, parents, social workers and boards of education.

The only source of information as to what medical inspection is and does, its history, its status, and the means and methods employed.

An important contribution to the cause of education.—*Journal of Education.*

Lucidly exhaustive and admirably arranged, the monograph will assist in the great work, scarcely begun, of supplying the sound body that is needed for the sound mind.—*The Nation.*

(Third Edition)
286 PAGES; 6 CHARTS; 64 FORMS; 31 TABLES. Price, Postpaid, $1.00

LAGGARDS IN OUR SCHOOLS

A STUDY OF RETARDATION AND ELIMINATION IN CITY SCHOOL SYSTEMS

By LEONARD P. AYRES, Ph.D.

FORMERLY GENERAL SUPERINTENDENT OF SCHOOLS FOR PORTO RICO AND CHIEF OF THE DIVISION OF STATISTICS OF THE INSULAR DEPARTMENT OF EDUCATION; SECRETARY OF THE BACKWARD CHILDREN INVESTIGATION OF THE RUSSELL SAGE FOUNDATION; CO-AUTHOR OF MEDICAL INSPECTION OF SCHOOLS, ETC.

A SIXTH of all the children in American city school systems are repeating grades, at an expense to the taxpayers of $27,000,000; large foreign populations do not produce the highest percentage of this "retardation"; physical defects account for only 9 per cent of it; irregular attendance is one of the largest factors; the child who starts youngest makes slowest progress, but stays longer in school—these are some of the striking points brought out by Mr. Ayres's study.

Your book, "Laggards in Our Schools," has rendered a most real service to public education in America.—WM. H. MAXWELL, *Supt. of Schools, New York City.*

(Third Edition)
252 PAGES; 106 TABLES; 38 DIAGRAMS. Price, Postpaid, $1.50

AMONG SCHOOL GARDENS

By M. LOUISE GREENE, M.Pd., Ph.D. (Yale)

AN exceedingly interesting and thoroughly practical book on "school gardens," including those conducted by associations in public parks and at the homes, as well as gardens carried on in connection with regular school work. Based upon personal study and observation, by the author, of school garden work throughout the United States and Canada. Beautifully illustrated.

One of the most important school books of the season.—*Journal of Education.*

A convincing document of the utility of making gardening a part of the school work.—*Washington Star.*

380 PAGES; 98 ILLUSTRATIONS
15 PLANS AND DIAGRAMS Price, Postpaid, $1.25

CHARITIES PUBLICATION COMMITTEE

105 EAST 22D STREET, NEW YORK

RUSSELL SAGE FOUNDATION PUBLICATIONS

HOUSING REFORM

A Handbook for Use in American Cities

By LAWRENCE VEILLER

Secretary Tenement House Commission of 1900; Deputy Commissioner New York Tenement House Department under Mayor Seth Low; Director Department for the Improvement of Social Conditions of the New York Charity Organization Society; Joint Author The Tenement Problem; Director National Housing Association.

As Mr. de Forest points out in the introduction, this book is written by "the person most competent by knowledge and experience to deal with the subject." Mr. Veiller is qualified as a reformer, as "a lobbyist in behalf of the common welfare," as a public official, to treat housing reform in a practical way. He tells not only the need but the remedy, and how to secure it.

CONTENTS

FOREWORD, BY ROBERT W. de FOREST

220 Pages; Price, Postpaid, $1.25

SOME SENTENCES FROM HOUSING REFORM

No growing American city, however free from tenements now, can afford to be without building regulations, to prevent dark rooms and unsanitary conditions.

No housing evils are necessary; none need be tolerated. Where they exist they are always a reflection upon the intelligence, rightmindedness and moral tone of the community.

Reforms not based upon carefully ascertained facts will be found to have no permanent value. The breastworks which defend the law are made of the materials dug out in the investigations.

CHARITIES PUBLICATION COMMITTEE

105 E. 22d Street, New York